Matters of Significance

Matters of Significance

Replication, translation, and academic freedom in developmental science

Marinus H. van IJzendoorn and
Marian J. Bakermans-Kranenburg

First published in 2024 by
UCL Press
University College London
Gower Street
London WC1E 6BT

Available to download free: www.uclpress.co.uk

Text © Authors, 2024
Images © Authors and copyright holders named in captions, 2024

The authors have asserted their rights under the Copyright, Designs and Patents Act 1988 to be identified as the authors of this work.

A CIP catalogue record for this book is available from The British Library.

Any third-party material in this book is not covered by the book's Creative Commons licence. Details of the copyright ownership and permitted use of third-party material is given in the image (or extract) credit lines. If you would like to reuse any third-party material not covered by the book's Creative Commons licence, you will need to obtain permission directly from the copyright owner.

This book is published under a Creative Commons Attribution-Non-Commercial 4.0 International licence (CC BY-NC 4.0), https://creativecommons.org/licenses/by-nc/4.0/. This licence allows you to share and adapt the work for non-commercial use providing attribution is made to the author and publisher (but not in any way that suggests that they endorse you or your use of the work) and any changes are indicated. Attribution should include the following information:

Van IJzendoorn, M. H. and Bakermans-Kranenburg, M. J. 2024. *Matters of Significance: Replication, translation, and academic freedom in developmental science*. London: UCL Press. https://doi.org/10.14324/111.9781800086500

Further details about Creative Commons licences are available at https://creativecommons.org/licenses/

ISBN: 978-1-80008-652-4 (Hbk)
ISBN: 978-1-80008-651-7 (Pbk)
ISBN: 978-1-80008-650-0 (PDF)
ISBN: 978-1-80008-653-1 (epub)
DOI: https://doi.org/10.14324/111.9781800086500

Note on the cover image: The spiralling, infinite stairs are a work of art by the Icelandic-Danish artist Olafur Eliasson. It is placed in Munich near the KPMG building and is titled 'Umschreibung', the German word for 'circumscription' or 'periphrasis'. It seems inspired by the impossible staircases of Penrose and Escher but it also reminds us of the double helix. In 2019 Eliasson was appointed Goodwill Ambassador for renewable energy by the United Nations Development Programme.

Contents

List of figures	vii
List of tables	xi
Preface	xiii
Acknowledgements	xv
Introduction: attachment theory in a nutshell	1
Part 1: The replication crisis and its remedies	7
1 Power failure in developmental research	9
2 A moratorium on self-reports	21
3 Meta-analyses searching for replicated evidence	33
Part 2: Translation to policy or practice	51
4 Video-feedback intervention (VIPP-SD) promotes sensitive parenting and secure attachment	53
5 Institutionalised child-rearing is structural neglect	63
6 Future generations can be saved from genocidal trauma: the case of the Holocaust	71
7 Jumping from 'is' to 'ought'?	81
8 Dubious effect size standards and cost-effectiveness criteria	89

Part 3: Busting myths is translation   99

9   It's all in the genome?   101

10   Attachment and parenting in the brain and hormones?   113

11   Is attachment culture specific?   125

12   Parenting shapes prosocial child development?   137

13   Is assessing attachment of individual children in applied practice valid?   151

14   SOS Children's Villages in the best interest of children?   161

15   Is adoption a modern, unethical in(ter)vention?   171

Part 4: Protecting academic freedom promotes replication and translation   185

16   Limits to participant, public, and policymaker involvement   187

17   Caution: personal conflicts of interest   201

18   Academic freedom in 'safe spaces'   211

     Epilogue: replication, translation, and academic freedom   225

Index   231

List of figures

0.0	Carla Kleekamp, *Signs of Spring* (Tekenen van het Voorjaar). Etching, 1983.	xii
0.1	Sergey Postnikov (1838–1880), *Farewell of Hector and Andromache*. Oil on canvas, 1863. The story of an attachment network told by Homer some 3,000 years ago in the *Iliad*.	4
0.2	Translation of scientific findings to practice or policy requires replicated results. A replication crisis implies a translational crisis.	7
1.1	Design of the L-CID study, a randomised accelerated cohort-sequential longitudinal twin intervention study.	13
2.1	Twin heritability of nonsensical Wildman items. In 8-year-old Dutch twin children we found substantial heritability of the bias to respond to nonsensical questions.	26
2.2	Response bias emerging in a questionnaire without questions.	27
3.1	The stages in primary empirical studies and in meta-analyses are largely overlapping, with similar requirements for reproducibility.	34
3.2	From primary empirical studies via secondary analysis and replications in the context of discovery to umbrella synthesis of meta-analyses and individual participant data meta-analysis in the context of justification.	42
0.3	Translation of scientific findings to practice and policy requires replicated results and academic freedom from external pressures. In addition, ethical reasoning to bridge the gap between means and ends and a suitable cost-benefit balance are required.	51

4.1	Potential active ingredients in Video-feedback Interventions to promote Positive Parenting and Sensitive Discipline (VIPP-SD).	55
4.2	Sessions of the Video-feedback Interventions to promote Positive Parenting and Sensitive Discipline (VIPP-SD).	57
5.1	Meta-analytic effects of institutionalisation are derived from all studies of the past 70 years covering more than 100,000 children in more than 60 countries.	65
6.1	Effects of the Holocaust on first-generation survivors in non-select samples underscore the extreme nature of Holocaust-related atrocities.	74
6.2	Effects of the Holocaust on first-, second-, and third-generation survivors in select and non-select samples. First-generation Holocaust survivors' traumatic stress did transmit to the second generation only in the presence of other risks and did not seem to be transmitted to the third generation.	76
7.1	Stairways to translational action and policy. Translation of replicated findings to practice and policy is increasingly complex and more value-laden.	86
8.1	Evaluating societal impact of interventions according to their (replicated) effects, costs in comparison to care-as-usual, and scalability to larger populations.	90
9.1	The basic twin design with monozygotic and dizygotic twin pairs to estimate the heritability of psychological traits.	102
9.2	Differential susceptibility to the environment for better *and* for worse. The dichotomy between susceptible (orchid-like) and non-susceptible (dandelion-like) individuals might in reality be a continuum.	107
10.1	The relations between neural activation in the brain, hormonal levels, and behavioural adaptations to environmental demands might be bidirectional.	114
10.2	The oxytocin molecule (oxygen replaced by hearts). Oxytocin is a nonapeptide hormone with a specific amino acid sequence acting as a neurotransmitter in the brain. Despite the hearts the term 'love hormone' is a misnomer.	115
11.1	A stele showing Akhenaten, Nefertiti, and three of their daughters. 18th dynasty, reign of Akhenaten. Limestone, ca. 1340 BC.	126

11.2	Percentages of secure infant-parent attachment relationships across the globe, derived from a meta-analysis of the first 20,000 Strange Situation Procedures.	129
13.1	Intercoder reliability of attachment measures is too low and chance of incorrect classifications too high for individual assessments or diagnoses. For individual children and their parents or caregivers, the attachment assessment will be wrong in at least one of every four cases.	156
14.1	Despite small-group care in SOS Children's Villages, meta-analytic evidence shows the delays of SOSCV children in physical and mental development compared to their peers raised in families (baseline, $d = 0$) or in large institutions.	164
15.1	International adoption is a child protective measure and a last resort to raise biologically or socially orphaned children without available parents or other (kin) caregivers in a safe, stable and shared (Triple S) caregiving environment.	177
15.2	The adoption triangle illustrates that in cases of possible adoption of abandoned children, the potential interests of at least three parties are at stake: adoptive parents, birth parents, and the child. Rawls' original position requires the readers to imagine that they do not know their role in the adoption triangle.	179
0.4	Academic freedom is required for scholars in their area of expertise. Individual academic freedom is not only under siege of powers outside academia but is also threatened by the university as a hierarchical organisation.	186
16.1	A Cooperative Practitioners-Researchers Model. Researchers are responsible for designing and conducting transparent and replicable research. Practitioners are involved in open communication about relevant research questions and about ethical implications of translating findings to policy or practice.	196
17.1	Full Conflict of Interest Disclosure Form of the Society for Research on Child Development.	203
0.5	Nested ovals displaying the relations between replication, translation, and academic freedom with their various components.	226

List of tables

3.1 Stages in the development of attachment theory as a Lakatosian research programme. A revival can be noted in the last decade with an emphasis on interdisciplinarity, collaboration, and transparency. 37

13.1 Assessing individual children for attachment insecurity or disorganisation should be evaluated according to the instrument's sensitivity and specificity which currently is insufficient for the existing attachment measures. 154

Figure 0.0 Carla Kleekamp, *Signs of Spring* (Tekenen van het Voorjaar). Etching, 1983. © Carla Kleekamp.

Preface

Attachment is, in a nutshell, the affective relationship of children to their parents and other caregivers. From its inception attachment theory has cherished high translational ambitions for applying findings to clinical practice and social policies. Can it deliver? Attachment theory has indeed become extremely popular among policymakers, child welfare professionals, and clinicians working in child and adolescent mental health care. Attachment measures and research results are embraced as solutions for complicated decisions about out-of-home placement, divorce disputes, parent coaching, and treatment of child behaviour problems.

Translation of scientific findings to policy or practice, however, requires a firm basis in replicated research. We argue that attachment research suffers from a replication crisis that also rages in the biomedical sciences. Inspired by our personal replication and translation experiences over the past 40 years, we present some replication problems and translation issues. Yet, despite the replication crisis, university administrators, policymakers, and funding agencies call ever louder for valorisation. In this book we argue that a replication crisis necessarily implies a translation crisis because translation requires replication.

Translating scientific findings to practice is usually conceptualised in a technical way. Knowing the causes of children's psychological distress might lead to manipulating the causal chain in order to optimise a developmental outcome. Parenting interventions are a prime example of such a technical approach for which replicated evidence from randomised controlled experiments is needed. We argue that two other considerations are important: the ethical justification of the intervention goals and the cost versus benefits balance.

An alternative, perhaps more viable way to apply developmental science is busting popular myths about parenting and child development. This can be done by using basic propositions, firmly grounded in decades of research and embedded in a lattice of supporting facts and plausible assumptions. A core evidence-based proposition of attachment theory identifies safe, stable, and shared (Triple S) care as a necessary condition of good-enough child rearing arrangements. Using this core proposition as criterion to criticise bad applied research and prevailing misconceptions and prejudices of parents, professionals, or policymakers, however, requires academic freedom, freedom from interference by stakeholders or administrators in the core stages of research.

We argue that research on child development is going through a replication crisis and that developmental researchers should practise translational caution by prioritising falsification of fake facts. Academic freedom is a paramount condition for this adversarial, critical role that might otherwise lead to side-lining or cancellation of the bearer of bad news. We submit that in terms of the challenges of replication and translation, attachment theory and research are exemplary for the problems facing researchers working in the broader domain of developmental science.

In this book our approach is personal; that is, we do not aim at discussing the vast literature on any topic addressed exhaustively. Instead, we focus on research we were personally involved in for several decades, and we want to articulate our insider perspective. Marinus started his research career in the 70s with studies on moral development, whereas Marian began to investigate attachment of parents and their children in the 1980s. They combined forces some 35 years ago, initially in an advisor-student relationship, and later as colleagues working in the same research programme on attachment and emotion regulation. Our personal experiences with theoretical, empirical, and meta-analytic work, debates, controversies, and publications are used as a source of reflections on the complicated relations between replication, translation, and academic freedom.

We wrote this book for graduate students, post-docs, and junior and senior researchers in the domain of developmental science. Because one of our central questions is whether, when, and how scientific findings can be translated to daily family life, clinical practice, or social policy, we might also serve some food for thought for professionals, social workers, clinicians, and policymakers. The chapters are ordered in four parts, on replication, translation, and academic freedom to reflect the connectedness and hierarchy between these dimensions. But each part or chapter can also be read on its own.

Note

We use 'translation' instead of 'valorisation' for the transition of science to policy or practice. Valorisation means adding value to a product more broadly. Translation is thus also valorisation, but with a more precise, scientific focus – the focus of interest to us.

Acknowledgements

We thank our wonderful and dedicated research collaborators from all parts of the world, first and foremost our PhD students and co-supervisors with whom we worked closely and enjoyably together over the past 40 years or so. They were most inspiring and showed the value of a world without borders. We also had the privilege to get thousands of pages of critical comments on our submitted manuscripts from (mostly anonymous) reviewers, making our work better with every revision. For the current book we want to mention Jay Belsky, Pehr Granqvist, and Robbie Duschinsky who each provided us with invaluable feedback and food for revising our thoughts and writings. Pat Gordon-Smith of UCL Press guided us in a most helpful and effective manner on our journey towards an Open Access digital book that can be downloaded without cost for the reader anywhere in the world. The work presented in this book has been generously supported by, among others, the Dutch Research Council (VIDI and VICI grants to Marian; Pioneer grant and Spinoza Prize to Marinus; Gravitation grant to both), by an Advanced Grant of the European Research Council to Marian, and by Leiden University. We thank Carla Kleekamp for allowing us to reprint her beautiful etching with watercolour 'Tekenen van het voorjaar' [Signs of spring]. It is the perfect representation of the collaborative process leading to this book.

Introduction: attachment theory in a nutshell

What is attachment on the species-specific level?

Attachment can be defined at two levels: the level of the species and the level of the dyad or individual (see Van IJzendoorn, 2021, for details of the following descriptions). On the level of the species, attachment is signifying an inborn bias to seek the protection of a conspecific in times of distress; in John Bowlby's words: 'To say of a child that he … has an attachment to someone means that he is strongly disposed to seek proximity to and contact with a specific figure and to do so in certain situations, notably when he is frightened, tired or ill' (John Bowlby, 1969/1982, p. 371). Somewhat confusing is the term *'a specific figure'* that Bowlby used to describe a person to whom a child becomes attached. This term has been wrongly interpreted as implying that there would be only one (not *a*) caregiver who might serve as an attachment figure, and this individual would be the biological mother who is responsible for taking care of the child.

However, attachment theory and research have amply documented the ability of infants and children to become attached to more than one parent or caregiver, in a network of attachment relationships (Bakermans-Kranenburg, 2021). From an evolutionary perspective this makes a lot of sense because in early times the risk of death of a mother during and after childbirth was rather high (and in some parts of the world this risk is still high). Without alternative attachment figures the infant would have perished and the parents' 'inclusive fitness' would have suffered accordingly (Hrdy, 2009). A biological tie between the attachment figure and the child is not a necessary condition for an attachment relationship. This has been documented in numerous studies on attachments in foster and adoptive families (Van IJzendoorn et al., 2020). Together with Harlow's infamous experiments on rhesus monkeys, adoption research also showed that feeding is not necessary for an attachment relationship to develop and that 'contact comfort' or protective proximity is the indispensable fuel for the development of attachments.

What is attachment on the individual level?

The inborn bias to become attached is comparable to the inborn ability of the human species to learn a language and to communicate with conspecifics, which facilitates cooperation, cultural transmission of expertise, and survival in general. What specific language children are going to master is dependent on the environment or language community in which they happen to find themselves. 'Inborn' does not mean that the social and physical environment would not matter. On the contrary, interactions with the world are needed to bring about the latent talents and turn the potential competence into a performance such as an adequate speech act in the correct syntax and context.

The same is true for attachment relationships. Every newborn comes into the world with the competence to develop an attachment relationship. Every infant will become attached to one or more caregivers who may be able to regulate the child's (di-)stress and anxieties when these become overwhelming. Attachment figures modulate feelings of discomfort and stress going beyond the capacity of the child to self-regulate. But the quality of the attachment relationships is dependent on the social environment that might provide more or less continuous, sensitive, or stimulating interactions. Most parents and other caregivers provide 'good-enough' care (Van IJzendoorn et al., 2020) which creates a safe haven in the sense of protection against harm. However, not all of them provide a secure base to freely explore the world (Van IJzendoorn & Bakermans-Kranenburg, 2021). Secure and insecure attachments might develop in such a caregiving arrangement, preparing the child for a specific future niche to which this individual child is expected to adapt.

It should be noted that the concepts of 'safe haven' and 'secure base' are often used in a somewhat confusing way. Safety is etymologically derived from the Latin word 'salvus', that is, the absence of injury, and security originates from 'se cura', that is, being without a care (Bowlby, 1969, as cited in Duschinsky, 2020; see also Chapter 7). That said, we submit that children have a species-specific innate bias to search for a safe haven but whether their individual attachments are secure or insecure at least partly depends on the quality of the care they receive.

Apart from the species-specific and individual levels of attachment, attachment at group level has been explored (e.g., attachment to school, religion, or state; see Granqvist, 2020; Marris, 1996; Ota, 2024), but currently this is very promising yet mostly preliminary work in progress that we will not discuss in this book.

Attachment networks: fathers and other caregivers

Attachment is not about the relationship between children and mothers specifically. About 3,000 years ago Homer described in the *Iliad* clear-cut attachment of Astyanax to his mother, father, and nurse. Homer narrates how Hector comes back from the battlefield with his shiny helmet and scares his son, who is on his mother's arm and huddles into her for safety (see Figure 0.1). Hector realises the cause of Astyanax's stress, pulls off his helmet, and gradually starts to interact. Astyanax soon becomes curious and initiates playful interaction with his father and nearby mother, Andromache. Not for long, however, because Hector must return to the battlefield to fight with Achilles who will defeat him and in a cruel way will drag his body around Troy in full view of his family and the other citizens (see also Chapter 6).

This tragic episode in the Trojan War makes clear that children become attached not only to their mother but also to their father, and possibly other caregivers such as nurses or nannies. Fathers have been neglected in developmental research in general and in attachment research as well, despite seminal work by Michael Lamb (2004). Due to societal changes like greater participation of women and mothers in the labour force, fathers' active involvement in raising their children has significantly increased in the past decades in most Western, industrialised nations, with a three- to six-fold increase in childcare involvement compared to their own fathers (Bakermans-Kranenburg et al., 2019). Parenting research lags behind this societal change, but the attention to fathers as parents is on the rise. While in the 1980s and 1990s 'inclusion' of both parents in studies often meant that the mother was observed in parent-child interactions and was asked to report on fathers' income, education, absence, or other characteristics that were then used as covariates in the analysis of mother's parenting and child outcomes, in the new century fathers themselves were more often observed. It is now acknowledged that fathers contribute independently from mothers to child development (e.g., Cowan et al., 2019; Perpetuo et al., 2023).

At the same time, this raises the question of how children deal with different attachment relationships (secure with one caregiver, insecure

Figure 0.1 Sergey Postnikov (1838–1880), *Farewell of Hector and Andromache*. Oil on canvas, 1863. The story of an attachment network told by Homer some 3,000 years ago in the *Iliad*. Public domain, Wikimedia Commons, https://commons.wikimedia.org/wiki/File:Postnikov_ProschGektora.jpg.

with the other, see Dagan et al., 2021) and, broader, how large a network of attachment relationships can be. We have argued that the attachment network may increase in size with the child's cognitive development. For the development of an attachment relationship, the child needs to be able to distinguish a specific caregiver from other adults and to have a mental representation of the caregiver when not present. Managing distinct cognitive models of a large number of attachment figures, with accompanying expectations about behavioural *dos* and *don'ts* in those specific relationships, requires complex cognitive processes and may thus only be feasible for somewhat older children. Having said that, not every caregiver is an attachment figure, and not every social relationship is an attachment relationship. Teachers have primarily an educational role, but in kindergarten the relationship of the child with the teacher may have attachment components. The limiting factor to the size of attachment networks may not be the number of caregivers, but the opportunities that a child has to learn contingencies in relationships that have an attachment component (Bakermans-Kranenburg, 2021).

Child maltreatment

Sometimes, however, a safe haven and secure base is not established, with detrimental consequences for the child's physical and mental health. The first condition that hampers attachment development is family violence leading to child maltreatment, and the second is structural neglect in institutional settings. From an evolutionary perspective, Bowlby argued that: 'the more the social environment in which a human child is reared deviates from the environment of evolutionary adaptedness (which is probably father, mother, and siblings in a social environment comprising grandparents and a limited number of other known families), the greater will be the risk of his developing maladaptive patterns of social behaviour' (Bowlby, 1969/1982, p. 166). During millennia of human evolution children have not evolved to endure social environments with very abusive parenting or fragmented and neglectful care by too many different (non–genetically related) caregivers. They will wither away more severely the more violent, neglecting, or discontinuous their social environment happens to be (see, e.g., Hamilton, 1964, and Trivers,1974, for the role of parent-offspring conflict).

The detrimental effects of institutional care and child maltreatment (Chapter 5) might teach us valuable lessons about the core propositions of attachment theory. The first lesson is that children need social interactions to grow up and develop their physical, social, and cognitive competences. Sufficient food and medical care are not enough to avoid serious developmental delays. Second, continuity of care arrangements is essential as fragmented care creates atypical attachments, growing insecurity, and increasing distrust in others. Third, children and their parents or caregivers need a small and reliable social network of individuals who offer the support they need in times of anxiety, stress, distress, or illness. Last, most children may recover from early issues with attachment (Chapter 14). A drastic change from a detrimental institutional environment to a supportive family environment leads to fast catch-up growth in most developmental domains, including attachment. According to attachment theory safe, stable and shared (Triple S) care is essential for child development.

References

Bakermans-Kranenburg, M. J. (2021). The limits of the attachment network. *New Directions for Child & Adolescent Development, 162*, 1–8. https://doi.org/10.1002/cad.20432

Bakermans-Kranenburg, M. J., Lotz, A. M., Alyousefi-an Dijk, K., & Van IJzendoorn, M. H. (2019). The birth of a father: Fathering in the first 1,000 days. *Child Development Perspectives, 13*, 247–253. https://doi.org/10.1111/cdep.12347

Bowlby, J. (1969/1982). *Attachment and Loss: Attachment*. Vintage.

Cowan, P. A., Cowan, C. P., Pruett, M. K., & Pruett, K. (2019). Fathers' and mothers' attachment styles, couple conflict, parenting quality, and children's behavior problems: An intervention test of mediation. *Attachment & Human Development, 21*, 532–550. https://doi.org/10.1080/14616734.2019.1582600

Dagan, O., Schuengel, C., Verhage, M. L., Van IJzendoorn, M. H., Sagi-Schwartz, A., Madigan, S., Duschinsky, R., Roisman, G. I., Bernard, K., Bakermans-Kranenburg, M., Bureau, J.-F., Volling, B. L., Wong, M. S., Colonnesi, C., Brown, G. L., Eiden, R. D., Fearon, R. M. P., Oosterman, M., Aviezer, O., Cummings, E. M., & The Collaboration on Attachment to Multiple Parents and Outcomes Synthesis. (2021). Configurations of mother-child and father-child attachment as predictors of internalizing and externalizing behavioral problems: An individual participant data (IPD) meta-analysis. *New Directions for Child and Adolescent Development, 180*, 67–94. https://doi.org/10.1002/cad.20450

Duschinsky, R. (2020). *Cornerstones of Attachment Research in the Twenty First Century*. Oxford University Press. https://doi.org/10.1093/med-psych/9780198842064.001.0001

Granqvist, P. (2020). *Attachment in Religion and Spirituality: A Wider View*. Guilford Press. https://psycnet.apa.org/record/2020-01351-000

Hamilton, W. D. (1964). The genetical evolution of social behaviour. *Journal of Theoretical Biology, 7*(1), 1–52. https://doi.org/10.1016/0022-5193(64)90038-4

Hrdy, S. (2009). *Mothers and Others: The Evolutionary Origins of Mutual Understanding*. Belknap Press. https://doi.org/10.2307/j.ctt1c84czb

Lamb, M. E. (Ed.) (2004). *The Role of the Father in Child Development*. John Wiley & Sons.

Marris, P. (1996). *The Politics of Uncertainty: Attachment in Private and Public Life*. Routledge. https://doi.org/10.4324/9780203360293

Ota, D. W. (2024). *Safe Passage for Attachment Systems: Can Attachment Security at International Schools Be Measured, and Is It at Risk?* Doctoral dissertation, Erasmus University Rotterdam, The Netherlands

Perpétuo, C., El-Sheikh, M., Diniz, E., & Veríssimo, M. (2023). Attachment to mother and father, sleep, and well-being in late middle childhood. *International Journal of Environmental Research and Public Health, 20*, 3399. https://doi.org/10.3390/ijerph20043399

Trivers, R. L. (1974). Parent-offspring conflict. *Integrative and Comparative Biology, 14*(1), 249–264. https://doi.org/10.1093/icb/14.1.249

Van IJzendoorn, M. H. (2021). Bindung und Entwicklungspsychopathologie. In K. H. Brisch (Ed.), *Bindung und psychische Storungen. Ursachen, Behandlung und Prävention* (pp. 122–132). Klett-Cotta.

Van IJzendoorn, M. H., Bakermans-Kranenburg, M. J., Duschinsky, R., & Skinner, G. C. M. (2020). Legislation in search of 'good-enough' care arrangements for the child: A quest for continuity of care. In J. G. Dwyer (Ed.), *The Oxford Handbook of Children and the Law* (pp. 129–153). Oxford University Press. https://doi.org/10.1093/oxfordhb/9780190694395.013.5

Part 1
The replication crisis and its remedies

In this section on the replication crisis, we show that Mary Ainsworth's pioneering but small attachment study on the development of infant crying during the first year of life did not replicate in an independent larger study with more reliable measures. The small study nevertheless led to the forceful and still popular advice to young parents to respond promptly to any crying of their infant. Small studies lead to lack of statistical power, and this 'power failure' is partly responsible for the problem of non-replicability, not only in attachment research but also in most other developmental and neurobiological studies. Additional stumbling blocks for replicability are the reliance on self-reports of observable behaviours and the so-called 'winner's curse', that is, the uncritical acceptance – even adoration – of impressively strong initial research results with a weak evidence base. Nevertheless, replication is a necessary prerequisite for translation (see Figure 0.2).

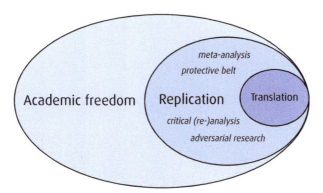

Figure 0.2 Translation of scientific findings to practice or policy requires replicated results. A replication crisis implies a translational crisis.
Source: Authors.

1
Power failure in developmental research

Replicating a famous study on response to infant crying

Translation requires replication, and a replication crisis implies a translational crisis. Replicability has been one of our main interests from the outset and remained an important focus throughout the past four decades of our research. The lack of replicability of some central research methods and findings of attachment theory has been disappointing. But even more frustrating is the defensive exclusion of non-replications from the collective memory of the community of researchers. A striking example may be the non-replication of the famous longitudinal Baltimore study of the influence of parental sensitive responsiveness on the development of infant crying.

Silvia Bell and Mary Ainsworth (1972) summarised the main result of their study as follows: 'the single most important factor associated with a decrease in frequency and duration of crying … is the promptness with which a mother responds to cries'. The Baltimore study on 26 families, intensively observed in their homes for a year, has been cited over 1,875 times (Google 5 May 2022) and had a great impact on the practice of childrearing and managing infant crying in the daily lives of young parents. The obituary of Ainsworth in the *New York Times* was telling: 'Though much of Dr. Ainsworth's research was for an academic audience, it also had a practical side. She argued, on the basis of her research, that picking up a crying baby does not spoil the child; rather, it reduces crying in the future' (*New York Times* 7 April 1999).

The finding that children would cry less when receiving immediate response to their distress signals not only was of practical significance but also seemed theoretically crucial in the competition between attachment theory and theories that emphasised classic or operant conditioning and the power of reinforcement in shaping behaviour (Gewirtz & Boyd, 1977; see Ainsworth & Bell, 1977, for a rebuttal; see Bosmans et al., 2020, 2022, for an integration of attachment and learning theories). At the start of the replication effort, almost 40 years ago, Marinus was still young, inexperienced, and ignorant of the opposition any falsification of a cherished proposition in a fledgling theory would trigger. Together with Frans Hubbard, he designed a longitudinal replication study with better, more reliable and more valid observational and recording measures and analytic strategies, and a twice as large sample of families compared to the Baltimore study. The results were totally unexpected. Parental prompt responding early in the infant's life did not reduce crying, but on the contrary increased the frequency of infant crying later in the first year, as conditioning theory would have predicted (Van IJzendoorn & Hubbard, 1987, 2000; Hubbard & Van IJzendoorn, 1991, 1994).

The replication study has been cited only about 50 times, mostly in paediatric journals, not in the attachment literature, and it has not been picked up in the popular parenting press. In fact, the failed replication was simply ignored and forgotten, probably because it did not fit in the prevailing narrative of an emerging attachment theory. We proposed differential responsiveness to crying as the hypothesis aligned with attachment theory as well as with our data (Van IJzendoorn & Hubbard, 1987), yet this suggestion was never admitted to the core of the research programme. To our satisfaction, the idea of responding promptly to crying as an expression of urgent attachment needs (e.g., hunger, thirst, illness, overwhelming distress) but ignoring fusses or crying out of boredom was later supported by neuro-endocrinological evidence (Riem et al., 2014).

Of course, one failed replication is insufficient to change the course of a scientific research programme and should not lead to a change of policy or practice recommendations, as we will argue below (Van IJzendoorn & Bakermans-Kranenburg, 2021). A research programme should protect itself against early falsifications (with a 'protective belt', Lakatos,1980; Meehl, 1990). Alternative interpretations of the failure to replicate can often make sense of the unexpected result (e.g., because a false measurement theory is incorporated in a measure; see the Duhem-Quine thesis, Quine, 1951). Unfortunately, however, in the last three decades no (exact, varied or conceptual) replications of the proposed association between caregivers' response to crying and infants' future crying frequency and duration have been conducted despite a core hypothesis with high practical relevance at stake. One of the hard personal lessons was that failure to replicate a foundational study runs the risk of eliciting blame and side-lining the messengers. For example, it was difficult to publish a paper on the non-replication in one of the major flagship journals of the American Psychological Association (*Developmental Psychology*) or the Society for Research on Child Development (*Child Development*).

Replication crisis in the cognitive neurosciences

Is lack of replicability an exclusive feature of attachment research and other so-called 'soft' developmental sciences or is it more widely spread, also among the 'hard' natural, biomedical and behavioural sciences? John Ioannidis' famous *PLOS Medicine* paper (2005), with the provocative title 'Why most published research findings are false', has been read more than three million times and cited more than 7,000 times. The paper played a pivotal role in the growing awareness of a replication issue – or even crisis – and made non-replicability a major issue in almost all empirical sciences (NAS, 2019). For example, of 112 pre-clinical cancer studies only 46% were found to be replicable, and nearly all effect sizes of the replication studies were smaller than those of the original studies (Errington et al., 2021).

Neuroscientific research using EEG or fMRI is tremendously popular with funding agencies, journals, newspapers and the wider public. This is probably because of the attractively coloured pictures of the brains that seem to disclose the colourful secrets of your inner mental life. The basic psychometrics of simple task-related imaging paradigms are a bit disappointing, however. With Rens Huffmeijer and Esther Heckendorf (Heckendorf et al., 2019) we found poor test–retest reliability across five weeks for a priming task showing faces with different expressions or familiarity. Only the rather uninteresting contrast of a real face versus a scrambled face did show stability over time in the Fusiform Face Area. Some years later, the study was included in a meta-analysis (Elliott et al., 2020) on 90 task-related fMRI experiments with in total 1,088 participants, documenting dramatically low reliabilities (average ICC = 0.40).

Moreover, the average number of participants (N = 20) in these experiments was below statistical par, which meant that studies were drastically underpowered with great risk of false positive results. In fact, low statistical power of neuroscientific studies is deemed to be a major cause for the non-replicability of their results. The diagnosis of Ioannidis and colleagues was 'power failure' in 85% of the publications, which may arguably be responsible for the lack of reliability of neuroscientific studies (Button et al., 2013). More recently, Marek et al. (2022) showed that brain-wide association studies examining individual differences in mental health or other complex traits require literally thousands of participants for robust, replicable results, whereas the average study in this area is based on only 25 subjects.

In rodent studies on maternal deprivation, such as those we did with Jiska Kentrop and Rixt van der Veen, a similarly catastrophic power failure can be observed (Bonapersona et al., 2019). This is partly due to ethics committees requiring a minimal number of animals to be sacrificed in those experiments, not realising that in underpowered studies all animals are needlessly wasted because no knowledge is gained. The remedy that Bonapersona et al. (2021) proposed is to use control groups from previous studies for a new experiment. That would indeed increase the number of animals, but it undermines any random assignment and thus jeopardises confounder comparability of experimental and control rodents (Hamaker et al., 2020).

More than ten years ago we initiated the Leiden-Consortium on Individual Development study (L-CID) to address some of the replicability issues confronting neurocognitive developmental research. We developed a randomised accelerated cohort-sequential longitudinal twin intervention study (see Figure 1.1) that includes about 1,000 children between ages of 3 and 13 years in two age cohorts with six partially overlapping measurement waves. Structural and functional MRI assessments were implemented in three waves on top of a series of observational measures on parenting and child behaviour development (Crone et al., 2020; Euser et al., 2016). The twin component of the design allows for internal replication of imaging results in highly similar sub-samples of children for optimal replication conditions; the cohort-sequential design enables replication in independent cohorts at the same age; and the longitudinal design feature allows for examination of reliability of imaging measures across time.

For most parts of this project, we pre-register the design and analytic plans; that is, before starting to explore the dataset we make our plans for statistical analyses public in some detail (e.g., Euser et al., 2016; Runze et al., 2022). Pre-registration of the data-collection and data-analysis plan is considered one of the major means to enhance replicability because it restricts the number of arbitrary choices for testing the hypotheses (Nosek et al., 2015). For reviewers and other readers of a paper it becomes possible to check whether the authors stuck to the original analysis plans or deviated from them in order to produce 'significant' results. In the biomedical sciences randomised clinical trials are required to be pre-registered since 1997 with an amendment

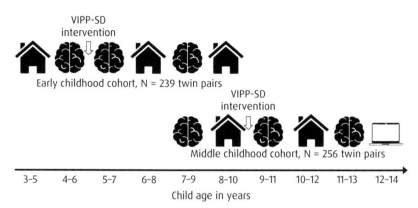

Figure 1.1 Design of the L-CID study, a randomised accelerated cohort-sequential longitudinal twin intervention study.
Source: Authors.

to the Food and Drug Act in the USA. For publication in major journals pre-registration is usually required since it decreases the so-called 'researcher degrees of freedom' to pick and choose some significant results from a large number of nonsignificant statistical tests (Simmons, Nelson & Simonsohn, 2011).

In L-CID, replication efforts for functional MRI results were only modestly successful, particularly for results concerning individual differences and brain–behaviour associations (e.g., Dobbelaar et al., 2022) and for results concerning stability over time of neural responses to tasks (Dobbelaar et al., 2023), but this is work in progress. The rather small genetic component in twin heritability estimates for functional MRI paradigms points in the same direction. More promising replicability might be expected for structural MRI measures like surface area and cortical thickness of brain regions. We found robust correlations for structural MRI measures within monozygotic twins, suggesting replicability across genetically similar individuals. Lower correlations for dizygotic twin pairs were found, resulting in rather substantial twin heritability estimates. Such results also point at replicability (e.g., Van der Meulen et al., 2020).

In a similar vein, resting state connectivity between brain regions appears to be more replicable and heritable than functional measures. We observed replicable brain connectivity patterns when comparing our two age-overlapping cohorts of 7- to 9-year-old children, both in whole brain analyses and in post hoc ROI analyses (Achterberg et al., 2018).

Russ Poldrack (2018) was right in concluding that 'we have to be very careful in our interpretation of published fMRI research studies' (Ch 6, eBook 120). This is certainly true for functional MRI. In large samples structural MRI features seem more robust across time and settings, and more promising in detecting neural differences in phenotypically different individuals.

Winner's curse or blessing in disguise?

Meta-analyses have some unexpected advantages beyond finding the common effect size, computing its variance and explaining this variance by moderators (Borenstein, 2019). Close reading of the Methods and Results sections of primary study reports is needed to conduct a meta-analysis. The meta-analyst often acts as a detective scrutinising statistics, tables and figures, stumbling across numerous statistical mistakes and misspellings. Confusion of standard errors and standard deviations is one of the more common mistakes; others are interpreting a one-sided $p < 0.05$ as significant in the conventional sense, swapping standardised and unstandardised betas or using different metrics for the Y-axes in figures that are meant to be compared at face value, to name just a few.

Most importantly, meta-analysis is a great detector of impossible outliers that end up constituting a winner's curse. An instructive example is the most prominent effect size Mary Ainsworth reported in her famous Baltimore study. She found an effect size of $r (24) = 0.78$ for the association between observed maternal sensitive responsiveness and infant attachment security (Ainsworth et al., 1978). Corrected for attenuation due to measurement errors, this correlation would be an impossible effect size of $r = 0.97$ (see Duschinsky, 2020, p. 121 for a possible explanation). In the meta-analysis with Marianne de Wolff on 21 studies exploring the association between parental sensitivity and infant attachment security a combined effect size of $r = 0.24$ was found for a total of 1,097 dyads (De Wolff & Van IJzendoorn, 1997). With Sheri Madigan and other colleagues, we updated this meta-analysis on 159 studies, including 21,483 mother-child dyads, and found a combined effect size in the same range, $r = 0.26$ (95% CI 0.22–0.29). Notably, the meta-analytic effect size for father-child dyads was similar in magnitude (Madigan et al., 2024).

Another outlier in a pioneering study of Ainsworth and Eichberg (1991) was uncovered in our meta-analysis of the association between unresolved attachment representation in parents, assessed with the Berkeley Adult Attachment Interview, and disorganised attachment in their children (Main, Kaplan & Cassidy, 1985). The puzzle of the inflated association in this pioneering study topping a long list of subsequent studies with much smaller effects (meta-analysed with Marije Verhage et al., 2016) might be explained by Ainsworth's post hoc corrections of some unresolved classifications which she mentioned in her chapter with Eichberg (Ainsworth & Eichberg, 1991, p. 164; also see Duschinsky, 2020).

To disabuse readers of the notion that outliers are unique for attachment research, an example of the association between genetic polymorphisms and brain volume is illustrative. In that meta-analysis carriers of the *met* variant of the brain derived neurotrophic factor (BDNF) polymorphism were shown not to have the expected smaller hippocampal volume despite impressive effect sizes reported in the first few studies (Molendijk et al., 2012). Molendijk asked Marinus for help in conducting this meta-analysis because in his own PhD study on BDNF he could not replicate the original result. He suspected that his finding was not exceptional because he felt he had done everything correctly. Similar null findings might be buried in the file drawers of frustrated fellow researchers. Indeed, it is not unusual to see young investigators blamed for unexpected or unwelcome results.

Almost 'anything goes' in search of bold conjectures

Is it bad science that leads to a winner's curse or should it be considered creative and generative exploratory work in the context of discovery? The example of the Baltimore study illustrates that inflated results in pioneering studies may be a blessing in disguise and were needed to set in train a collective investment in a research programme with the promise of smaller but robust and useful findings, even if it takes some decades of slow science. In other words, if most findings in developmental behavioural and neurosciences are indeed false at the current point in time (in line with the Ioannidis, 2005, proposition), they may contain important leads for programmatic work in the future. Research programmes need bold conjectures about strong associations, some of which survive scrutiny albeit almost always in a weaker form.

Against the background of the replication crisis, we have just scratched the surface of the potential evidence base in most developmental research domains. But the almost blind search for potentially fruitful hypotheses might turn out to be a necessary step towards hypothesis testing in the context of justification. In our view, as long as we are conscious and transparent of working in a preliminary stage of the search for bold conjectures, in a context of discovery, 'anything goes' as Paul Feyerabend stated in his epistemology (Feyerabend, 1975, 1995), with the exception of fraudulent behaviour. Feyerabend, however, incorrectly generalised this anarchistic opposition 'against method' to the whole scientific enterprise. Unfortunately, quite a few students and popularisers of attachment and other developmental researchers seemingly work like Feyerabend anarchists, pretending to produce replicable and valid knowledge with exploratory non-replicated studies. They deem their results ready for translation to guidelines for policy and practice, without any fraudulent intention or motivation but with potentially bad consequences for science and practice.

That said, in the context of discovery we may allow ourselves more researcher degrees of freedom (Simmons et al., 2011; Simonsohn et al., 2014) than in the context of justification, to leave open the possibility of stumbling across generative hypotheses and serendipitous findings. Playing with a piece of Scotch tape and peeling a thin layer of carbon from a pencil led Andre Geim and Konstantin Novoselov to their discovery of the one-carbon-atom-thick graphene that was super thin and strong at the same time, and with great electrical conductivity. Such free play was custom in their lab on Friday afternoons, meant to leave room for chance and to create a genuine 'safe space' for serendipity (Day, 2010). This habit brought them the Ig Nobel Prize in 2000 for their pitiful frog floating in a magnetic field and won them the real Nobel Prize in 2010 for their generative graphene discovery.

Another example is the discovery of organoids developing from stem cells that Hans Clevers and his team brought worldwide fame (https://nihrecord.nih.gov/2022/06/10/pioneer-field-describes-industrious-organoids). It just happened serendipitously that one of the many growth experiments with stem cells was hitting the target because of a special gel that enabled three-dimensional growth of the cells. Organoids mimicking real human organs, including parts of the brain, are now used for experimental tests of drugs for all kinds of diseases. They make personalised medical treatments, for example, of cancer, more than just a far-fetched promise. It should be noted that Clevers left Utrecht University for the Swiss pharmaceutical firm Roche. He was frustrated by new policies for evaluating research performances and grant proposals without quantitative impact data ('Erkennen en Waarderen'). He was also targeted in the media with accusations of belonging to the class of white old males dominating the field of biomedical science in the Netherlands (see also Chapter 18).

In a Darwinian view of philosophy of science, room for a multitude of variations is needed, as well as stringent selection of the most adaptive variants for fruitful reproduction and dissemination (Campbell, 1960; Hofhuis, 2022). Ainsworth's outliers might post hoc be considered examples of forcing her observations of naturally occurring family interactions in a straitjacket of theoretical expectations to make narrative sense of otherwise chaotic family life. Mary Main's intrinsic curiosity about the effects of autobiographical memory of parents on attachment relationships in their offspring and her interest in language as verbal behaviour led her to develop generative coding systems for attachment representations in an intuitive way (Main et al., 1985; Hesse, 2016). As Louis Pasteur quipped: 'chance favors only the prepared minds'. In Popper's World 3 (Popper, 1978) publicly available research reports become independent of the author, so any self-identification as discoverers of truth instead of producers of fruitful hypotheses is irrelevant.

The tragedy of the winner's curse though falls on young researchers who are eager to follow the promising lead and try to replicate and extend the original ideas but are getting stuck in failed attempts blaming themselves in the process or – maybe worse – being blamed by the leaders in the field. In the case of the Baltimore findings on parental sensitivity it became clear after several decades that intergenerational transmission of attachment is a robustly replicated insight with an important role for sensitive, responsive parenting. In our meta-analyses we were able to quantify a 'transmission gap', identifying what 'known unknowns' remain to be studied (Van IJzendoorn, 1995; Verhage et al., 2016). This documents the heuristic role of meta-analysis in identifying gaps in our knowledge (see also Chapter 3).

References

Achterberg, M., Bakermans-Kranenburg, M. J., Van IJzendoorn, M. H., Van der Meulen, M., Tottenham, N., & Crone, E. A. (2018). Distinctive heritability patterns of subcortical-prefrontal cortex resting state connectivity in childhood: A twin study. *Neuroimage, 175*, 138–149. https://doi.org/10.1016/j.neuroimage.2018.03.076

Ainsworth, M. D. S., & Bell, S. M. (1977). Infant crying and maternal responsiveness: A rejoinder to Gewirtz and Boyd. *Child Development, 48*(4), 1208–1216. https://doi.org/10.2307/1128477

Ainsworth, M., Blehar, M., Waters, E., & Wall, S. (1978). *Patterns of Attachment: A Psychological Study of the Strange Situation.* Lawrence Erlbaum Associates. https://doi.org/10.4324/9780203758045

Ainsworth, M. D. S., & Eichberg, C. G. (1991). Effects on infant-mother attachment of mother's experience related to loss of an attachment figure. In C. M. Parkes, J. Stevenson-Hinde, & P. Marris (Eds.), *Attachment across the Life Cycle* (pp. 160–183). Routledge.

Bell, S. M., & Ainsworth, M. D. S. (1972). Infant crying and maternal responsiveness. *Child Development, 43*(4), 1171–1190. https://doi.org/10.2307/1127506

Bonapersona, V., Hoijtink, H., RELACS Consortium, Sarabdjitsingh, R. A., & Joëls, M. (2021). Increasing the statistical power of animal experiments with historical control data. *Nature Neuroscience, 24*(4), 470–477. https://doi.org/10.1038/s41593-020-00792-3

Bonapersona, V., Kentrop, J., Van Lissa, C. J., Van Der Veen, R., Joels, M., & Sarabdjitsingh, R. A. (2019). The behavioral phenotype of early life adversity: A 3-level meta-analysis of rodent studies. *Neuroscience and Biobehavioral Reviews, 102*, 299–307. https://doi.org/10.1016/j.neubiorev.2019.04.021

Borenstein, M. (2019). *Common Mistakes in Meta-analysis and How to Avoid Them.* Biostat Inc.

Bosmans, G., Bakermans-Kranenburg, M. J., Vervliet, B., Verhees, M. W. F. T., & Van IJzendoorn, M. H. (2020). Learning theory of attachment: Unraveling the black box of attachment development. *Neuroscience and Biobehavioral Reviews, 113*, 287–298. https://doi.org/10.1016/j.neubiorev.2020.03.014

Bosmans, G., Van Vlierberghe, L., Bakermans-Kranenburg, M. J. Kobak, R., Hermans, D., & Van IJzendoorn, M. H. (2022). A learning theory approach to attachment theory: Exploring clinical applications. *Clinical Child Family Psychology Review.* https://doi.org/10.1007/s10567-021-00377-x

Button, K. S., Ioannidis, J. P. A., Mokrysz, C., Nosek, B. A., Flint, J., Robinson, E. S. J., & Munafo', M. R. (2013). Power failure: Why small sample size undermines the reliability of neuroscience. *Nature Reviews Neuroscience, 14*, 365–376. https://doi.org/10.1038/nrn3475

Campbell, D. T. (1960). Blind variation and selective retentions in creative thought as in other knowledge processes. *Psychological Review, 67*(6), 380–400. https://doi.org/10.1037/h0040373

Crone, E. A., Achterberg, M., Dobbelaar, S., Euser, S., Van den Bulk, B., Van der Meulen, M., Van Drunen L., Wierenga, L., Bakermans-Kranenburg, M. J., Van IJzendoorn, M. H. (2020). Neural and behavioral signatures of social evaluation and adaptation in childhood and adolescence: The Leiden Consortium on Individual Development (L-CID). *Developmental Cognitive Neuroscience, 45*, 100805, ISSN 1878–9293, https://doi.org/10.1016/j.dcn.2020.100805.

Day, C. (October 5 2010). Andre Geim and Konstantin Novoselov win 2010 Physics Nobel for graphene. *Physics Today.* https://doi.org/10.1063/PT.4.0866

De Wolff, M. S., & Van IJzendoorn, M. H. (1997). Sensitivity and attachment: A meta-analysis on parental antecedents of infant attachment. *Child Development, 68*(4), 571–591. https://doi.org/10.1111/j.1467-8624.1997.tb04218.x

Dobbelaar, S., Achterberg, M., Van Drunen, L., Van Duijvenvoorde, A. C. K., Van IJzendoorn, M. H., & Crone, E. A. (2022). Development of social feedback processing and responses in childhood: An fMRI test-replication design in two age cohorts. *Social Cognitive and Affective Neuroscience*, nsac039. https://doi.org/10.1093/scan/nsac039

Dobbelaar, S., Achterberg, M., Van Duijvenvoorde, A. C. K., Van IJzendoorn, M. H., & Crone, E. A. (2023). Developmental patterns and individual differences in responding to social feedback: A longitudinal fMRI study from childhood to adolescence. *Developmental Cognitive Neuroscience, 62*, 101264. https://doi.org/10.1016/j.dcn.2023.101264

Duschinsky, R. (2020). *Cornerstones of Attachment Research in the Twenty First Century.* Oxford University Press. https://doi.org/10.1093/med-psych/9780198842064.001.0001

Elliott, M. L., Knodt, A. R., Ireland, D., Morris, M. L., Poulton, R., Ramrakha, S., Sison, M. L., Moffitt, T. E., Caspi, A., & Hariri, A. R. (2020). What is the test-retest reliability of common task-functional MRI measures? New empirical evidence and a meta-analysis. *Psychological Science, 31*(7), 792–806. https://doi.org/10.1177/0956797620916786

Errington, T. M., Mathur, M., Soderberg, C. K., Denis, A., Perfito, N., Iorns, E., & Nosek, B. A. (2021). Investigating the replicability of preclinical cancer biology. *eLife, 10*, e71601. https://doi.org/10.7554/eLife.71601

Euser, S., Bakermans-Kranenburg, M. J., Van den Bulk, B. G., Linting, M., Damsteegt, R. C., Vrijhof, C. I., Van Wijk, I. C., Crone, E. A., & Van IJzendoorn, M. H. (2016). Efficacy of the video-feedback intervention to promote positive parenting and sensitive discipline in twin families (VIPP-Twins): Study protocol for a randomized controlled trial. *BMC Psychology 4*(1), 33. https://doi.org/10.1186/s40359-016-0139-y

Feyerabend P. (1975). *Against Method: Outline of an Anarchistic Theory of Knowledge.* New Left Books. https://doi.org/10.1007/bf02383263

Feyerabend P. (1995). *Killing Time: The Autobiography of Paul Feyerabend.* University of Chicago Press. https://doi.org/10.1086/357492

Gewirtz, J. L., & Boyd, E. F. (1977). Does maternal responding imply reduced infant crying? A critique of the 1972 Bell and Ainsworth report. *Child Development, 48*(4), 1200–1207. https://doi.org/10.2307/1128476

Heckendorf, E., Bakermans-Kranenburg, M. J., Van IJzendoorn, M. H., & Huffmeijer, R. (2019). Neural responses to children's faces: Test-retest reliability of structural and functional MRI. *Brain and Behavior*, e01192. https://doi.org/10.1002/brb3.1192

Hesse, E. (2016). The Adult Attachment Interview: Protocol, method of analysis, and empirical studies: 1985–2015. In J. Cassidy & P. R. Shaver (Eds.), *Handbook of Attachment: Theory, Research, and Clinical Applications* (3rd ed.). The Guilford Press.

Hofhuis, S. (2022). *Qualitative Darwinism: An Evolutionary History of Witch-Hunting*. [Doctoral thesis 1 (Research UU/Graduation UU), Universiteit Utrecht]. Utrecht University. https://doi.org/10.33540/1460

Hubbard, F. O., & Van IJzendoorn, M. H. (1991). Maternal unresponsiveness and infant crying across the first nine months: A naturalistic longitudinal study. *Infant Behavior and Development, 14*(3), 299–312. https://doi.org/10.1016/0163-6383(91)90024-M

Hubbard, F. O. A., & Van IJzendoorn, M. H. (1994). Does maternal unresponsiveness increase infant crying? A critical replication of the 1972 Bell and Ainsworth study. In R. van der Veer, M. H. Van IJzendoorn, & J. Valsiner (Eds.), *On Reconstructing the Mind. Replicability in Research on Human Development* (pp. 255–270). Ablex.

Ioannidis, J. P. A. (2005). Why most published research findings are false. *PLOS Medicine, 2*(8), e124. https://doi.org/10.1371/journal.pmed.0020124

Lakatos, I. (1980). *The Methodology of Scientific Research Programmes. Philosophical Papers* (Volume I). Cambridge University Press.

Madigan, S., Deneault, A. A., Duschinsky, R., Bakermans-Kranenburg, M. J., Schuengel, C., Van IJzendoorn, M. H., Ly, A., Fearon, R. M. P., Eirich, R., & Verhage, M. L. (2024). Maternal and paternal sensitivity: Key determinants of child attachment security examined through meta-analysis. *Psychological Bulletin*.

Main, M., Kaplan, N., & Cassidy, J. (1985). Security in infancy, childhood, and adulthood: A move to the level of representation. In I. Bretherton & E. Waters (Eds.), *Growing Points of Attachment Theory and Research*. Monographs of the Society for Research in Child Development, *50*(1–2, Serial No. 209) (pp. 66–104). https://doi.org/10.2307/3333827

Marek, S., Tervo-Clemmens, B., Calabro, F. J., Montez, D. F., Kay, B. P., Hatoum, A. S., Donohue, M. R., Foran, W., Miller, R. L., Hendrickson, T. J., Malone, S. M., Kandala, S., Feczko, E., Miranda-Dominguez, O., Graham, A. M., Earl, E. A., Perrone, A. J., Cordova, M., Doyle, O., ... Dosenbach, N. U. F. (2022). Reproducible brain-wide association studies require thousands of individuals. *Nature, 603*(7902), 654–660. https://doi.org/10.1038/s41586-022-04492-9.

Meehl, P. E. (1990). Appraising and amending theories: The strategy of Lakatosian defense and two principles that warrant it. *Psychological Inquiry, 1*(2), 108–141. https://doi.org/10.1207/s15327965pli0102_1.

Molendijk, M. L., Bus, B. A. A., Spinhoven, P., Kaimatzoglou, A., Oude Voshaar, R. C., Penninx, B. W. J. H., Van IJzendoorn, M. H., & Elzinga, B. M. (2012) A systematic review and meta-analysis on the association between BDNF val66met and hippocampal volume: A genuine effect or a winner's curse? *American Journal of Medical Genetics Part B: Neuropsychiatric Genetics, 159b*, 731–740. https://doi.org/10.1002/ajmg.b.32078

National Academies of Sciences, Engineering, and Medicine. (2019). *Reproducibility and Replicability in Science*. National Academies Press. https://doi.org/10.17226/25303

Nosek, B. A., Alter, G., Banks, G. C., Borsboom, D., Bowman, S. D., Breckler, S. J., Buck, S., Chambers, C. D., Chin, G., Christensen, G., Contestabile, M., Dafoe, A., Eich, E., Freese, J., Glennerster, R., Goroff, D., Green, D. P., Hesse, B., Humphreys, M., ... Yarkoni, T. (2015). Promoting an open research culture. *Science, 348*(6242), 1422–1425. https://doi.org/10.1126/science.aab2374

Poldrack, R. A. (2018). *The New Mind Readers: What Neuroimaging Can and Cannot Reveal about Our Thoughts*. Princeton University Press. https://doi.org/10.2307/j.ctvc77ds2

Popper, K. (1959). *The Logic of Scientific Discovery*. Routledge. https://doi.org/10.4324/9780203994627

Popper, K. (1978). *Three Worlds*. The Tanner Lecture on Human Values. University of Michigan.

Quine, W. V. (1951). Two dogmas of empiricism. *The Philosophical Review, 60*(1), 20–43. https://doi.org/10.2307/2181906

Riem, M. M. E., Voorthuis, A., Bakermans-Kranenburg, M. J., & Van IJzendoorn, M. H. (2014). Pity or peanuts? Oxytocin induces different neural responses to the same infant crying labeled as sick or bored. *Developmental Science, 17,* 248–256. https://doi.org/10.1111/desc12103

Runze, J., Pappa, I., Van IJzendoorn, M. H., & Bakermans-Kranenburg, M. J. (2022). Conduct problems and hair cortisol concentrations decrease in school-aged children after VIPP-SD: A randomized controlled trial in two twin cohorts. *International Journal of Environmental Research and Public Health, 19*(22), 15026. https://doi.org/10.3390/ijerph192215026

Simmons, J. P., Nelson, L. D., & Simonsohn, U. (2011). False-positive psychology: Undisclosed flexibility in data collection and analysis allows presenting anything as significant. *Psychological Science, 22*(11), 1359–1366. https://doi.org/10.1177/0956797611417632

Simonsohn, U., Nelson, L. D., & Simmons, J. P. (2014). P-curve: A key to the file-drawer. *Journal of Experimental Psychology General, 143*(2), 534–547. https://doi.org/10.1037/a0033242

Van der Meulen, M., Wierenga, L. M., Achterberg, M., Drenth, N., Van IJzendoorn, M. H., & Crone, E. A. (2020). Genetic and environmental influences on structure of the social brain in childhood. *Developmental Cognitive Neuroscience, 45,* 100822. https://doi.org/10.1016/j.dcn.2020.100822

Van IJzendoorn, M. H. (1995). Adult attachment representations, parental responsiveness, and infant attachment: A meta-analysis on the predictive validity of the Adult Attachment Interview. *Psychological Bulletin, 117,* 387–403. https://doi.org/10.1037//0033-2909.117.3.387

Van IJzendoorn, M. H., & Bakermans-Kranenburg, M. J. (2021). Replication crisis lost in translation? On translational caution and premature applications of attachment theory. *Attachment & Human Development, 23,* 422–437. https://doi.org/10.1080/14616734.2021.1918453

Van IJzendoorn, M. H., & Hubbard, F. O. A. (1987). De noodzaak van replicatie-onderzoek naar gehechtheid [The necessity of replication research on attachment]. *Nederlands Tijdschrift voor Psychologie, 42*(3), 291–298.

Van IJzendoorn, M. H., & Hubbard, F. O. A. (2000). Are infant crying and maternal responsiveness during the first year related to infant-mother attachment at 15 months? *Attachment and Human Development, 2,* 386–406. https://doi.org/10.1080/14616730010001596

Verhage, M. L., Schuengel, C., Madigan, S., Fearon, R. M. P., Oosterman, M., Cassibba, R., Bakermans-Kranenburg, M. J., & Van IJzendoorn, M. H. (2016). Narrowing the transmission gap: A synthesis of three decades of research on intergenerational transmission of attachment. *Psychological Bulletin, 142*(4), 337–366. https://doi.org/10.1037/bul0000038

2
A moratorium on self-reports

Quick but dirty questionnaires

Among the most widely used instruments of developmental science are self-report questionnaires. Even behavioural phenomena such as attachment relationships or externalising behaviour problems are often assessed by asking respondents to choose from multiple choice options the best fitting one as if they would have privileged knowledge of themselves or the relationship with their children and would provide unbiased answers.

We and others have conducted a multitude of studies showing a big gap between what people say in response to questionnaires and what they do according to independent observations. Furthermore, questionnaires with absurd items trigger answers that show heritability in our twin studies and in our molecular genetics work. Questionnaires run the risk of producing systematically biased data and inflated results. We keep using such measures because they are easy to complete and to process. Yet, the large amount of data also leads to 'data dredging' and non-replicable chance results.

In cohort studies non-replicability may often be caused by a lavish use of researcher degrees of freedom in big datasets (Simmons, Nelson, & Simonsohn, 2011). When there are a multitude of options for selecting variables and for analytic strategies to process the data, researchers might select those variables and strategies that show the most impressive results. The almost obsessive-compulsive fixation on the magic alpha level of 0.05 also stimulates this dredging the data for significant associations. Although a slow change is visible in recent years, it still is much easier to get a paper accepted for publication when its main result is statistically significant. From our experiences as researchers and mentors it comes as no surprise that anticipating the risk of rejection, researchers are inclined to keep fishing for significant results in large datasets until they accidentally catch one. This is called *p*-hacking and it becomes quite literally visible with a pile of p-values just below the conventional threshold of 0.05. But some 35 years ago, Rosnow and Rosenthal (1989) already speculated that: 'surely, God loves the .06 nearly as much as the .05. Can there be any doubt that God views the strength of evidence for or against the null as a fairly continuous function of the magnitude of p?'

Unfortunately, many principal investigators, PhD advisors, and journal editors still seem to doubt God's statistical wisdom and leave doctoral students desperately looking for significant results that support a favourite hypothesis. They follow the lead of the late Susan Goldberg, attachment researcher, stating with some wry humour: 'I tortured the data but they did not give way'. Maybe Goldberg should have continued her beating around the data bush to get a significant result because other investigators with more persistence were successful. Regarding studies on event-related potentials (ERPs), that is, the measured brain response to a specific sensory, cognitive, or motor event, Luck and Gaspelin (2017) published *'How to get statistically significant effects in any ERP experiment (and why you shouldn't)'* showing numerous arbitrary choices with shifting time windows for ERPs, selective use of electrodes, and inclusion of multiple moderators. With Rens Huffmeijer we demonstrated that validity of ERPs is far from self-evident because a high number of electrodes is critically important for getting reliable results (Huffmeijer et al., 2014).

In behavioural and developmental sciences fishing expeditions might be especially tempting when several quick-but-dirty (self-report) questionnaires are used with arbitrary choices of measures in one and the same study. Even well-established and widely used questionnaires such as the famous Strengths and Difficulties Questionnaire (SDQ; Goodman, 1997) targeting externalising and internalising behaviour problems and prosociality, and cited more than 10,000 times, are invalid at face value. For example, numerous questions have ambiguous content and are probably confusing for respondents: 'I try to be nice to other people. I care about their feelings'. Or: 'I am nervous in new situations. I easily lose confidence'. In a study with Claudia Vrijhof (Vrijhof et al., 2016) we split five SDQ items with double content into ten separate questions and found that the means of the two versions aggregating the separate questions differed half a standard deviation from the original combined questions, with only 20% overlap in variance between the two versions.

The SDQ has nevertheless also been used as a mapping instrument for computation of generic Quality of Life Years or QALYs (see Chapter 8). In health economics the theory and measurement of quality of life took centre stage in recent years (Kwon et al., 2018). The idea is to define and quantify improvement in quality of life due to medical treatments, behavioural interventions, or policy measures, and to compare the revenues of these interventions in terms of one and the same 'currency', the QALYs. In times of scarce resources to be distributed across a large variety of interventions, the ultimate goal is to spend less money on larger QALY gains. But what are larger or smaller gains in quality of life? Health economists provide decision-makers with the tools to make difficult decisions between, for example, spending more money on cancer curation and the treatment of depression. The criteria for what counts as an improvement in QALYs are based on large surveys with brief self-report questionnaires.

One of those measures is the EQ-5D-Y questionnaire with questions about five domains of functioning: mobility; looking after yourself; doing usual activities; having pain or discomfort; and feeling worried, sad, or unhappy. Several EQ-5D-Y questions contain multiple content such as 'Having pain or discomfort' (I have *no, some, a lot* of pain or discomfort), or 'feeling worried, sad or unhappy' (I am *not, a bit, very* worried, sad or unhappy). Ambiguous content such as worry/sadness/unhappiness produces ambiguous answers to each one of the feelings or any combination of two of them, or all of them. In fact, here a pile of seven questions is packed in one. Such nugatory, invalid questionnaires are determining choices between different drugs for cancer treatment or between various parenting coaching programmes to prevent child maltreatment (see Chapter 8 for discussion of other weaknesses of this health economy approach).

Even worse, when child-specific data on a QALY measure are not available, an alternative method currently used to compute QALYs for children is mapping some existing assessment of child functioning such as the SDQ on the EQ-5D-Y or a similar questionnaire (e.g., the CHU-9D, Mukuria, Rowen, Harnan et al., 2019). In a study conducted by Furber et al. (2015), 200 caregivers of Australian children aged 5–17 years receiving mental health services completed the SDQ and the CHU-9D. The CHU-9D utility criteria were determined using a linear multiple regression function based on the five SDQ sub-scales for emotions, conduct, peer relations, prosociality, and hyperactivity (see Van IJzendoorn & Bakermans-Kranenburg, 2020, for details). These sub-scales accounted for about 28% of the variance in CHU-9D scores. While the inclusion of the conduct problems and prosociality sub-scales is a positive aspect of this proxy utility function (see Chapter 8), the small sample size and wide age range of children aged 5–17 years make it difficult to generalise these findings to the broader (clinical or non-clinical) population and use the resulting estimates of QALYs for costly decisions between treatments or interventions. Extending the proxy utility function to children aged 0–5 years would be even more problematic (Shearer et al., 2018).

Ambiguous SDQ questions exacerbate the invalidity of QALY measures with equally ambiguous questions.

Another problem is divergence of self-report and proxy reports. Based on a review of the convergence between self-reported and proxy-reported utilities, Khadka et al. (2019) concluded that there is a significant gap between the ratings of different individuals. For example, in their survey exploring self-report and proxy-report quality-of-life measures for 726 people living with dementia in 50 care homes, Griffiths et al. (2020) found low agreement between patient, staff, and relatives. Most disturbingly, residents reported experiencing higher quality of life than staff or relatives did.

Parents often differ in their description of child problems from children's self-reported problems, and they differ both from staff- and teacher-reported child functioning. Usually, such discrepancies are explained by referring to the different settings in which parents and teachers observe the child's behaviour, while the report of one of the respondents is subsequently used to operationalise the child's problem behaviour in general. In our Generation R team Alex Neumann developed a more sophisticated model for the General P Factor in relation to white matter microstructure by having a separate latent construct for informant-related variance (Neumann et al., 2020). Such an approach, however, is still limited by the input of error-prone questionnaires with ambiguous questions and simplistic response categories.

The same is true for attachment. Attachment security is not defined as being secure or insecure only in the eyes of the beholder. An early study showed no overlap between parental reports of their infants' attachment security and attachment security observed by trained raters in the Strange Situation Procedure (Van Dam & Van IJzendoorn, 1988). After a decade of hard labour with Berkeley colleagues Mary Main and Erik Hesse on a self-report questionnaire assessing adult attachment representations we had to give up. Promising results in the first round were non-replicable in next rounds of robustness tests (Hesse & Van IJzendoorn, 1991; Van IJzendoorn, 1993). The construct of attachment is too complicated to be assessed with self-report questionnaires. The gold standard for measuring adult attachment representations is the Adult Attachment Interview (Main, Kaplan & Cassidy, 1985). The transcript of the interview is coded by trained raters on formal features of the participant's verbal behaviour (see Bakermans-Kranenburg & Van IJzendoorn, 1993; Hesse, 2016). Self-rated and trained coder-rated attachment qualifications diverge drastically (see Roisman et al., 2007, for a meta-analysis).

Several researchers, however, developed a set of self-report items claiming to measure attachment with sufficient internal overlap to show a palatable Cronbach's alpha. But they did not invest much time in testing important psychometrics such as test-retest reliability, convergent and discriminant validity with interview or observational measures, and other pertinent psychometrics. Such questionnaires became hugely popular. The IPPA (Armsden & Greenberg, 1987), for example, was cited almost 7,000 times (Google Scholar, consulted on 12 February 2023). Despite lack of basic psychometrics, numerous self-report questionnaires, often on the same construct and in short form, are used within the same cohort study because their application is cheap and easy. The wide choice in the analysis of questionnaire data, however, elevates the chance of finding false positives, which are easier to publish but undermine the trustworthiness of a research programme and its application to policy or practice. Observational assessments of attachment such as the Strange Situation Procedure (Ainsworth et al., 1978) still leave room for researcher degrees of freedom but they require much more investment in time and other resources to collect and to code than questionnaires. This restricts the multiplication of observational measures in large cohort studies.

Heritability of response bias

It may be considered alarming that respondents' trust in science and scientists is so strong that they are willing to answer any question, even if asked to rate the applicability of nonsense items such as 'I have headaches that are so severe that my feet hurt'. With Nhu Tran we were surprised to see that in her sample of 2,342 Vietnamese adolescents about 25% responded affirmatively to this nonsensical item (Tran et al., 2017). In a study with Jana Runze on 8-year-old Dutch twin children we found a similar bias to respond to a set of Wildman-type (Wildman & Wildman, 1999) quaint questions ('When I am stressed, I can feel it in my feet') as if the content was reasonable. Importantly, we found that the bias to support nonsensical content is heritable according to the classic ACE modelling of behavioural genetics research. In the parents, using a child-based twin design, the heritability was estimated to be 76% (see Runze & Van IJzendoorn, 2023). In the regular twin design monozygotic twins, sharing 100% of their genome, responded more similarly to nonsensical questions (correlation $r = 0.52$) than did dizygotic twins (with a correlation of $r = 0.17$), who share on average only 50% of their genes. Additive (A) heritability was estimated to be 44% with unique environmental

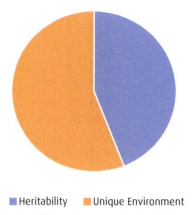

Figure 2.1 Twin heritability of nonsensical Wildman items. In 8-year-old Dutch twin children we found substantial heritability of the bias to respond to nonsensical questions.

influences or error (E) explaining the rest of the variance – see Figure 2.1 (Runze & Van IJzendoorn, 2023).

In addition to ACE modelling, we also applied a molecular genetics approach based on polygenic scores in the same sample, also involving the parents of the twins. Polygenic scores are increasingly being used in developmental and clinical research to predict an individual's genetic predisposition for a wide range of complex traits and diseases, including height, academic achievement, depression, or cardiovascular disease risk (see Chapter 9). A polygenic score is a statistical measure that combines the (regression) effects of multiple genetic variants (single nucleotide polymorphisms, SNPs) on a particular trait or disease. These genetic variants may each have tiny individual effects, but combined in an aggregated polygenic score, they may explain a substantial part of the variance in a trait or disease risk. Beta weights for polygenic scores have been published in large-scale genome-wide association studies (GWAS) with sufficient statistical power to identify SNPs that are associated with a particular trait or disease risk.

From these GWASs we derived the weights for polygenic scores of educational attainment, IQ, and family income, and we computed the polygenic scores for each of our study participants, parents, and children, based on the analysis of their DNA extracted from saliva. The three polygenic scores correlated substantially with each other, so a latent variable 'EDINQ' was constructed. In a structural equation model, we examined the association between this polygenetic latent variable of the parents and the children on the one hand and the response to the nonsensical Wildman-type questions on the other hand. We found that higher scores on the polygenetic EDINQ component predicted lower scores on the nonsensical items, with effect sizes ranging from –0.22 to –0.37. Polygenic scores for educational attainment and income were particularly predictive of the variance in Wildman responses. The polygenic score for IQ did not contribute much to explaining the variance (Runze & Van IJzendoorn, 2023). The results suggest a polygenetic basis (primarily related to educational attainment and family income) for an acquiescence response bias that might elicit agreeable answers to ambiguous items.

Not only do nonsense questions reveal response biases, but individuals are even inclined to respond in a systematically biased way to answers without questions (see Figure 2.2), with a preference for 'yes' instead of 'no', 'sometimes' instead of 'always' or 'never', or 'agree' instead of 'indifferent' or 'disagree' (Van IJzendoorn, 1984). If one is opposed to the ever-increasing number of university staff in public relation offices one would better ask, 'Should the number of university staff in public relation offices be reduced? Agree or Disagree' than 'Should the number of university staff in public relation offices be increased? Agree or Disagree'. Commercial public opinion polls know how to make use of such response biases. Support

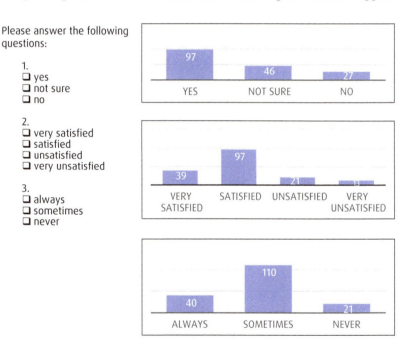

Figure 2.2 Response bias emerging in a questionnaire without questions.
Source: Authors.

for affirmative action in the USA was found in 62% of respondents in a 2021 Gallup poll, whereas a Pew Research Center 2022 poll estimated that 74% of Americans voted *against* affirmative action in college admissions. Context, framing, and sampling may create large differences.

As a consequence, any GWAS of complex psychological or psychiatric traits measured with questionnaires should consider such heritable bias as a potential confounder. GWAS research on complex psychiatric or psychological traits is notorious for the use of self-report questionnaires for the phenotypes and nevertheless harvests plenty of publicity with such overly simplistic phenotyping. A recent example was the publicity about the heritability of happiness (Ward et al., 2022). More than 100,000 participants from the UK Biobank were asked one single question: 'In general, how happy are you?' Response options ranged from extremely happy to extremely unhappy. SNP heritability, that is, the variance attributed to genetic factors computed by comparing the similarity in genotype with the similarity in phenotype in a large sample, amounted to 0.8%, which was sufficient for numerous happy headlines in major newspapers (Ward et al., 2022). Single-item measures are, however, notoriously unreliable because even the built-in replication of a multiple-item instrument is lacking in such measures (Prince et al., 2020).

One of the reasons for the almost endemic use of questionnaires with dubious validity as proxies for behaviour is the need for large samples to detect the tiny genetic signals in millions of data points. GWAS research is exemplary for its emphasis on statistical power, correction for multiple testing, and stringent replication criteria, but the balance between detailed genotyping and superficial, sloppy phenotyping got worse in the process of massification of the studies. Harmonising phenotypic measures across many cohorts in large consortia like Eagle or PACE (Felix et al., 2018) often results in choosing the least common multiple, that is, the few items shared across various cohorts. Alternatively, one resorts to combining cohort results meta-analytically with the risk that the largest cohorts with often the weakest measures dominate.

Primatologist Frans de Waal is outspoken about the use of questionnaires in developmental and behavioural research: 'The study of human psychology usually relies on the use of questionnaires which are heavy on self-reported feelings and light on actual behaviour. But I favor the reverse. We need more observations of actual human social affairs' (De Waal, 2022, see also De Waal, 2019). One of the *Trio of Concerns* Jerome Kagan addressed at the end of his productive career as a researcher of the biological underpinnings of child inhibition had to do with questionnaires: 'Because the questionnaire data are too crude an index of the psychological correlates of a genetic feature, biochemical profile, or brain state, this strategy is unlikely to reveal strong relations between the biological and psychological measures. This asymmetry in the sensitivity of the two measures is analogous to using an atomic clock to determine if a person is walking 'very slowly, slowly, moderately fast, or very fast'. Self-report questionnaires about complex psychological traits should be avoided. For it is true what Friedrich Nietzsche (1887) more than a century ago pointedly wrote in *On the Genealogy of Morals*: 'we are personally ignorant about ourselves', which is of course the very reason why we need developmental science to make sense of our emerging selves in social context. Our field of inquiry, targeting our mental life, deserves better, even if it takes as much resources as a James Webb telescope to explore extra-terrestrial life. It is time to announce a moratorium on the use of questionnaires in serious developmental research and leave its (mis-)use to public opinion polls.

References

Armsden, G. C., & Greenberg, M. T. (1987). The inventory of parent and peer attachment: Individual differences and their relationship to psychological well-being in adolescence. *Journal of Youth & Adolescence, 16*, 427–454. https://doi.org/10.1007/BF02202939

Bakermans-Kranenburg, M. J., & Van IJzendoorn, M. H. (1993). A psychometric study of the Adult Attachment Interview: Reliability and discriminant validity. *Developmental Psychology, 29*, 870–880. https://doi.org/10.1037//0012-1649.29.5.870

De Waal, F. B. M. (2019). *Mama's Last Hug: Animal Emotions and What They Tell Us about Ourselves*. W. W. Norton & Company. https://doi.org/10.1215/0961754x-8723129

De Waal, F. B. M. (2022). *Different: Gender through the Eyes of a Primatologist*. W. W. Norton & Company. https://doi.org/10.1126/science.abo1569

Felix, J., Joubert, B., Baccarelli, A., et al. (2018). Cohort profile: Pregnancy and Childhood Epigenetics (PACE) Consortium. *International Journal of Epidemiology, 47*(1), 22–23u. https://doi.org/10.1093/ije/dyx190

Furber, G., Segal, L., Leach, M., et al. (2015). Preventing mental illness: Closing the evidence-practice gap through workforce and services planning. *BMC Health Services Research, 15*, 283. https://doi.org/10.1186/s12913-015-0954-5

Goodman R (1997) The Strengths and Difficulties Questionnaire: A research note. *Journal of Child Psychology and Psychiatry, 38*, 581–586.

Griffiths, A. W., Smith, S. J., Martin, A., Meads, D., Kelley, R., & Surr, C. A. (2020). Exploring self-report and proxy-report quality-of-life measures for people living with dementia in care homes. *Quality of Life Research: An International Journal of Quality of Life Aspects of Treatment, Care and Rehabilitation, 29*(2), 463–472. https://doi.org/10.1007/s11136-019-02333-3

Hesse, E. (2016). The Adult Attachment Interview: Protocol, method of analysis, and empirical studies: 1985–2015. In J. Cassidy & P. R. Shaver (Eds.), *Handbook of Attachment: Theory, Research, and Clinical Applications* (3rd ed.). The Guilford Press.

Hesse, E., & Van IJzendoorn, M. H. (April 17–20, 1991). Developing the Berkeley-Leiden Adult Attachment Questionnaire (BLAAQ). Poster presented at the Biennial Meeting of the Society for Research in Child Development, Seattle, WA.

Huffmeijer, R., Bakermans-Kranenburg, M. J., Alink, L. R. A., & Van IJzendoorn, M. H. (2014). Reliability of event-related potentials: The influence of number of trials and electrodes. *Physiology & Behavior, 130*, 13–22. https://doi.org/10.1016/j.physbeh.2014.03.008

Khadka, J., Lang, C., Ratcliffe, J., Corlis, M., & Vagenas, D. (2019). Trends in the utilisation of aged care services in Australia, 2008–2016. *BMC Geriatrics, 19*, 213. https://doi.org/10.1186/s12877-019-1209-9.

Kwon, J., Kim, S. W., Ungar, W. J., Tsiplova, K., Madan, J., & Petrou, S. (2018). Systematic review and meta-analysis of childhood health utilities. *Medical Decision Making, 38*(3), 277–305. https://doi.org/10.1177/0272989x17732990

Luck, S. J., & Gaspelin, N. (2017). How to get statistically significant effects in any ERP experiment (and why you shouldn't). *Psychophysiology, 54*, 146–157. https://doi.org/10.1111/psyp.12639

Main, M., Kaplan, N., & Cassidy, J. (1985). Security in infancy, childhood, and adulthood: A move to the level of representation. *Monographs of the Society for Research in Child Development, 50*(1/2), 66–104. https://doi.org/10.2307/3333827

Mukuria, C., Rowen, D., Harnan, S., Rawdin, A., Wong, R., Ara, R., & Brazier, J. (2019). An updated systematic review of studies mapping (or cross-walking) measures of health-related quality of life to generic preference-based measures to generate utility values. *Applied Health Economics and Health Policy, 17*(3), 295–313. https://doi.org/10.1007/s40258-019-00467-6.

Neumann, A., Muetzel, R. L., Lahey, B. B., Bakermans-Kranenburg, M. J., Van IJzendoorn, M. H., Jaddoe, V. W., Hilligers, M. H. J., White, T., & Tiemeier, H. (2020). White matter microstructure and the General Psychopathology Factor in children. *Journal of the American Academy of Child and Adolescent Psychiatry*. DOI: 10.1016/j.jaac.2019.12.006

Nietzsche, F. (1887). *On the Genealogy of Morals* (W. Kaufmann & R. J. Hollingdale, Translation). Vintage Books.

Prince, S. A., Cardilli, L., Reed, J. L., et al. (2020). A comparison of self-reported and device measured sedentary behaviour in adults: A systematic review and meta-analysis. *International Journal of Behavioral Nutrition and Physical Activity, 17*, 31. https://doi.org/10.1186/s12966-020-00938-3.

Roisman, G. I., Holland, A., Fortuna, K., Fraley, R. C., Clausell, E., & Clarke, A. (2007). The Adult Attachment Interview and self-reports of attachment style: An empirical rapprochement. *Journal of Personality and Social Psychology, 92*(4), 678–697. https://doi.org/10.1037/0022-3514.92.4.678

Rosnow, R. L., & Rosenthal, R. (1989). Statistical procedures and the justification of knowledge in psychological science. *American Psychologist, 44*(10), 1276–1284. https://doi.org/10.1037/0003-066X.44.10.1276

Runze, J., & Van IJzendoorn, M. H. (2023). Response bias is genetically biased: Another argument for Kagan's philippic against questionnaires in developmental psychology. *Developmental Psychology*. https://dx.doi.org/10.1037/dev0001614

Shearer, J., Papanikolaou, N., Meiser-Stedmann, R., McKinnon, A., Dalgleish, T., Smith, P., & Byford, S. (2018). Cost-effectiveness of cognitive therapy as an early intervention for posttraumatic stress disorder in children and adolescents: A trial-based evaluation and model. *Journal of Child Psychology and Psychiatry, 59*, 773–780.

Simmons, J. P., Nelson, L. D., & Simonsohn, U. (2011). False-positive psychology: Undisclosed flexibility in data collection and analysis allows presenting anything as significant. *Psychological Science, 22*(11), 1359–1366. https://doi.org/10.1177/0956797611417632

Tran, N. K., Van Berkel, S. R., Van IJzendoorn, M. H., & Alink, L. R. A. (2017). The association between child maltreatment and emotional, cognitive, and physical health functioning in Vietnam. *BMC Public Health, 17*. https://doi.org/10.1186/s12889-017-4258-z

Van Dam, M., & Van IJzendoorn, M. H. (1988). Measuring attachment security: Concurrent and predictive validity of the parental attachment Q-set. *Journal of Genetic Psychology, 149*, 447–457. https://doi.org/10.1080/00221325.1988.10532172

Van IJzendoorn, M. H. (1984). Answers without questions. A note on response style in questionnaires. *Perceptual and Motor Skills, 59*, 827–831. https://doi.org/10.2466/pms.1984.59.3.827

Van IJzendoorn, M. H. (1993, March). The BLAAQ Inventory for assessing attachment organization in Dutch and US samples: Reliability, stability, and convergent validity. Paper presented at the symposium on 'Adolescent attachment organization: Findings from the BLAAQ self-report inventory, and relations to absorption and dissociation' (Chair: M. Main). 60th Anniversary Meeting of the Society for Research in Child Development, New Orleans, Louisiana, p. 140.

Van IJzendoorn, M. H., & Bakermans-Kranenburg, M. J. (2020). Problematic cost–utility analysis of interventions for behavior problems in children and adolescents. *New Directions for Child and Adolescent Development*, 89–102. https://doi.org/10.1002/cad.20360

Vrijhof, C. I., Van den Bulk, B. G., Overgaauw, S., Lelieveld, G.-J., Engels, R. C. M. E., & Van IJzendoorn, M. H. (2016). The Prosocial Cyberball Game: Compensating for social exclusion and its associations with empathic concern and bullying in adolescents. *Journal of Adolescence*, *52*, 27–36. https://doi.org/10.1016/j.adolescence.2016.07.005

Ward, J., Lyall, L., Cullen, B., Strawbridge, R. J., Zhu, X., Stanciu, I., Aman, A., Niedzwiedz, C. L., Anderson, J., Bailey, M. E. S., Lyall, D. M., & Pell, J. (2022). The genetics of happiness: Consistent effects across the lifespan and ancestries in multiple cohorts. *European Neuropsychopharmacology, 63,* e282 https://doi.org/10.1016/j.euroneuro.2022.07.501

Wildman, R. W., & Wildman, R. W. (1999). The detection of malingering. *Psychological Reports, 84*, 386–388. https://doi.org/10.2466/pr0.1999.84.2.386

3
Meta-analyses searching for replicated evidence

Reproducibility and replicability

What could be done to solve the replication crisis and pave the way for responsible translation to policy and practice? The National Academy of Sciences, Engineering, and Medicine (NAS) published an e-book titled *Reproducibility and Replicability in Science* (2019, free access), in which a helpful differentiation between reproducibility and replicability was proposed. Reproducibility was defined as obtaining consistent results using the same input data, computational steps, methods, and code, and conditions of analysis. Replicability was described as obtaining consistent results across studies aimed at answering the same scientific question, each of which has obtained its own data.

For reproducibility it is critical to have publicly available datasets and codes or syntax of published papers to enable independent researchers to try and reproduce the reported findings. This seems a superfluous step because it is self-evident that analytic procedures must reproduce, but in a 1994 chapter on replicability one of us already argued for the need to test reproducibility of primary studies as a secondary analysis of the original dataset (Van IJzendoorn, 1994). Unfortunately, the same dataset may lead to very different 'findings'. Botvinik-Nezer et al. (2020) asked 70 independent teams to analyse the same raw fMRI dataset and test nine *a priori* hypotheses. Analytic approaches diverged in almost all cases and conclusions about the truth-value of the hypotheses differed substantially. Other disappointing replications of such non-reproducibility have also been reported, for example, in the multi-lab reproducibility study on the facial feedback hypothesis by the Many Smiles Collaboration (Coles et al., 2022).

The bright spot of the deplorable reproducibility results that Botvinik-Nezer et al. (2020) revealed was the convergence of the image-based meta-analysis across all team results, despite the large variation between the results of the individual teams. The NAS authors suggest that meta-analysis is an important tool to help solve the reproducibility and replication crisis (NAS, 2019), and we agree wholeheartedly with this recommendation. In his inaugural lecture 40 years ago, Marinus called for a more quantitative instead of a subjective narrative synthesis of developmental research with help of replicable meta-analytic methods (Van IJzendoorn, 1983, p. 26). Given the abundance of empirical research in most research areas, it was argued that the task of critical analysis and integration had to be carried out more methodically than was usually the case. Widely cited 'state-of-the-art' reviews were often non-replicable subjective interpretations of a researcher's personal impressions of a large number of research reports with diverging results. An emerging trend towards formalising literature reviews was noted, labelled 'meta-analysis', showing that quantitative procedures for integrating empirical results often give a more realistic and at least more reproducible image of the literature than the traditional approach (Glass et al., 1981).

Here we define a meta-analysis as the three-step identification of (i) an overall quantitative summary of the effect sizes of a set of empirical studies in the same field of inquiry, (ii) the variation around this estimate of an overall outcome, and (iii) the explanation of this variation using study characteristics as moderators (Van IJzendoorn et al., 2011). Any meta-analysis should examine the robustness of its results by testing the influence of outlying studies and unpublished research, and whether the quality

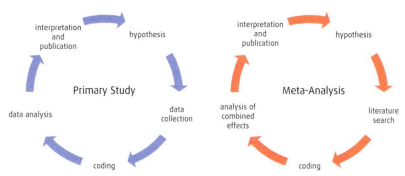

Figure 3.1 The stages in primary empirical studies and in meta-analyses are largely overlapping, with similar requirements for reproducibility.
Source: Authors.

of the primary studies is associated with the size of the effects. In essence, the process model of meta-analysis is very similar to that of primary studies, with the main difference in the phase of data collection. The phase of recruitment and observation of participants in primary studies is replaced by literature search and screening in meta-analysis (see Figure 3.1).

Development of meta-analysis

Narrative reviewers are more likely to make type II errors (i.e., failing to reject a null hypothesis despite being false). In a pioneering study by Rosenthal (1991), 41 graduate students and senior researchers were asked to review a set of 7 studies examining the relation between sex and persistence in completing tedious tasks. Half of the reviewers were randomly assigned to a course on meta-analysis. Of the narrative reviewers without training 73% found no association, while only 32% of the meta-analysts reached this conclusion. The correct conclusion was that women were significantly more persistent in completing boring tasks than men. Specifically, when studies show nonsignificant trends, the overall effect size across these studies tends to be underestimated (for another example, see Bushman & Wells, 2001).

Despite this superiority of meta-analysis, it took quite some time for the quantitative approach to become popular. At the beginning of the last century Karl Pearson (1904) reported already on one of the first known meta-analyses of four studies on typhus vaccinations, but only by the end of that century did the approach become part of the so-called evidence-based medical science. It was the educational researcher Glass (1976) who introduced the term 'meta-analysis', and with Smith he conducted one of the most controversial meta-analytic studies ever on 375 psychotherapy studies concluding that no specific treatment was superior, but all had substantial positive effects (Smith & Glass, 1977). Psychoanalytic psychotherapy, for example, seemed equally effective as cognitive behaviour therapy and level of training of therapists did not matter, illustrating the Dodo Bird verdict: 'Everybody has won, and all must have prizes' (Carroll, 1893). Notably, this result seems to stand the test of time (e.g., Van Os et al., 2019).

One of the first meta-analyses on attachment examined cross-cultural patterns of attachment and found that intra-country differences in attachment distributions were larger than between-country distributions (Van IJzendoorn & Kroonenberg, 1988). This counter-intuitive finding triggered a heated debate on the cross-cultural validity of the

Strange Situation Procedure that is still ongoing (Madigan et al., 2023; see Chapter 11). Soon more meta-analyses on attachment-related studies followed, a majority of which were conducted by our research team (Schuengel et al., 2021). Attachment research lends itself to meta-analyses because of the use of a strong theoretical framework rooted in established evolutionary theory, a core set of constructs and hypotheses, and standard measures of central variables like attachment and parental sensitive responsiveness. This creates more homogeneity in study designs than in most other developmental areas. In fact, for those reasons attachment can be considered a Lakatosian research programme (Van IJzendoorn & Tavecchio, 1987).

Attachment research as a Lakatosian research programme

Attachment theory can be broadly characterised as a research programme in the sense of Lakatos (1978) because of two main features. First, attachment researchers share a core set of fundamental principles that form the basis for their empirical investigations. A key component is the idea that attachment is the result of an innate, evolution-based bias in newborns to seek proximity to a protective conspecific. Second, the research programme places a strong emphasis on detailed protocolised and generally accepted ways of measuring key concepts, such as attachment and sensitivity. These concepts are most often assessed through observations of verbal and non-verbal interactive behaviour that indicate the quality of relationships or their cognitive representation in terms of a secure base.

In Table 3.1, we present the five stages and four levels within these stages of attachment theory as a Lakatosian research programme. Attachment researchers have sometimes been called the 'attachment mafia' which is a pejorative label for a scientific community that has organised itself in a (quasi-secret) society, i.e., the Society for Emotion regulation and Attachment Studies (SEAS), with a biennial conference (International Attachment Conference, IAC), a journal (*Attachment & Human Development*), a *Handbook of Attachment*, and some consensus statements uniting many attachment researchers (Forslund et al., 2022; Granqvist et al., 2017).

Such communicative platforms strengthen social bonds between researchers but also codify what is counted as attachment and as acceptable attachment measures. At its start, any research programme is vulnerable to attacks from competing programmes. In the case of attachment theory, one may think of the clashes between attachment and

Table 3.1 Stages in the development of attachment theory as a Lakatosian research programme. A revival can be noted in the last decade with an emphasis on interdisciplinarity, collaboration, and transparency. (Adapted from Van IJzendoorn & Bakermans-Kranenburg, 2021)

Level	Formulation	Construction	Saturation	Exhaustion	Alternative
Content	Theoretical framework (Bowlby, 1969)	Normal science Empirical research (Ainsworth et al., 1978)	Diminishing returns Meta-analytic convergence (De Wolff & Van IJzendoorn, 1997)	Cumulation of anomalies, replication crisis (Verhage et al., 2016)	Attachment Theory 2.0: Move to level of context, integration of learning theory (Bosmans et al., 2020)
Methodology	Speculative, programmatic	Context of discovery, exploratory research (Sroufe et al., 2005)	Context of justification, hypothesis testing	Protective belt, auxiliary hypotheses	Absorption of old theory into a broader interdisciplinary framework
Communication	Almost absent	Informal (papers in general journals & symposia at general conferences) (CD, SRCD)	Formal exchange in societies, special conferences, journals (SEAS, IAC, AHD)	Organised in research institutes and handbook syntheses	Open science, cooperation in global consortia and IPD (CATS/ CARS)
Policy/Practice	Heuristic practice ↔ theory	Data source practice → theory	Application practice ← theory	Integration practice ↔ theory	Heuristic 2.0 practice ↔ theory

temperament theories, or between attachment theory and conditioning paradigms. Within the various platforms for debates (societies, conferences, journals) the 'protective belt' of auxiliary hypotheses is discussed. This aims at saving the core propositions from refutation and premature abandonment and fortifies the theory before entering the wider scientific forum (e.g., Padron et al., 2014). In this respect the social organisation of attachment researchers is not unique in the domain of developmental science. It would only deserve a bad reputation as a mafia if there was no room for criticism and new developments.

We notice, however, that after more than 30 years a fifth stage with new and exciting developments seems to emerge (e.g., Schuengel et al., 2021), with emphasis on even more interdisciplinarity than in the past, on open science and transparency, and on global cooperation in response to the replication crisis and the call for larger samples and collaboration in consortia (e.g., CATS, Verhage et al., 2016; and CASCADE, Madigan et al., 2023). These developments illustrate the openness to new approaches and the absence of dogmatic resistance against modification. New (neurobiological) methods such as molecular genetics and imaging are welcomed, and other evolutionary theories such as life history theory and differential susceptibility models have been integrated. Temperamental differences between children are acknowledged as shedding light on differential effects of parenting and parenting interventions on attachment development (Van IJzendoorn & Bakermans-Kranenburg, 2015) despite the controversy between attachment and temperament theories in the last quarter of the previous century (Sroufe, 1985; Kagan, 1984; Fox, 1995; Van IJzendoorn, 1995b). Even conditioning theories are now introduced and combined with attachment theory in a more fine-grained theory of the emergence of internal working models and scripts (Bosmans et al., 2020; 2022).

The roles of meta-analysis in a research programme

Meta-analyses fulfil different roles depending on the stage of the research programme. In the first stage of attachment research, meta-analyses produced outstanding questions and hypotheses to be tested in further, more detailed and focused empirical studies. An example is the meta-analysis identifying a gap between the transmission of attachment from parents to their children when only parental sensitivity is taken into account (Van IJzendoorn, 1995a; Van IJzendoorn & Bakermans-Kranenburg, 2019). We labelled this the so-called *'transmission gap'* that over time has become smaller, perhaps due to better designs and measurements in more recent studies. The meta-analytic finding of a quantified gap triggered numerous empirical studies on factors that might bridge this gap by measuring other dimensions of parenting or the wider social contexts (see Verhage et al., 2016; 2020).

At the end of a research programme, meta-analysis may show that an originally promising result after several attempts does not replicate and should be considered a dead-end. In a pioneering study on the role of the oxytocin receptor genotype in determining level of sensitive parenting we found that parents with the AA or AG variant of the oxytocin receptor gene OXTR rs53576 showed lower levels of sensitive responsiveness to their toddlers than the non-carriers of these variants (Bakermans-Kranenburg & Van IJzendoorn, 2008). Studies on candidate genes were within reach of research groups and studies on oxytocin were 'hot', which resulted in a substantial number of studies on the oxytocin receptor gene in social, personality, and parenting research in less than a decade. Six years later we conducted a meta-analysis on the effects of the two most popular SNPs of the OXTR gene, rs 53576 and rs 2254298 (with combined sample sizes of 17,559 and 13,547, respectively) on social responsiveness in various domains of human functioning (Bakermans-Kranenburg & Van IJzendoorn, 2014). We failed to find effect sizes significantly different from zero for both genotypes. Our initial finding was a so-called 'winner's curse', with results that could not be replicated in later work. The time was ripe for another approach, away from single genes to genome-wide analyses and polygenic scores, that are based on many genes and summarise an individual's genetic liability to a particular trait.

A cumulative meta-analysis, adding new study outcomes every year, might detect at an early stage when a line of research is saturated and should lead to a change of course. Our meta-analysis on BDNF with effect sizes of underpowered studies converging closer to zero with each replication attempt is an example of such a cumulative meta-analysis (Molendijk et al., 2012). Cumulative meta-analysis might save lots of material and human resources if it flags at an early stage exhaustion of the possibilities to make an originally promising hypothesis work.

Meta-analyses, IPD, and umbrella syntheses

As defined at the beginning of this chapter, a meta-analysis is basically a three-step identification of (i) an overall quantitative summary of the effect sizes of a set of empirical studies; (ii) the variation around this estimate; and, maybe most importantly, (iii) the explanation of this variation using study characteristics as moderators (Van IJzendoorn et al., 2011). Meta-analyses differ from systematically conducted narrative reviews only in the data-analytic stage, in which study outcomes are quantified and weighted according to the size of the sample, a proxy for the precision of the estimate.

Even more powerful than the conventional meta-analysis is the Individual Participant Data (IPD) meta-analysis, in which the raw data of several studies are combined after harmonisation of variables that are assessed in the relevant studies (Verhage et al., 2018; 2020). The advantage of an IPD meta-analysis is the increase in power because meta-analytic study-level variables such as age can be included for each participant in all studies separately rather than the mean age in a specific sample, empowering moderator analyses. Multilevel modelling makes it possible to examine study- and participant-level variables predicting an outcome simultaneously (see Roisman & Van IJzendoorn, 2018). In an IPD meta-analysis we found that the transmission of attachment from parents to their children was weakened by ecological constraints such as very low education, single parenthood, or adolescent parenthood (Verhage et al., 2018). It should be noted that the number of studies included in an IPD meta-analysis will usually be smaller than those included in a regular meta-analysis, due to difficulties in getting access to data and in harmonising variables on the individual participant level. However, it is possible to include study-level statistics in a hybrid sort of IPD to enhance its power (Riley, Tierney, & Stewart, 2021).

At the highest level, the umbrella synthesis approach might be used to analyse and integrate multiple meta-analyses on a specific topic (Ioannidis, 2009). This involves systematically collecting and evaluating meta-analytic results using a uniform approach for comparison. The approach leads to estimates of effect sizes across several meta-analyses, an evaluation of heterogeneity and potential biases, a systematic stratification of evidence, and sensitivity analyses to identify reporting biases (Fusar-Poli & Radua, 2018). The quality of published meta-analyses is systematically assessed, taking into account factors such as the completeness and transparency of the search strategy, number of studies, coding procedures and intercoder agreements, and tests for publication bias.

The goal of this approach is to create the best possible evidence base for further research on gaps in a specific research domain, potential applications for clinical practice, or translation to policy. Our first umbrella synthesis focused on the large meta-analytic literature on precursors of child maltreatment and (preventive) maltreatment interventions (Van IJzendoorn et al., 2020). With the umbrella synthesis of thousands of studies on almost 1.5 million participants we were able to quantify the associations of maltreatment with the following risk factors: parental experience of maltreatment in his or her own childhood ($d = 0.47$), low socioeconomic status of the family ($d = 0.34$), dependent and aggressive parental personality ($d = 0.45$), intimate partner violence ($d = 0.41$), and higher baseline autonomic nervous system activity ($d = 0.24$). Interventions to prevent or reduce child maltreatment were not very effective ($d = 0.27$ for diagnosed maltreatment cases). A second umbrella synthesis on child maltreatment led by Barry Coughlan focused on mental health sequelae of maltreatment in more than 11 million participants (Coughlan et al., 2022). Surprisingly, we identified comparable associations for different forms of maltreatment, suggesting common mechanisms linking various types of maltreatment across the measured spectrum of mental ill health.

A process model of research programmes

In our process model of primary studies, replications, meta-analyses, and umbrella syntheses, no single empirical study would play a crucial role in changing the course of a research programme or in translating scientific findings to policy or practice. The reason is that a single study implements only one of the many possible sampling procedures, operationalisations, times of assessments, and types of statistical analyses and produces only one of the many possible effect estimates, each of which has large confidence intervals (Hamaker et al., 2020; Van IJzendoorn, 2019).

For example, Wadhwa and Cook (2019) discussed the assumptions of randomised controlled trials inherent to the combination of units, outcomes, settings, and historical times ('*utosti*'). They argued that the traditional focus on randomising only participants and neglecting the randomisation of experimental stimuli, settings, and times may have contributed to the current replication crisis and the numerous disappointing replication efforts (Klein et al., 2014; Open Science Collaboration, 2015; see Chapter 1). Every single random sample of respondents is only one potential representation of the population, but statistical theory relies on the assumption that numerous randomly drawn samples will converge on an unbiased representation of the population. The same is true for questionnaire and test items and the number and time points of assessments that never are drawn from a universe of possible 'utosti' combinations (see also Van IJzendoorn & Van der Veer, 1983 on similar critical

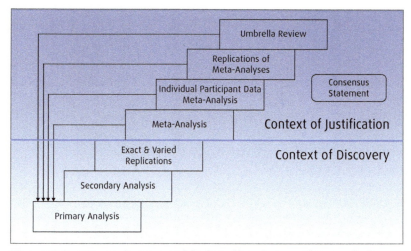

Figure 3.2 From primary empirical studies via secondary analysis and replications in the context of discovery to umbrella synthesis of meta-analyses and individual participant data meta-analysis in the context of justification.
Source: Authors.

analyses of experimental research by Klaus Holzkamp). The multiverse of analytic approaches to test the same hypothesis has only recently come to the fore and is increasingly studied and applied (Steegen et al., 2016).

If single empirical studies are insufficient for progress in science or practice, the replicable synthesis of numerous studies addressing the same hypothesis in different utosti configurations would be critical. This is illustrated in our process model of a cumulative research programme; see Figure 3.2. This model starts with primary studies, followed by secondary analysis (similar to checking the reproducibility) and exact and varied replications in a next step. This first stage is in Karl Popper's (1959) philosophy of science, the so-called context of discovery or the stage of producing numerous bold conjectures. In the next stage, called the 'context of justification', meta-analytic synthesis of the various replication studies takes place, searching for commonalities as well as differences between the studies that point to systematic moderators.

Because meta-analyses are also based on a variety of analytic choices (as Lytton, 1994, elegantly demonstrated) replications of meta-studies would be important, and because meta-analyses might not always have sufficient statistical power for moderator analyses, Individual Participant Data (IPD) meta-analysis may be required (Roisman & Van IJzendoorn, 2018; Verhage et al., 2020; Riley et al., 2021). Meta-analyses might lead to the need for testing auxiliary hypotheses that save some core hypotheses of a research programme, and IPDs may be better fitted to this task because of their increased power for moderation and related analyses. Ultimately, in the updated version of the process model of replications (Van IJzendoorn & Bakermans-Kranenburg, 2021) an umbrella synthesis might uncover the common denominator of thousands of studies including hundreds of thousands of participants (for example, on sequelae of child maltreatment, see Coughlan et al., 2022) and lead to justifiable translation to policy or practice if cost-benefit and ethical considerations have been taken into account (see Chapters 7 and 8).

Although meta-analyses are conducted to find the best evidence in an active field of research, they still are dependent on quality of the primary studies. Garbage In, Garbage Out only produces GIGO bytes of information. Careful quality ratings of primary studies are therefore necessary, and a special focus on the best primary studies in interpreting meta-analytic results is advisable (Simonsohn et al., 2022; see Chapter 5 for an example of our institutionalisation meta-analysis, Van IJzendoorn et al., 2020). However, a major problem with *a priori* excluding 'bad' studies is the problem of determining which studies are below par. An experiment with independent evaluations of research designs proposed by NIH R01 grant proposals showed that 10 or more reviewers would be required to have modest interrater agreement (Forscher et al., 2019). In our experience meta-analyses that start out being inclusive and cast a wide net searching for primary studies deliver the most robust and replicable evidence base. Moderator analysis can be used to test whether the quality of studies is related to effect size.

As an example, in our meta-analysis of attachment-based parenting interventions we included both randomised controlled studies and studies with weaker designs (such as quasi-experimental studies and studies without a control group). We found that the combined effect size for randomised controlled studies ($d = 0.36$) was significantly smaller than the combined effect size for studies with weaker designs ($d = 0.61$). By including studies with various designs, we showed meta-analytically that non-randomised designs produce inflated effect sizes for intervention efficacy (Bakermans-Kranenburg et al., 2003).

The availability of pertinent studies is another threat to the conclusion validity of meta-analyses. The 'file drawer' with studies that remain unpublished because their null results are less attractive for publication potentially inflates meta-analytic outcomes. But statistical methods to estimate its influence are becoming more and more sophisticated (Carter et al., 2019). Pre-registration of study designs and a lower bonus on statistical significance of results will also help in getting more valid meta-analytic findings (Lakens et al., 2016). Unpublished dissertations tend to show smaller effect sizes than similar studies in the same area (Rosenthal, 1991). Such dissertations often seem to fail to convince editors and reviewers of their contribution to the scientific debate, but they have been screened for quality by advisors and reading committees. These studies are of course critical to be included in meta-analyses to deflate meta-analytic results. Inclusive meta-analyses save the investments of blood, sweat, and tears of disappointed PhD students from oblivion.

Beyond umbrella syntheses, a final step in spiralling ever closer to the truth might consist in consensus statements. Consensus statements result from intensive discussions in the forum of experts in a specific field who try to find common ground for advice to policymakers or practitioners. Meta-analytic evidence and umbrella studies are often used to find such common ground, but they also identify outstanding questions still to be settled. In the medical sciences consensus statements present preferred protocols for treatment of diseases or policy guidelines for prevention of ill health. The *Lancet* editors commission consensus statements on a regular basis in various areas of the (mental) health sciences. Our work on causes and consequences of (de-)institutionalisation of children without available parents was meant to create an evidence-based consensus about the state of the relevant research (Goldman et al., 2020; Van IJzendoorn et al., 2020). In the natural sciences one of the major examples is the United Nations–installed Intergovernmental Panel on Climate Change (IPCC) that brings together scientists from around the world to assess the state of knowledge on climate change and its impacts.

In developmental science consensus statements are rare, maybe because there is much dissensus about adequate theories, valid methods, and interpretation of results. In a roundtable discussion some 35 years ago, representatives of four different temperamental theories strived for consensus about defining and measuring children's temperamental features and the origins of temperamental differences (Goldsmith et al., 1987). In recent years some 70 attachment researchers brought attachment theory 'to the court'. Their goal was to find the common core of propositions and findings that everyone could subscribe to for social work around family court and child protection cases (Forslund et al., 2022). The resulting consensus statement was quickly translated into different languages (among others Spanish, Italian, Chinese, Japanese) and reached a wide readership with around 100,000 downloads in two years after publication (status on 03 July 2023 counted at www.tandfonline.com/doi/pdf/10.1080/14616734.2020.1840762?needAccess=true&fbclid=IwAR3km-qtinIKBrhv11QiGbNmJ-MoTxRaQBEINO3pvSJ8EADLCjvJ4x6e4PrQ). This consensus statement of attachment researchers from various countries, ages, genders, ethnicities, and disciplinary backgrounds might fulfil the two criteria for future-proof scientific findings: (1) 95% of the relevant scientific community must be signing up for the statement of fact, and (2) the relevant scientific community must be large and represent great diversity of perspectives (Vickers, 2023). Of course, people can suffer from groupthink and a herd mentality, and scientists sometimes really look like typical people. But a reasoned consensus after lots of hot debates between usually dissenting experts in a field might be some guarantee for the validity of the findings.

This leads to one final warning at the end of this chapter. So-called rapid (Tricco et al., 2015) and scoping reviews (Munn et al., 2018) threaten to replace slow but replicable meta-analyses, quantitative umbrella reviews, and consensus statements. Instead, we advocate 'slow science' including replications and quantitative syntheses, with a clear division of roles and responsibilities between researchers and practitioners (see Chapter 16) to establish first a strong evidence base and only subsequently strive for translation to policy or practice in close collaboration with practitioners, clinicians, and policymakers.

References

Bakermans-Kranenburg, M. J., & Van IJzendoorn, M. H. (2008). Oxytocin receptor (OXTR) and serotonin transporter (5-HTT) genes associated with observed parenting. *Social Cognitive and Affective Neuroscience*, *3*, 128–134. https://doi.org/10.1093/scan/nsn004

Bakermans-Kranenburg, M. J., & Van IJzendoorn, M. H. (2014). A sociability gene? Meta-analysis of oxytocin receptor (OXTR) genotype effects in humans. *Psychiatric Genetics*. https://doi.org/10.1097/YPG.0b013e3283643684

Bakermans-Kranenburg, M. J., Van IJzendoorn, M. H., & Juffer, F. (2003). Less is more: Meta-analyses of sensitivity and attachment interventions in early childhood. *Psychological Bulletin*, *129*, 195–215. https://doi.org/10.1037/0033-2909.129.2.195

Bosmans, G., Bakermans-Kranenburg, M. J., Vervliet, B., Verhees, M. W. F. T., & Van IJzendoorn, M. H. (2020). A learning theory of attachment: Unraveling the black box of attachment development. *Neuroscience & Biobehavioral Reviews*, *113*, 287–298. https://doi.org/10.1016/j.neubiorev.2020.03.014

Bosmans, G., Van Vlierberghe, L., Bakermans-Kranenburg, M. J., Kobak, R., Hermans, D., & Van IJzendoorn, M. H. (2022). A learning theory approach to attachment theory: Exploring clinical applications. *Clinical Child Family Psychology Review*. https://doi.org/10.1007/s10567-021-00377-x

Botvinik-Nezer, R., Holzmeister, F., Camerer, C. F., et al. (2020). Variability in the analysis of a single neuroimaging dataset by many teams. *Nature*, *582*, 84–88. https://doi.org/10.1038/s41586-020-2314-9

Bushman, B. J., & Wells, G. L. (2001). Narrative impressions of literature: The availability bias and the corrective properties of meta-analytic approaches. *Personality and Social Psychology Bulletin*, *27*(9), 1123–1130. https://doi.org/10.1177/0146167201279000527

Carroll, L. (1893). *Alice's Adventures in Wonderland*. Macmillan. https://doi.org/10.1515/9781400874262

Carter, E. C., Schönbrodt, F. D., Gervais, W. M., & Hilgard, J. (2019). Correcting for bias in psychology: A comparison of meta-analytic methods. *Advances in Methods and Practices in Psychological Science*, *2*, 115–144. https://doi.org/10.1177/2515245919847196

Coles, N. A., March, D. S., Marmolejo-Ramos, F., et al. A multi-lab test of the facial feedback hypothesis by the Many Smiles Collaboration. *Nature Human Behaviour*, 6, 1731–1742 (2022). https://doi.org/10.1038/s41562-022-01458-9

Coughlan, B., Duschinsky, R., Bakermans-Kranenburg, M., Bakkum, L., Skinner, G., Markham, A., Beckwith, H., & Van IJzendoorn, M. H. (December 19, 2022). Sequelae of Child Maltreatment: Umbrella synthesis on mental health correlates in over 11 million participants. *PsyArXiv*. https://doi.org/10.31234/osf.io/zj7kb

Fanelli, D. (2018). Opinion: Is science really facing a reproducibility crisis, and do we need it to? *Proceedings of the National Academy of Sciences*, *115*(11), 2628–2631. https://doi.org/10.1073/pnas.1708272114

Fanelli, D., & Larivière, V. (2016). Researchers' individual publication rate has not increased in a century. *PLOS One*, *11*, e0149504. https://doi.org/10.1371/journal.pone.0149504

Forscher, P. S., Brauer, M., Azevedo, F., Cox, W. T. L., & Devine, P. G. (April 9, 2019). How many reviewers are required to obtain reliable evaluations of NIH R01 grant proposals? *PsyArXiv*. https://doi.org/10.31234/osf.io/483zj

Fusar-Poli, P., & Radua, J. (2018). Ten simple rules for conducting umbrella reviews. *Evidence-based Mental Health*, *21*(3), 95–100. https://doi.org/10.1136/ebmental-2018-300014

Fox, N. A. (1995). Of the way we were: Adult memories about attachment experiences and their role in determining infant-parent relationships: A commentary on Van IJzendoorn (1995). *Psychological Bulletin*, *117*(3), 404–410. https://doi.org/10.1037/0033-2909.117.3.404

Glass, G. V. (1976). Primary, secondary, and meta-analytic analysis of research. *Educational Researcher*, *5*, 3–8. https://doi.org/10.3102/0013189x005010003

Glass, G. V., McGaw, B., & Smith, M. L. (1981). *Meta-Analysis in Social Research*. Sage Publications.

Goldman, P. S., Bakermans-Kranenburg, M. J., Bradford, B., et al. (2020). Institutionalisation and deinstitutionalisation of children 2: Policy and practice recommendations for global, national, and local actors. *The Lancet Child & Adolescent Health*, *4*(8), 606–633. https://doi.org/10.1016/s2352-4642(20)30060-2

Goldsmith, H. H., Buss, A. H., Plomin, R., Rothbart, M. K., Thomas, A., Chess, S., Hinde, R. A., & McCall, R. B. (1987). Roundtable: What is temperament? Four approaches. *Child Development*, *58*(2), 505–529. https://doi.org/10.2307/1130527

Granqvist, P., Sroufe, L. A., Dozier, M., Hesse, E., Steele, M., Van IJzendoorn, M., Solomon, J., Schuengel, C., Fearon, P., Bakermans-Kranenburg, M., Steele, H., Cassidy, J., Carlson, E., Madigan, S., Jacobvitz, D., Foster, S., Behrens, K., Rifkin-Graboi, A., Gribneau, N., Spangler, G., Ward, M. J., True, M., Spieker, S., Reijman, S., Reisz, S., Tharner, A., Nkara, F., Goldwyn, R., Sroufe, J., Pederson, D., Pederson, D., Weigand, R., Siegel, D., Dazzi, N., Bernard, K., Fonagy, P., Waters, E., Toth, S., Cicchetti, D., Zeanah, C. H., Lyons-Ruth, K., Main, M., & Duschinsky, R. (2017). Disorganized attachment in infancy: A review of the phenomenon and its implications for clinicians and policy-makers. *Attachment & Human Development*, *19*, 534–558. https://doi.org/10.1080/14616734.2017.1354040.

Hamaker, E. L., Mulder, J. D., & Van IJzendoorn, M. H. (2020). Description, prediction and causation: Methodological challenges of studying child and adolescent development. *Developmental Cognitive Neuroscience*, *46*, 100867. https://doi.org/10.1016/j.dcn.2020.100867.

Ioannidis, J. P. (2009). Integration of evidence from multiple meta-analyses: A primer on umbrella reviews, treatment networks and multiple treatments meta-analyses. *CMAJ: Canadian Medical Association Journal = journal de l'Association medicale canadienne*, *181*(8), 488–493. https://doi.org/10.1503/cmaj.081086

Forslund, T., Granqvist, P., Van IJzendoorn, M. H., Sagi-Schwartz, A., Glaser, D., Steele, M., Hammarlund, M., Schuengel, C., Bakermans-Kranenburg, M. J., Steele, H., Shaver, P. R., Lux, U., Simmonds, J., Jacobvitz, D., Groh, A. M., Bernard, K., Cyr, C., Hazen, N. L., Foster, S., Psouni, E., Cowan, P. A., Cowan, C. P., Rifkin-Graboi, A., Wilkins, D., Pierrehumbert, B., Tarabulsy, G. M., Carcamo, R. A., Wang, Z., Liang, X., Kázmierczak, M., Pawlicka, P., Ayiro, L.,

Chansa, T., Sichimba, F., Mooya, H., McLean, L., Verissimo, M., Gojman-de-Millán, S., Moretti, M. M., Bacro, F., Peltola, M. J., Galbally, M., Kondo-Ikemura, K., Behrens, K. Y., Scott, S., Rodriguez, A. F., Spencer, R., Posada, G., Cassibba, R., Barrantes-Vidal, N., Palacios, J., Barone, L., Madigan, S., Mason-Jones, K., Reijman, S., Juffer, F., Fearon, R. P., Bernier, A., Cicchetti, D., Roisman, G. I., Cassidy, J., Kindler, H., Zimmerman, P., Feldman, R., Spangler, G., Zeanah, C. H., Dozier, M., Belsky, J., Lamb, M. E., & Duschinsky, R. (2022). Attachment goes to court: Child protection and custody issues. *Attachment & Human Development*, 24, 1–51. https://doi.org/10.1080/14616734.2020.1840762.

Kagan, J. (1984). *The Nature of the Child*. Basic Books.

Klein, R. A., Ratliff, K. A., Vianello, M., et al. (2014). Investigating variation in replicability: A 'many labs' replication project. *Social Psychology*, 45, 142–152. https://doi.org/10.1027/1864-9335/a000178

Kvarven, A., Strømland, E., & Johannesson, M. (2020). Comparing meta-analyses and preregistered multiple-laboratory replication projects. *Nature Human Behaviour*, 4(4), 423–434. https://doi.org/10.1038/s41562-019-0787-z

Lakatos, I. (1978). Falsification and the methodology of scientific research programmes. In J. Worrall & G. Currie (Eds.), *The Methodology of Scientific Research Programmes: Philosophical Papers* (pp. 8–101). Cambridge University Press.

Lakens, D., Hilgard, J., & Staaks, J. (2016). On the reproducibility of meta-analyses: Six practical recommendations. *BMC Psychology*, 4, 24. https://doi.org/10.1186/s40359-016-0126-3.

Lytton, H. (1994). Replication and meta-analysis: The story of a meta-analysis of parents' socialization practices. In R. van der Veer, M. H. Van IJzendoorn, & J. Valsiner (Eds.) *Reconstructing the Mind: Replicability in Research on Human Development* (pp. 117–149). Ablex Publ. Company.

Madigan, S., Fearon, R. M. P., Van IJzendoorn, M. H., Duschinsky, R., Schuengel, C., Bakermans-Kranenburg, M. J., Ly, A., Cooke, J. E., Deneault, A.-A., Oosterman, M., & Verhage, M. L. (2023). The first 20,000 strange situation procedures: A meta-analytic review. *Psychological Bulletin*, 149(1–2), 99–132. https://doi.org/10.1037/bul0000388

Munn, Z., Peters, M. D. J., Stern, C., Tufanaru, C., McArthur, A., & Aromataris, E. (2018). Systematic review or scoping review? Guidance for authors when choosing between a systematic or scoping review approach. *BMC Medical Research Methodology*, 18, 143. https://doi.org/10.1186/s12874-018-0611-x

Molendijk, M. L., Bus, B. A. A., Spinhoven, P., Kaimatzoglou, A., Oude Voshaar, R. C., Penninx, B. W. J. H., Van IJzendoorn, M. H., & Elzinga, B. M. (2012) A systematic review and meta-analysis on the association between BDNF val66met and hippocampal volume: A genuine effect or a winner's curse? *American Journal of Medical Genetics Part B: Neuropsychiatric Genetics*, 159b, 731–740. https://doi.org/10.1002/ajmg.b.32078

National Academy of Sciences, Engineering, and Medicine. (2019). *Reproducibility and Replicability in Science*. Washington, DC: The National Academies Press.

Open Science Collaboration. (2015). Estimating the reproducibility of psychological science. *Science*, 349, 4716. https://doi.org/10.1126/science.aac4716

Padrón, E., Carlson, E. A., & Sroufe, L. A. (2014). Frightened versus not frightened disorganized infant attachment: Newborn characteristics and maternal caregiving. *American Journal of Orthopsychiatry*, 84(2), 201–208. https://doi.org/10.1037/h0099390

Popper, K. (1959). *The Logic of Scientific Discovery*. Routledge. https://doi.org/10.2307/2550489

Popper, K. (1978). *Three Worlds: The Tanner Lecture on Human Values*. The University of Michigan. https://doi.org/10.4324/9781315182872-15

Pearson, K. (1904). Report on certain enteric fever inoculations statistics. *British Medical Journal*, 3, 1243–1246. https://doi.org/10.1016/s0140-6736(01)34830-4

Riley, R. D., Tierney, J. F., & Stewart, L. A. (Eds.). (2021). *Individual Participant Data Meta-analysis. Handbook for Healthcare Research*. Wiley. https://doi.org/10.1002/9781119333784

Roisman G. I., & Van IJzendoorn, M. H. (2018). Meta-analysis and individual participant data synthesis in child development: Introduction to the special section. *Child Development*, 89, 1939–1942.

Rosenthal, R. (1991). *Meta-analytic Procedures for Social Research*. Sage Publications. https://doi.org/10.4135/9781412984997

Rosnow, R. L., & Rosenthal, R. (1989). Statistical procedures and the justification of knowledge in psychological science. *American Psychologist*, 44, 1276–1284. https://doi.org/10.1037/0003-066x.44.10.1276

Schuengel, C., Verhage, M. L., & Duschinsky, R. (2021). Prospecting the attachment research field: A move to the level of engagement. *Attachment & Human Development, 23*(4), 375–395. https://doi.org/10.1080/14616734.2021.1918449

Simonsohn, U., Simmons, J., & Nelson, L. D. (2022). Above averaging in literature reviews. *Nature Psychology Reviews, 1*, 551–552. https://doi.org/10.1038/s44159-022-00101-8

Smith, M. L., & Glass, G. V. (1977). Meta-analysis of psychotherapy outcome studies. *American Psychologist, 32*(9), 752–760. https://doi.org/10.1037/0003-066X.32.9.752

Sroufe, L. A. (1985). Attachment classification from the perspective of infant-caregiver relationships and infant temperament. *Child Development, 56*(1), 1–14.

Steegen, S., Tuerlinckx, F., Gelman, A., & Vanpaemel, W. (2016). Increasing transparency through a multiverse analysis. *Perspectives on Psychological Science, 11*(5), 702–712. https://doi.org/10.1177/1745691616658637

Tricco, A. C., Antony, J., Zarin, W., et al. (2015). A scoping review of rapid review methods. *BMC Medicine, 13*, 224. https://doi.org/10.1186/s12916-015-0465-6

Van IJzendoorn, M. H. (1983). *Van wijsgerige naar theoretische pedagogiek. Over de taken van de theoretische pedagogiek bij onderzoek naar vroegkinderlijke opvoeding (oratie)*. Van Loghum Slaterus.

Van IJzendoorn, M. H. (1994). Process model of replication studies: On the relations between different types of replication. In R. van der Veer, M. H. Van IJzendoorn, & J. Valsiner (Eds.), *On Reconstructing the Mind: Replicability in Research on Human Development* (pp. 57–70). Ablex.

Van IJzendoorn, M. H. (1995a). Adult attachment representations, parental responsiveness, and infant attachment: A meta-analysis on the predictive validity of the Adult Attachment Interview. *Psychological Bulletin, 117*, 387–403. https://doi.org/10.1037//0033-2909.117.3.387

Van IJzendoorn, M. H. (1995b). Of the way we are: On temperament, attachment and the transmission gap: A rejoinder to Fox. *Psychological Bulletin, 117*, 411–415.

Van IJzendoorn, M. H., & Bakermans-Kranenburg, M. J. (2015). Integrating temperament and attachment: The differential susceptibility paradigm. In M. Zentner & R. L. Shiner (Eds.), *Handbook of Temperament* (pp. 403–424). Guilford Press.

Van IJzendoorn, M. H. (2019). Addressing the replication and translation crises taking one step forward, two steps back? A plea for slow experimental research instead of fast 'participatory' studies. In S. Hein & J. Weeland (Eds.), *Alternatives to Randomized Controlled Trials (RCTs) in Studying Child and Adolescent Development in Clinical and Community Settings* (pp. 133–140). *New Directions for Child and Adolescent Development, 167*. https://doi.org/10.1002/cad.20308

Van IJzendoorn, M. H., & Bakermans-Kranenburg, M. J. (2019). Bridges across the intergenerational transmission of attachment gap. *Current Opinion in Psychology, 25*, 31–36. https://doi.org/10.1016/j.copsyc.2018.02.014

Van IJzendoorn, M. H., & Bakermans-Kranenburg, M. J. (2021). Replication crisis lost in translation? On translational caution and premature applications of attachment theory. *Attachment & Human Development, 23*, 422–437. https://doi.org/10.1080/14616734.2021.1918453

Van IJzendoorn, M. H., Bakermans-Kranenburg, M. J., & Alink, L. R. A. (2011). Meta-analysis in developmental science. In B. Laursen, T. D. Little, & N. A. Card (Eds.), *Handbook of Developmental Research Methods* (pp. 667–686). Guilford.

Van IJzendoorn, M. H., Bakermans-Kranenburg, M. J., Coughlan, B., & Reijman, S. (2020). Child maltreatment antecedents and interventions: Umbrella synthesis and differential susceptibility perspective on risk and resilience. *Journal of Child Psychology and Psychiatry, 61*, 272–290. https://doi.org/10.1111/jcpp.13147

Van IJzendoorn, M. H., Bakermans-Kranenburg, M. J., Duschinsky, R., Goldman, P. S., Fox, N. A., Gunnar, M. R., Johnson, D. E., Nelson, C. A., Reijman, S., Skinner, G. C. M., Zeanah, C. H., & Sonuga-Barke, E. J. S. (2020). Institutionalisation and deinstitutionalisation of children I: A systematic and integrative review of evidence regarding effects on development. *The Lancet Psychiatry, 7*, 703–720. https://doi.org/10.1016/S2215-0366(19)30399-2

Van IJzendoorn, M. H., & Kroonenberg, P. M. (1988). Cross-cultural patterns of attachment. A meta-analysis of the Strange Situation. *Child Development, 59*, 147–156. doi:10.2307/1130396

Van IJzendoorn, M. H., & Tavecchio, L. W. C. (1987). The development of attachment theory as a Lakatosian research program: In L. W. C. Tavecchio & M. H. van IJzendoorn (Eds.), *Attachment in Social Networks: Contributions to the Bowlby-Ainsworth Attachment Theory* (pp. 3–31). Elsevier Science Publishers. https://doi.org/10.1016/s0166-4115(08)61071-7

Van IJzendoorn, M. H., & Van der Veer, R. (1983). Holzkamp's critical psychology and the functional-historical method: A critical appraisal. *Storia e Critica della Psicologia, 4*, 5–26.

Van Os, J., Guloksuz, S., Vijn, T. W., Hafkenscheid, A., & Delespaul P. (2019). The evidence-based group-level symptom-reduction model as the organizing principle for mental health care: Time for change? *World Psychiatry, 18*(1), 88–96. https://doi.org/10.1002/wps.20609

Verhage, M. L., Schuengel, C., Madigan, S., Fearon, R. M. P., Oosterman, M., Cassibba, R., Bakermans-Kranenburg, M. J., & Van IJzendoorn, M. H. (2016). Narrowing the transmission gap: A synthesis of three decades of research on intergenerational transmission of attachment. *Psychological Bulletin, 142*(4), 337–366.

Verhage, M. L., Fearon, R. M. P., Schuengel, C., Van IJzendoorn, M. H., Bakermans-Kranenburg, M. J., Madigan, S., Roisman, G. I., Oosterman, M., Behrens, K. Y., Wong, M. S., Mangelsdorf, S., Priddis, L. E., Brisch, K. H., & Collaboration on Attachment Transmission Synthesis. (2018). Constraints on the intergenerational transmission of attachment via Individual Participant Data Meta-analysis. *Child Development, 89*, 2023–2037. https://doi.org/10.1111/cdev.13085

Verhage, M. L., Schuengel, C., Duschinsky, R., Van IJzendoorn, M. H., Fearon, R. M. P., Madigan, S., Roisman, G. I., Bakermans–Kranenburg, M. J., & Oosterman, M. (2020). The Collaboration on Attachment Transmission Synthesis (CATS): A move to the level of individual-participant-data meta-analysis. *Current Directions in Psychological Science, 29*(2), 199–206. https://doi.org/10.1177/0963721420904967

Vickers, P. (2023). *Identifying Future-Proof Science*. Oxford: Oxford University Press.

Wadhwa, M., & Cook, T. D. (2019). The set of assumptions randomized control trials make and their implications for the role of such experiments in evidence-based child and adolescent development research. *New Directions for Child and Adolescent Development, 167*, 17–37. https://doi.org/10.1002/cad.20313

Part 2
Translation to policy or practice

Only scientific results which have been successfully replicated multiple times and for which meta-analytic evidence or quantitative synthesis is available may responsibly be translated into recommendations for policy or practice (see Figure 0.3). From our attachment research programme we selected three projects with multiple empirical studies and meta-analytic evidence that makes them feasible for translation to policy or (clinical) practice. Our work on attachment-based parenting support, on institutionalised care of children without available parents, and on genocidal trauma caused by the Holocaust illustrates that translatable research is slow science.

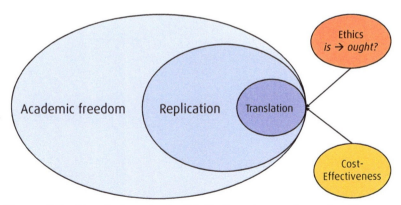

Figure 0.3 Translation of scientific findings to practice and policy requires replicated results and academic freedom from external pressures. In addition, ethical reasoning to bridge the gap between means and ends and a suitable cost-benefit balance are required. Source: Authors.

4
Video-feedback intervention (VIPP-SD) promotes sensitive parenting and secure attachment

Development of the intervention

If the quality of parenting, more specifically caregiver sensitivity, predicts security of the child-parent attachment relationship, intervention programmes supporting sensitive caregiving are an effective means to establish secure attachments in children. In this chapter we describe the evidence-based development of an intervention programme: the Video-feedback Intervention to promote Positive Parenting and Sensitive Discipline (VIPP-SD). Around thirty years ago, we started to discuss the development of an early parenting intervention designed to promote positive parent-child interactions with our colleague Femmie Juffer. Femmie had some intervention experience supporting adoptive parents in the first year after adopting a child from abroad. Marinus was an expert in attachment research but had been disappointed with a previous parenting intervention that used videoclips to model sensitive parent-child interactions. Compared to brochures with information on sensitive parenting, the effects of using video-clips with model parents and children – very innovative at the time – were nil. He suspected that parents had difficulties identifying with the model parent or did not recognise their own infants' behaviour in that of the videotaped infant. Marian just had her first infant, providing firsthand parent-child interactions for piloting interventions.

The VIPP-SD was developed in conjunction with a meta-analytical study of attachment-based parenting interventions (Bakermans-Kranenburg et al., 2003). This study analysed 88 attachment-based interventions and found, somewhat to our surprise, that longer interventions were not more effective than shorter ones. On the contrary, interventions with more than 16 sessions turned out to be less effective in promoting caregiver sensitivity than interventions with shorter duration, even in parents with multiple problems. Part of the explanation of this somewhat counterintuitive finding may be that longer interventions run the risk of discontinuity of interveners. Such discontinuities due to job changes, parental leave, etc., are in the way of establishing a relationship between caregiver and intervener in which the caregiver feels secure enough to trust the intervener and try out new behaviour. Based on this finding, the VIPP-SD intervention programme was designed to be brief.

The meta-analysis also showed that interventions focusing on sensitive parenting behaviours, that is, the ability to promptly and adequately respond to child signals, were more effective than those that also addressed general support, attachment representations, or traumatic experiences. The VIPP-SD intervention was therefore structured to focus on behaviours of parents/caregivers in interaction with their child. It may be combined with treatments that focus on specific caregiver conditions, for example, cognitive behaviour treatment in a group of mothers with bulimic eating disorders (Stein et al., 2006).

In addition, the use of video-feedback was identified in the meta-analysis as an effective approach to supporting positive parenting. Meta-analytically, interventions using video-feedback to support positive parenting were more effective than interventions without video-feedback. Filming a child's play, birthday, or interaction with a parent or grandparent has become more common over the years. Yet, it has lost none of its strengths in the process of enhancing sensitive parenting and gentle discipline, and video-feedback is a key feature of VIPP-SD.

The VIPP-SD toolbox

As part of the video-feedback method, stilling, repeating, and commenting on fragments are powerful tools in the VIPP-SD toolbox (see Figure 4.1 for what we think are active ingredients of VIPP-SD). It allows caregivers to see their interactions with their children more clearly and to better understand their children's signals and behaviours than during live interaction. Repeating a fragment enables the caregiver to see child signals that went unnoticed, either because the caregiver's focus was on something else or because the signals were subtle. Seeing child signals is a prerequisite for a sensitive response and it can be trained with video-feedback. Caregivers are also asked to take their child's perspective by providing 'subtitles' for their child's behaviour. Such speaking for the child stimulates taking the child's perspective.

Furthermore, video-feedback helps caregivers become aware of the feedback their child is providing during interactions (Bakermans-Kranenburg et al., 2019). Recognising this feedback may start a positive feedback loop and improve their interactions with their child. This may be why short-term interventions can be effective in the long term. Additionally, highlighting a child's efforts to comply with difficult tasks or demands can foster parental empathy, leading to a more sensitive and understanding response. Reviewing video fragments of inappropriate parenting and discussing alternative responses can help caregivers reframe their thoughts and beliefs, increasing their capacity for reflective functioning. These 'corrective messages' are given in a supportive environment that acknowledges the caregiver's knowledge and competence as a parent by also showing and repeating positive interaction episodes.

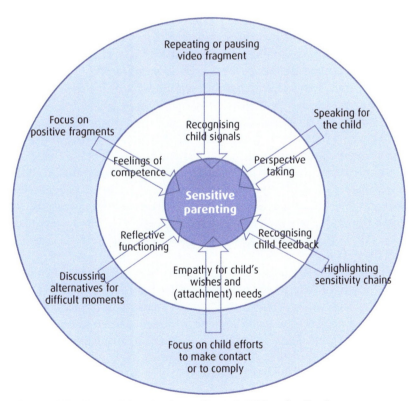

Figure 4.1 Potential active ingredients in Video-feedback Interventions to promote Positive Parenting and Sensitive Discipline (VIPP-SD). Adapted from Van IJzendoorn, Schuengel, Wang, and Bakermans-Kranenburg (2023).

The VIPP-SD method is both standardised and individualised. It is standardised in that it follows a manual with designated themes per session (Figure 4.2) and type of settings to be recorded, and individualised in that the feedback is driven by what the recordings of this specific caregiver-child dyad show. Before each intervention session, the intervener has prepared a 'script' documenting the messages that the intervener wants to convey at specific time codes of the recording, based on the themes and guidelines in the VIPP-SD manual. During the session the intervener also invites the parent to contribute to the conversation by asking her questions or by encouraging the parent to comment on the child's behaviour.

Integrating attachment theory and social learning theory

The VIPP-SD intervention is based on attachment theory, with a focus on caregiver sensitivity, and on social learning theory, in particular Gerald Patterson's work on coercive cycles that should be avoided in effective parent-child interaction. The VIPP-SD method consists of six intervention sessions, and a baseline visit to make recordings for feedback during the first intervention session. Three phases can be distinguished in the trajectory. In the first phase (sessions 1 and 2), the focus is on building a working alliance, and the video-feedback concentrates on child behaviour and signals, and on the caregiver's strengths. In the second phase (sessions 3 and 4), the focus is more on improving parenting behaviours. In addition to highlighting effective parenting behaviour, moments of ineffective parenting are now discussed, suggesting alternatives for these moments while showing empathy for the parent and repeating video fragments where the caregiver's strategy was adequate. The final phase (sessions 5 and 6) consists of two booster sessions, during which interveners repeat the themes and messages from the previous sessions. They reinforce sensitive caregiver-child interactions and positive parenting strategies and support caregivers' reflecting on their video-recorded behaviour. In all sessions, caregivers are explicitly acknowledged as the expert on their child, which is essential for building rapport and boosting the caregiver's feelings of competence. Only then can caregivers explore new strategies and try out different parenting behaviour.

Each intervention session in the VIPP-SD programme follows specific themes for both the sensitivity and the discipline dimension (see Figure 4.2). The themes related to the sensitivity dimension are (1) the distinction between child's explorative versus attachment behaviour;

(2) taking the child's perspective using 'speaking for the child'; (3) awareness of sensitivity chains consisting of a child signal, the caregiver's response, and the child's reaction to that response; and (4) sharing emotions as a way of affect attunement. The discipline dimension is addressed with the following themes per session: (1) distraction and induction as non-coercive responses to difficult child behaviour, (2) positive reinforcement, praising the child for positive behaviour and ignoring negative attention seeking, (3) using a sensitive interaction pause to de-escalate conflicts or temper tantrums (not a time-out as punishment for the child), and (4) showing empathy and understanding for the child while maintaining clear and consistent limit setting. As an example, one specific setting is a clean-up task, which can trigger opposition in children and anger in parents and offers an opportunity for caregivers to stick to the rules while showing empathy for the child. In the booster sessions, all themes are repeated, with some emphasis on what seems most relevant for the individual dyad and filmed fragments.

In all sessions, a central focus is the caregiver's ability to notice and understand the child's signals, respond appropriately to both positive and negative signals, and adjust their pace to the child's needs. This includes introducing breaks, 'waiting and seeing', giving directions and explanations in a sensitive way, showing empathy and understanding accompanying clear limit setting, encouraging eye contact, and engaging in open, playful communication.

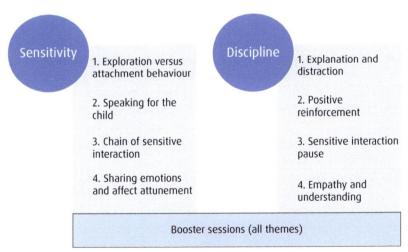

Figure 4.2 Sessions of the Video-feedback Interventions to promote Positive Parenting and Sensitive Discipline (VIPP-SD).
Source: Authors.

Meta-analysis of 25 VIPP-SD randomised controlled trials

Our first randomised controlled trials to test the effectiveness of the intervention showed positive effects on sensitive parenting and discipline as well as effects on child attachment security and behaviour problems in specific groups (Klein Velderman et al., 2006; Van Zeijl et al., 2006). To determine whether the positive outcomes of VIPP-SD are retained over time and contexts, a meta-analysis was conducted combining the results of all randomised controlled studies of the programme. It is important to consider whether earlier studies may have been particularly effective due to the involvement of the developers or other factors that may not be replicable in later trials. Additionally, the widespread use of video recordings may have reduced the effectiveness of video-feedback over time.

In addition to these practical considerations, studying the effects of interventions like VIPP-SD that aim to enhance positive parenting and secure child-parent attachment relationships can also contribute to theory building. It is generally accepted that sensitive parenting leads to more secure attachment in children, but this association is usually demonstrated through correlational studies, which cannot prove causality. It is possible that other factors, such as easy temperament or shared genetics, may explain the correlation between parental sensitivity and attachment quality. However, when an intervention leads to improved sensitivity in caregivers and this is associated with improved attachment security in the intervention group, it suggests that promoting sensitivity leads to more secure attachment in a causal way, supporting attachment theory. Meta-analyses can also identify the circumstances under which an intervention is most effective in improving caregiver behaviour or caregiver-child relationships, and when its effects are minimal. Thus, meta-analysis serves as a way to evaluate an intervention's viability and applicability over time and can inspire improvements for targeting specific groups.

In total, 25 studies comprising more than 2,000 parents and caregivers were included in the meta-analysis (Van IJzendoorn et al., 2023). The sample sizes ranged from 40 to 300 and included biological parents, foster parents, adoptive parents, and professional caregivers. The children in the studies exhibited externalising problem behaviour, were diagnosed with autism or had a sibling with autism, or experienced parental insensitivity, maltreatment, or environmental risks such as poverty. All of the studies were randomised controlled trials and the majority included checks for fidelity of intervention implementation as part of the VIPP-SD protocol guidelines. Ensuring that the intervention was implemented as intended allows for easier comparison and combination of the individual studies.

After the intervention, caregiver-child interaction was always observed and rated by observers who were unaware of whether the specific dyad had received the VIPP-SD intervention or had been in the control group. The combined effect size for sensitive parenting and discipline was $d = 0.38$, meaning that caregivers who participated in VIPP-SD were more than a third of a standard deviation more sensitive in their interaction with the child or in their limit-setting behaviours. This is a large effect size compared to the average effect sizes in the field of educational and family interventions. Additionally, the intervention promoted positive cognitions about sensitivity and sensitive discipline, with a combined effect size of $d = 0.33$. These changed cognitions may contribute to the stability of changes in caregiving behaviours and may be a mechanism of change in caregiving behaviours. Children in the intervention group showed a decrease in externalising behaviour ($d = 0.14$) and an increase in attachment security of nearly half a standard deviation ($d = 0.48$). These effects were independent of specific risks of the parents or children involved and thus indicate the potential generic impact of VIPP-SD across a variety of psychological problems.

We included quality ratings of the individual studies. Studies can be considered of higher quality – and thus lower risk of bias – if they are pre-registered; have low attrition rates; use intent-to-treat analysis, checks on fidelity of the programme delivery, outcome measures rated or completed by individuals who do not know whether the case belongs to the control group or the intervention group; and are conducted without involvement of the programme developers. In the set of VIPP-SD studies, a third were pre-registered and two-thirds used intent-to-treat analyses, while the vast majority reported on fidelity checks and 'blind' coding of outcome measures (except for externalising behaviour that is usually parent-reported). The developers of the VIPP-SD programme were not involved in 13 trials. Attrition rates varied between 0% and 42% (the latter in a study on improving centre-based day-care), with an average of 12%. An aggregated score for risk of bias based on the six indicators was not associated with study effect sizes but shows that there is room for improvement in individual studies. No evidence for p-hacking was detected in the meta-analyses for parenting and child outcomes. Together, the examination of these quality indicators and their influence on meta-analytic results supports the idea that the intervention effects are replicable.

The positive evaluation of our VIPP-SD has been supported by the Home Visiting Evidence of Effectiveness (HomVEE) review in 2023. The HomVEE review was launched in 2009 with sponsorship from the Administration for Children and Families (ACF) Office of Planning, Research, and Evaluation (OPRE) within the U.S. Department of Health and Human Services (HHS) (Sama-Miller et al., 2020). HomVEE concluded that VIPP-SD and its various adaptations to specific target populations were meeting the U.S. Department of Health and Human Services criteria for an evidence-based early childhood home visiting service delivery model. To our surprise, HomVEE considers only studies conducted in high-income countries. Of course, we were excited about the positive HomVEE evaluation of our VIPP-SD suite of parenting intervention programmes, even without excellent VIPP-SD studies in Turkey (Alsancak-Akbulut et al., 2021) and Colombia (Barone et al., 2021). Nevertheless, we argue elsewhere that their criteria for effects including quasi-experimental designs, but conducted in wealthy countries only, and documenting statistical significance instead of effect sizes are not satisfactory from a scientific perspective as presented in this book (see Chapter 8).

Increased sensitive parenting and limit-setting promote attachment security

The meta-analytic effect sizes for changes in child behaviour are especially noteworthy, considering that the child is never directly addressed in the intervention, meaning that any effect on child behaviour is an indirect effect via changes in caregiver behaviour. Indeed, increases in positive parenting were associated with increased attachment security, so studies with larger effects on sensitive parenting and limit setting also had more effect on child attachment security.

The association between sensitive parenting and secure attachment has often been documented in correlational studies. A recent meta-analysis combined the 230 available studies with in total almost 23,000 child-parent dyads (Madigan et al., 2024) and found a combined effect size of $r = 0.25$. Intervention studies complement correlational studies, and convergence of findings corroborate tentative conclusions. In theory, VIPP-SD might enhance other caregiver behaviour than sensitive parenting, and this other (unmeasured) caregiver behaviour might promote children's attachment security. Yet, the more parsimonious interpretation of our meta-analytic finding of an association between intervention effects on parenting and effects on child attachment security is that the caregiver's sensitivity influences the child's attachment behaviour. This emphasises the crucial importance of supporting parents and other caregivers in promoting secure attachment relationships.

References

Alsancak-Akbulut, C., Sahin-Acar, B., & Sumer, N. (2021). Effect of video-feedback intervention on Turkish mothers' sensitivity and physical intrusiveness: A randomized control trial. *Attachment & Human Development, 23*, 795–813. https://doi.org/10.1080/14616734.2020.1753085

Barone, L., Carone, N., Salazar, J. G., & Jenny, A. (2021). Enhancing food habits via sensitivity in rural low-SES mothers of children aged 1–3 living in Colombia: A randomized controlled trial using video-feedback intervention. *Attachment & Human Development, 23*, 831–852. https://doi.org/10.1080/ 14616734.2020.1784243

Bakermans-Kranenburg, M. J., Van IJzendoorn, M. H., & Juffer, F. (2003). Less is more: Meta-analyses of sensitivity and attachment interventions in early childhood. *Psychological Bulletin, 129*, 195–215. https://doi.org/10. 1037/0033-2909.129.2.195

Bakermans-Kranenburg, M. J., Juffer, F., & Van IJzendoorn, M. H. (2019). Reflections on the mirror: On video-feedback to promote positive parenting and infant mental health. In Ch.H. Zeanah (Ed.), *Handbook of Infant Mental Health* (4th ed., pp. 527–542). Guilford Press.

Juffer, F., Bakermans-Kranenburg, M. J., & Van IJzendoorn, M. H. (2017). Pairing attachment theory and social learning theory in video-feedback intervention to promote positive parenting. *Current Opinion in Psychology, 15*, 189–194. https://doi.org/10.1016/j.copsyc.2017.03.012

Klein Velderman, M., Bakermans-Kranenburg, M. J., Juffer, F., & Van IJzendoorn, M. H. (2006a). Effects of attachment-based interventions on maternal sensitivity and infant attachment: Differential susceptibility of highly reactive infants. *Journal of Family Psychology, 20*, 266–274. https://doi.org/10.1037/0893-3200.20.2.266

Klein Velderman, M., Bakermans-Kranenburg, M. J., Juffer, F., Van IJzendoorn, M. H., Mangelsdorf, S. C., & Zevalkink, J. (2006b). Preventing preschool externalizing behavior problems through video-feedback intervention in infancy. *Infant Mental Health Journal, 27*(5), 466–493. https://doi.org/10.1002/imhj.20104

Madigan, S., Deneault, A. A., Duschinsky, R., Bakermans-Kranenburg, M. J., Schuengel, C., Van IJzendoorn, M. H., Ly, A., Fearon, R. M. P., Eirich, R., & Verhage, M. L. (2024). Maternal and paternal sensitivity: Key determinants of child attachment security examined through meta-analysis. *Psychological Bulletin*.

Sama-Miller, E., Lugo-Gil, J., Harding, J., Akers, L., & Coughlin, R. (2020). *Home Visiting Evidence of Effectiveness (HomVEE) Systematic Review: Handbook of Procedures and Evidence Standards, Version 2*. OPRE Report # 2020–151. Office of Planning, Research, and Evaluation, Administration for Children and Families, U.S. Department of Health and Human Services.

Stein, A., Woolley, H., Senior, R., Hertzmann, L., Lovel, M., Lee, J., & Fairburn, C. G. (2006). Treating disturbances in the relationship between mothers with bulimic eating disorders and their infants: A randomized, controlled trial of video feedback. *American Journal of Psychiatry, 163*(5), 899–906. https://doi.org/10.1176/ajp.2006.163.5.899

Van IJzendoorn, M. H., Schuengel, C., Wang, Q., & Bakermans-Kranenburg, M. J. (2023). Improving parenting, child attachment and externalizing behaviors: Meta-analysis of the first 25 randomized controlled trials on the effects of Video-feedback Intervention to promote Positive Parenting and Sensitive Discipline. *Development & Psychopathology, 35*, 241–256. https://doi.org/10.1017/S0954579421001462

Van Zeijl, J., Mesman, J., Van IJzendoorn, M. H., Bakermans-Kranenburg, M. J., Juffer, F., Stolk, M. N., Koot, H. M., & Alink, L. R. A. (2006). Attachment-based intervention for enhancing sensitive discipline in mothers of 1- to 3-year-old children at risk for externalizing behavior problems: A randomized controlled trial. *Journal of Consulting and Clinical Psychology, 74*(6), 994–1005. https://doi.org/https://doi.org10.1037/0022-006X.74.6.994

5
Institutionalised child-rearing is structural neglect

Institutionalisation

Children should not grow up in institutions. We argue that institutionalisation of (biological or social) orphans is structural neglect, defined as emotional neglect embedded in the structure of what Ervin Goffman called a total institution, regulating all facets of life, including food intake, sleep, schooling, and 'free time'. Staff turnover is endemic because the caregiver job in institutions is not valued in the wider society; it is underpaid and emotionally exhausting. However, the number of children living in institutional settings amounts to a staggering 7.52 million, which is almost 0.4% of the children worldwide (the most plausible estimate from Desmond et al., 2020). This number is expected to grow in the coming years, due to COVID-19 and destructive wars, because more children will lose the care of their (allo-)parents due to poverty or death. The number of orphans because of COVID-19 is estimated to be more than 5 million (Hillis et al., 2021).

In the past four decades we conducted research in Greece, Ukraine, and India in collaboration with our colleague Femmie Juffer. For example, daily life of children in an institutional setting in India was video-recorded with spot observations of one minute every 10 minutes, targeting each individual child from 9 a.m. to 2 p.m. Distressingly, no interactions at all happened in 80% of the observations, and in only 5% of the observations some interaction between a caregiver and child took place. The children in this overcrowded and understaffed setting showed stunted physical growth, with almost two standard deviations of weight, height, and head circumference below the norm, and an average IQ somewhat below 70 (Juffer et al., 2017a). In Ukraine some institutionalised pre-schoolers had already experienced 40 different caregivers by the time they were four years old. This is the exemplification of fragmented care (Dobrova-Krol et al., 2008; 2017).

Of course, the few empirical studies we conducted in India, Ukraine, and Greece are insufficient to conclude that the findings would be replicable and causal, despite their convergence with similar studies finding large developmental delays for institutionalised children compared to their luckier peers growing up in families. For such a conclusion a meta-analysis of studies in various institutions in different parts of the world is necessary. We conducted a series of meta-analyses combining all available studies on the effects of institutionalisation and de-institutionalisation, including more than 100,000 children in more than 60 countries. The combined effect sizes for physical growth were larger than a standard deviation, and cognitive development lagged behind by 0.80 standard deviations (see Figure 5.1). Focusing on attachment of institutionalised children, an almost two times higher prevalence of attachment insecurity and an almost four times higher prevalence of disorganised or unclassifiable attachments were observed (Van IJzendoorn et al., 2020).

There are two arguments to interpret these delays in development as causal consequences of institutionalisation. First, the meta-analytic findings converged with the unique randomised controlled trial comparing institutionalised children with their peers in foster care in the Bucharest Early Intervention Project (described in *Romania's abandoned children*, Nelson et al., 2014). The findings cannot, therefore, be explained away by pointing at the possibility of pre-existing delays specifically serious for children who remained in institutional settings while their less delayed and more fortunate peers left the institution for an adoptive or foster family (Van IJzendoorn et al., 2020). In fact, this comparison of correlational meta-analytic findings with the RCT results accommodates Simonsohn et al.'s (2022) requirement to use the best-designed studies as a yardstick for meta-analytic evidence.

Second, the series of meta-analyses published in *The Lancet Psychiatry* documented the extremely large developmental delays suffered by institutionalised children in a dose-response manner: longer stays in orphanages created more severe delays, with varying degrees in domains such as physical, cognitive, and socio-emotional development. We also examined research on de-institutionalisation and found that catch-up growth and development were impressive, maybe not for all children but certainly for most of those who made the transition to a regular family-type childrearing arrangement, such as

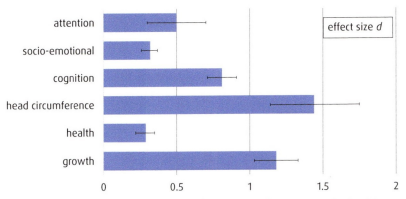

Figure 5.1 Meta-analytic effects of institutionalisation are derived from all studies of the past 70 years covering more than 100,000 children in more than 60 countries.
Source: Van IJzendoorn et al. (2020).

foster care or (domestic or international) adoption. And again, these results converged with the BEIP randomized trial that showed how beneficial foster family life turned out to be for the Romanian children involved.

Prevention and de-institutionalisation needed

In the policy paper published in *The Lancet Child and Adolescent Health,* we therefore insisted on a transition of all children away from institutional settings to family life (Goldman et al., 2020a). Two sets of recommendations for policy and practice at the local, national, and international level were detailed. The first set pertained to prevention of out-of-home placements of children into institutions. Strengthening of support for families that are at risk of falling apart because of poverty, traumatic stress, or social violence was proposed, and direct coaching of such families recommended, with concrete suggestions for evidence-based programmes (e.g., Bakermans-Kranenburg, 2019; Juffer et al., 2017b). In many low- and middle-income countries (LMICs) a reliable and robust system for monitoring safety of children and protection against maltreatment and neglect is absent and should be prioritised. Developing such an infrastructure might take time and investments and is less visible than the bricks and mortar that constitute institutional settings. But in the long run it will lead to cost-effectiveness and, more importantly, to fewer mental health issues and a better life for the children involved (Goldman et al., 2020a).

The second set of recommendations proposed involved curative remediation through de-institutionalisation in an organised and well-monitored way. The COVID-19 pandemic has led to hastily dissolving some institutions because of fear that professional staff would get infected in the crowded institutional environment (Goldman et al., 2020b). But placement in alternative, family-type environments such as foster and adoptive families, kafalah, or kinship care should be monitored and supported by clinically trained professionals to create the best possible match between the child and the receiving family and to coach the parents in getting used to the sometimes seemingly rejecting or indifferent attachment behaviours of children who are traumatised by their experiences in the institutions. Evidence-based support for foster and adoptive parents is critical to avoid separations between these parents and the children in their care. Children who carry the scars of institutional care are expecting separations more often than children raised in typical families, but they are least capable of coping with such cumulative separations that they experience as rejections of themselves as individuals not worthy of good-enough care.

From the perspective of developmental psychopathology, we might learn some valuable lessons from research on institutional care. The first lesson is that children need social interactions to grow up and develop their competences. Sufficient food and medical care are not enough to avoid serious developmental delays. Social interactions with significant others belong to the core needs of the developing child. Second, continuity of care arrangements is essential, and fragmented care should be avoided because it creates atypical attachments with fleeting attention and attention deficits of the children involved. Indiscriminate friendliness might for many children be the defence mechanism to cope with recurring separations (Bakermans-Kranenburg et al., 2011; 2012). Third, children and their parents or caregivers need a small, transparent, and reliable social network of individuals who can give them the support they need in times of anxiety, stress, distress, or illness. In short, children need safe, stable and shared (Triple S) care in family-type arrangements. Parenting children with experiences of structural neglect is a difficult task and a great responsibility but the benefits for the children involved and the society at large are huge.

Orphanages against infanticide

From an evolutionary perspective institutional care falls outside the range of the environments of evolutionary adaptedness (Bowlby, 1969) in which the human species is supposed to have evolved over millennia (Van IJzendoorn et al., 2020; Van IJzendoorn & Bakermans-Kranenburg, 2021). This is not because of bad intentions or lack of abilities in staff or management. Professional group care is unique across evolutionary times (Hrdy, 2009) and the institutions' organisation is atypical for any known environment for care of offspring. Some typical characteristics of institutions are their regimented nature with strictly monitored day and night routines of sleeping, eating, playing, schooling, and free time; the high child-to-caregiver ratios compared to a regular family; the multiple shifts needed to cover 24/7 care; and the high staff turnover because of the heavy workload, low levels of payment, incompatibility with raising children of their own, and low social respect for the profession.

These components in various constellations result in discontinuous, fragmented care arrangements with too many separations and too little opportunity to establish attachment relationships in an organised way and to feel safe and grow into an adaptive adult. Operating as total institutions (Goffman, 1961), on the one hand they show high levels of violence between peers and between residents and staff (Euser et al., 2014; 2016), and on the other hand they lack meaningful activities and interactions during the most part of the day as we described above (Juffer et al., 2017). Structural neglect characterises the typical institution (Van IJzendoorn et al., 2011).

If institutional care is so bad for children, why did orphanages emerge at all? Why would institutional childcare have flourished if it is outside any environment of evolutionary adaptedness in which the human species evolved over millennia of variations, selection pressures, and replications? We submit the hypothesis that orphanages (partly) replaced infanticide (Van IJzendoorn & Bakermans-Kranenburg, 2021). Throughout evolutionary times infanticide existed at a rather high rate, for different reasons. First, extreme lack of social and physical resources forced parents to choose between their offspring, saving some and at the same time letting others starve to death (Scheper-Hughes, 1993). Second, the struggle for dominance within and between groups caused infanticide by the new alpha males or leaders to increase their chances of having their own offspring (Hrdy, 1999). Last, (perceived) constitutional vulnerabilities or disabilities were seen as a liability of growing up and becoming adult without the capability to create offspring and transmit the gene pool into the next generation (DeVries, 1984).

Basically the 'goal' of neo-Darwinian evolution is offspring survival into procreative age followed by enhanced inclusive fitness. Hamilton's rule might be considered to be the hidden law behind this process of adaptation (Hamilton, 1964; Trivers, 1974). It states that costs (C) of providing care should be lower than the benefits (B) of that provision of care weighted by the degree of genetic relatedness (r) of those cared for; in short, $C < B*r$. If the (foreseen) costs become much larger than these weighted benefits ($C >> B*r$) infanticide might be the (unintended or culturally 'acceptable') consequence. Scheper-Hughes (1993), for example, describes how infanticide was made culturally and religiously acceptable because babies in their first year of life were seen as angels instead of human beings and, when they died, would go straight back to heaven.

But if abandonment would lower the costs of infanticide and (ever so slightly) elevate the chance of benefits by survival of the abandoned offspring, then the equation of $C > B*r$ might change in a positive direction. Because too many newborns were drowned in the Tiber, in 1198 Pope Innocent III decreed that 'foundling wheels' should be installed to give young mothers a chance to deliver their newborns anonymously to institutional care. Until today so-called 'baby hatches' still exist in many countries, for example in Germany, which is estimated to have 100 of such facilities. If there is even a slight chance of survival into procreative adulthood, it would make evolutionary sense to use foundling wheels and institutional care that might lead to foster care, adoption, or kafalah at a later stage. This might be an example of gene-culture coevolution in the service of inclusive fitness (Laland, 2017).

Conclusion

One of the most important universal children's rights is the right to grow up in a family. Most countries around the world (except for the USA and some other countries) signed up for this by ratifying the United Nations Convention on the Rights of the Child. Since John Bowlby's World Health Organization report (Bowlby, 1951), more than 70 years of research on the damaging effects of institutionalisation on child development have provided a firm basis for his advocacy to abolish institutions. Recent scandals about massive child abuse and neglect in Irish and Canadian institutions and documented child abuse in SOS Children's Villages (see Chapter 14) show the risks of residential care for children born healthy but in dire circumstances. De-institutionalisation has been proven to be a powerful intervention for unparalleled improvement of children's physical and mental health even after their stay in an institution in the earliest years of their lives. In Chapter 15 we discuss local and international adoption as one way to enhance de-institutionalisation if no other alternatives for children are available. After 825 years of demonstrating their shortcomings, it is time for institutions to be torn down.

References

Bakermans-Kranenburg, M. J., Juffer, F., & Van IJzendoorn, M. H. (2019). Reflections on the mirror: On video-feedback to promote positive parenting and infant mental health. In Ch.H. Zeanah (Ed.), *Handbook of Infant Mental Health* (4th ed., pp. 527–542). Guilford Press.

Bakermans-Kranenburg, M. J., McCreery Bunkers, K., Dobrova-Krol, N. A., Engle, P., Fox, ... Zeanah, C. H. (2012). The development and care of institutionally reared children. *Child Development Perspectives*, 6, 174–180. https://doi.org/10.1111/j.1750-8606.2011.00231.x

Bakermans-Kranenburg, M. J., Steele, H., Zeanah, C. H. Muhamedrahimov, R. J., Vorria, P., Dobrova-Krol, N. A., Steele, M., Van IJzendoorn, M. H., Juffer, F., & Gunnar, M. R. (2011). Attachment and emotional development in institutional care: Characteristics and catch-up. *Monographs of the Society for Research in Child Development*, 76(4), 62–91. https://doi.org/10.1111/j.1540-5834.2011.00628.x

Bowlby, J. (1951). *Maternal Care and Mental Health*. World Health Organization.

Bowlby, J. (1969). *Attachment and Loss, Vol. 1: Attachment*. Penguin. https://doi.org/10.2307/2798963.

Desmond, C., Watt, K., Saha, A., Huang, J., & Lu, C. (2020). Prevalence and number of children living in institutional care: Global, regional, and country estimates. *The Lancet Child & Adolescent Health*, 4(5), 370–377. https://doi.org/10.1016/s2352-4642(20)30022-5

DeVries, M. W. (1984). Temperament and infant mortality among the Masai of East Africa. *American Journal of Psychiatry*, 141(10), 1189–1194. https://doi.org/10.1176/ajp.141.10.1189

Dobrova-Krol, N. A., Van IJzendoorn, M. H., Bakermans-Kranenburg, M. J., Cyr, C., & Juffer, F. (2008). Physical growth delays and stress dysregulation in stunted and non-stunted Ukrainian institution-reared children. *Infant Behavior & Development*, 31, 539–553. https://doi.org/10.1016/j.infbeh.2008.04.001

Dobrova-Krol, N. A., & Van IJzendoorn, M. H. (2017). Institutional care in Ukraine: Historical underpinnings and developmental consequences. In A. V. Rus, S. R. Parris, & E. Stativa (Eds.), *Child Maltreatment in Residential Care: History, Research, and Current Practice* (pp. 219–240). Springer International Publishing. https://doi.org/10.1007/978-3-319-57990-0_11

Euser, S., Alink, L. R. A., Tharner, A., Van IJzendoorn, M. H., & Bakermans-Kranenburg, M. J. (2014). Out of home placement to promote safety? The prevalence of physical abuse in residential and foster care. *Child Youth Services Review*, 37, 64–70. https://doi.org/10.1016/j.childyouth.2013.12.002

Euser, S., Alink, L. R. A., Tharner, A., Van IJzendoorn, M. H., & Bakermans-Kranenburg, M. J. (2016). The prevalence of child sexual abuse in out-of-home care: Increased risk for children with a mild intellectual disability. *Journal of Applied Research in Intellectual Disabilities*, 29(1), 83–92. https://doi.org/10.1111/jar.12160.

General Assembly of the United Nations. (2019). Resolution adopted by the General Assembly on 18 December 2019. *Rights of the Child*. (Resolution No. 74/133). https://undocs.org/en/A/RES/74/133

Goffman, E. (1961). *Asylums: Essays on the Social Situation of Mental Patients and Other Inmates*. Doubleday. https://doi.org/10.1007/978-3-476-05871-3_38.

Goldman, P. S., Bakermans-Kranenburg, M. J., Bradford, B., et al. (2020a). Institutionalisation and deinstitutionalisation of children 2: Policy and practice recommendations for global, national, and local actors. *The Lancet Child & Adolescent Health*, *4*(8), 606–633. https://doi.org/10.1016/s2352-4642(20)30060-2

Goldman, P. S., Van IJzendoorn, M. H., & Sonuga-Barke, E. J. S. on behalf of the Lancet Institutional Care Reform Commission Group (2020b). The implications of COVID-19 for the care of children living in residential institutions. *The Lancet Child & Adolescent Health* (Correspondence) April 21. https://doi.org/10.1016/ S2352-4642(20)30130-9

Hamilton, W. D. (1964). The genetical evolution of social behaviour. *Journal of Theoretical Biology*, *7*(1), 1–52. https://doi.org/10.1016/0022-5193(64)90038-4

Hillis, S. D., Unwin, H. J. T., Chen, Y., Cluver, L., Sherr, L., Goldman, P. S., Ratmann, O., Donnelly, C. A., Bhatt, S., Villaveces, A., Butchart, A., Bachman, G., Rawlings, L., Green, P., Nelson, C. A., 3rd, & Flaxman, S. (2021). Global minimum estimates of children affected by COVID-19-associated orphanhood and deaths of caregivers: A modelling study. *Lancet*, *398*(10298), 391–402. https://doi.org/10.1016/S0140-6736(21)01253-8

Hrdy, S. B. (1999). *Mother Nature: A History of Mothers, Infants, and Natural Selection*. Pantheon Books. https://doi.org/10.1017/s073093840000556

Hrdy, S. (2009). *Mothers and Others: The Evolutionary Origins of Mutual Understanding*. Belknap Press. https://doi.org/10.2307/j.ctt1c84czb

Juffer, F., Van IJzendoorn, M. H., & Bakermans-Kranenburg, M. J. (2017a). Structural neglect in orphanages: Physical growth, cognition, and daily life of your institutionalized children in India. In A. V. Rus, S. R. Parris, & E. Stativa (Eds.), *Child Maltreatment in Residential Care: History, Research, and Current Practice* (pp. 301–322). Springer International Publishing AG. https://doi.org/10.1007/978-3-319-57990-0.

Juffer, F., Bakermans-Kranenburg, M. J., & Van IJzendoorn, M. H. (2017b). Pairing attachment theory and social learning theory in video-feedback intervention to promote positive parenting. *Current Opinion in Psychology*, *15*, 189–94. https://doi.org/10.1016/j.copsyc.2017.03.012

Laland, K. N. (2017). *Darwin's Unfinished Symphony*. Princeton University Press. https://doi.org/10.15581/009.52.36810

Nelson, C. A., Fox, N. A., & Zeanah, C. H. (2014). *Romania's Abandoned Children: Deprivation, Brain Development, and the Struggle for Recovery*. Harvard University Press. https://doi.org/10.4159/harvard.9780674726079

Scheper-Hughes, N. (1993). *Death without Weeping: The Violence of Everyday Life in Brazil*. University of California Press. https://doi.org/10.1525/9780520911567

Simonsohn, U., Simmons, J., & Nelson, L. D. (2022). Above averaging in literature reviews. *Nature Psychology Reviews*, *1*, 551–552. https://doi.org/10.1038/s44159-022-00101-8.

Trivers, R. L. (1974). Parent-offspring conflict. *Integrative and Comparative Biology*, *14*(1), 249–264. https://doi.org/10.1093/icb/14.1.249

Van IJzendoorn, M. H., & Bakermans-Kranenburg, M. (2021, April 8). 'Tear down your institutions': Empirical and evolutionary perspectives on institutional care in SOS Children's Villages. *PsyArxiv*. https://doi.org/10.31234/osf.io/ye7jh

Van IJzendoorn, M. H., Bakermans-Kranenburg, M. J., Duschinsky, R., Goldman, P. S., Fox, N. A., Gunnar, M. R., Johnson, D. E., Nelson, C. A., Reijman, S., Skinner, G. C. M., Zeanah, C. H., & Sonuga-Barke, E. J. S. (2020a). Institutionalisation and deinstitutionalisation of children I: A systematic and integrative review of evidence regarding effects on development. *The Lancet Psychiatry*, *7*, 703–720. https://doi.org/10.1016/S2215-0366(19)30399-2.

Van IJzendoorn, M. H., Bakermans-Kranenburg, M. J., Coughlan, B., & Reijman, S. (2020b). Child maltreatment antecedents and interventions: Umbrella synthesis and differential susceptibility perspective on risk and resilience. *Journal of Child Psychology and Psychiatry*, *61*, 272–290. https://doi.org/10.1111/jcpp.13147

Van IJzendoorn, M. H., Palacios, J., Sonuga-Barke, E. J. S., et al. (2011). Children in institutional care: Delayed development and resilience. *Monographs of the Society for Research in Child Development*, *76*(4), 8–30. https://doi.org/10.1111/j.1540-5834.2011.00626.x

6
Future generations can be saved from genocidal trauma: the case of the Holocaust

Surviving war and genocide

War and atrocities are from all times. In the Introduction of this book, we referred to how 3,000 years ago Homer described in the *Iliad* the end of the Trojan War, with a glimpse into the momentary peaceful lives and attachment relationships of Hector, Andromache, their nanny, and their son Astyanax. The story, however, ends with a series of truly traumatic events. Hector plays with his son before he returns to the battlefield. Unbeknownst to the happy family then, Achilles will defeat him. As done in those days, at least in the epic poems, the victor drags the victim's body around the city in full view of his family. This must have been a traumatic experience for Andromache and Astyanax. We read that Andromache responds with great outbursts of grief and continues to commemorate Hector after her remarriage. The impact of the trauma on Astyanax in later life is unknown, because the child is thrown from the walls for fear that he would avenge his father.

Unfortunately, reality is not more peaceful than Homer's *Iliad*. The past century has seen wars and genocides in many countries, including Armenia, Rwanda, former Yugoslavia, Ukraine, Cambodia, and Nigeria. The one that is outstanding for its scale is the Holocaust, aimed at the extermination of the Jewish people in Europe in World War II. This was not the first time that they were persecuted (see Elon, 2002), but it was the most devastating, with the murder of six million Jews. They were hunted down and slain; their living conditions in concentration camps were horrendous; they experienced starvation, diseases, and daily death threats (Eitinger & Major, 1993). Outside the concentration camps they were living in hiding under false identities in constant stress or fighting alongside the partisans in primitive and inhuman conditions (Ben-Zur & Zimmerman, 2005; Yehuda et al., 1997). It left those who survived with atrocious memories of camps and hiding places, and often without loved ones. Families, houses, and possessions were lost. Is it possible to resume daily life, coping with the experiences, and protect the next generations from the burden of what happened?

Studies of the Holocaust: select and non-select sampling

The traumatic experiences of Holocaust survivors led to in-depth studies of the long-term consequences of trauma, with diverging hypotheses and outcomes. Some researchers suggested that after such experiences, psychopathological disorders such as chronic anxiety or depression are inevitable (e.g., Niederland, 1968). Too often survivors were confronted with new stressors after the war (including being blamed for their fate, losing their premises, and realising that they had lost most of their family), resulting in secondary traumatisation (Keilson, 1979). Others submitted that only a minority would suffer from continuing psychological impairment, while the majority would be able to have successful and productive lives notwithstanding the horror they had endured (e.g., Leon et al., 1981; Sigal, 1998). A meta-analytic combination of empirical studies of survivors' mental and physical health can estimate the impact of the genocide and reveal factors that explain differences in study outcomes. The same can be done for the second and third generation of Holocaust survivors, those who did not experience the atrocities themselves, but had parents or grandparents who survived the trauma of the Holocaust. We conducted meta-analyses on the aftermath of the Holocaust in first-, second-, and third-generation survivors of the Holocaust.

Variation in research questions and paradigms as well as variation in methodological features of studies on the Holocaust may explain positive or rather negative outcomes for long-term adaptation. Important methodological issues are the selection of the target population (e.g., the specific group of concentration camp survivors versus survivors with diverging experiences during the Holocaust) and the sampling strategy. In the corpus of Holocaust studies two main sampling methods have been used to recruit participants, namely select and non-select sampling. Non-select sampling procedures involve large populations that include Holocaust survivors or draw participants from all Jewish households in a given area (e.g., Eaton et al., 1982). In non-select sampling Holocaust survivors are not studied as a group; instead, participants are recruited from a larger community with and without Holocaust experiences. Select sampling procedures employ convenience sampling methods. The snowball method of personal referral may be used, or participants from survivors' organisations or gatherings may be approached for participating in research (e.g., Shmotkin & Lomranz, 1998). It is conceivable that these two different sampling methods lead to different groups being studied, different results, and different conclusions. This can be empirically tested by using sampling method as a moderator in the meta-analyses.

The first generation

The long-term consequences in the first generation of survivors have been documented in more than 70 studies with in sum almost 13,000 participants (Barel et al., 2010). Combining these studies, we found an effect size for overall adjustment of $d = 0.36$, after correction for publication bias $d = 0.24$, meaning that Holocaust survivors were less well functioning than comparisons. Effect sizes were similar for studies focusing on men or women, respectively, but were larger in the set of studies with select sampling methods ($d = 0.45$) than when non-select sampling methods were used ($d = 0.28$). Generally speaking, for those who were children during the Holocaust effects were stronger ($d = 0.41$) than for those who experienced the Holocaust as adults ($d = 0.17$). One might expect that living in Israel after the Holocaust would support coping with the Holocaust experiences, because of a shared past and felt safety in a predominantly Jewish community (Van IJzendoorn et al., 2003). However, living in Israel could also be considered a risk to the psychological well-being of survivors, as they were expected to be silent about their suffering and put their energy into the building of the new nation (Kahana et al., 1988; Segev, 1992). In addition, wars and political instability in the Middle East may actually have threatened feelings of safety for Holocaust survivors residing in Israel. We found no difference between the two groups; studies conducted among survivors in Israel and in other countries showed similar effect sizes except for psychological well-being. Living in Israel rather than elsewhere served as a protective factor against lowering of well-being (Barel et al., 2010).

Zooming in on specific outcomes in the studies with non-select sampling methods, we found relatively small effects for later physical health, psychological well-being, and cognitive functioning ($ds < 0.17$), and by far the largest effects for post-traumatic stress symptoms ($d = 0.72$); see Figure 6.1. For neurobiological effects only select studies were available (e.g., Yehuda et al., 2002; 2005). To make sense of this

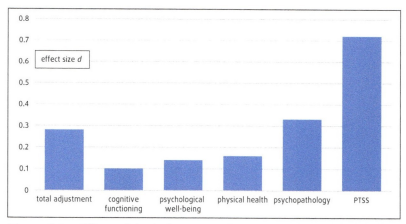

Figure 6.1 Effects of the Holocaust on first-generation survivors in non-select samples underscore the extreme nature of Holocaust-related atrocities.
Source: Authors.

pattern of results, it should be noted that a variety of measures of PTSS were used; participants were not necessarily clinically diagnosed as having PTSD when they reported post-traumatic stress symptoms. Yet, the high prevalence of post-traumatic stress symptoms in Holocaust survivors, even decades after the experience, underscores the extreme nature of Holocaust-related atrocities, and one may wonder how survivors managed to adapt relatively successfully in later life. It has been suggested that successful denial mechanisms helped survivors in repressing their traumatic experiences, focusing on active adaptation, establishing new homes, and raising new families (Mazor et al., 1990; Shanan & Shahar, 1983). In a similar vein, increased dismissal of attachment-related issues in survivors might serve as a defensive strategy to protect against vulnerability in close relationships (Sagi et al., 2002). Alternatively, survivors' resilience in the domains of physical health and cognitive functioning may play a role in successful adaptation to family life and work, despite elevated symptoms of post-traumatic stress.

The finding that negative effects for survivors were weaker when they were adults during the Holocaust than when they experienced the Holocaust as children may point to the protective effect of a childhood undisturbed by trauma. Rutter (1992) suggested that the foundation of protective mechanisms lies in self-esteem and self-efficacy. Such capacities are mainly formed through supportive interpersonal relationships during childhood and adolescence (Bowlby, 1988). Stable and secure attachment relationships with parents can be expected to foster resilience when forced to cope with traumatic events later in life, increasing the chances of adaptation in survivors with a relatively undisturbed childhood. A natural subsequent question is whether survivors in turn were able to provide a secure base for their own offspring and raise their children without transmitting the traumas of their past. Is the second generation of Holocaust survivors affected by the first generation's traumatic experiences?

The second generation

Post-traumatic stress with periods of reexperiencing the trauma, avoidance of trauma-related stimuli, and increased hypervigilance or irritability may cause impairments in social functioning, affect family life, and be in the way of sensitive parenting. This idea stimulated researchers such as Danieli (1998) to examine the intergenerational transmission of traumatic experiences to children of Holocaust survivors born after the war. This would be caused by the strains and stresses of the survivors who cannot prevent the trauma from trickling down to the next generation (Keilson, 1979). Indeed, clinical studies have reported disturbed family relations of Holocaust survivors (Barocas & Barocas, 1973; 1980), which is in line with the large effect size for post-traumatic stress symptoms in the first generation. But intergenerational transmission of the trauma may either be true of a minority of survivors' families or be very common among them.

Meta-analytic results ($k = 32$, $N = 4,418$) revealed an important difference: In studies with select sampling procedures, with participants recruited through, e.g., Holocaust survivor meetings or advertisements, secondary traumatisation was found ($d = 0.35$), but not in non-select groups of Holocaust survivor families ($d = 0.18$, not significant). This pattern was found for all types of outcomes, for general mental health or adaptation, for post-traumatic stress symptoms, and for other psychopathological symptomatology such as anxiety and depression (Van IJzendoorn et al., 2003). It made no difference whether one or both of their parents were Holocaust survivors. In non-select studies, secondary traumatisation emerged only in studies on clinical participants, who were stressed for other reasons such as a life-threatening disease or military stress. We may conclude that in general the second generation was not hindered by their parents' traumatisation. Only under conditions of severe stress does a latent vulnerability become visible in children of

Holocaust survivors. For them, the accumulation of stressful events may tip the balance.

The third generation

The absence of psychological problems in the children of Holocaust survivors in non-select studies fuels the expectation that the grandchildren will not be affected either. Nevertheless, the idea of the trauma 'running through the families' of Holocaust survivors is part of the beliefs of some professionals and the wider community. Moreover, it has been suggested that intergenerational transmission of traumas might skip a generation and be present in the grandchildren of the survivors. The corpus of studies on the third generation ($k = 13$, $N = 1012$) is smaller than those for the first and second generations, hampering thoroughly testing differential effects in studies with select and non-select sampling procedures. But in both sets of studies the combined effect sizes were small and nonsignificant, $d = 0.07$ in select studies and $d = 0.03$ in non-select studies (Sagi-Schwartz et al., 2008). The third generation shows no evidence of tertiary traumatisation; see Figure 6.2.

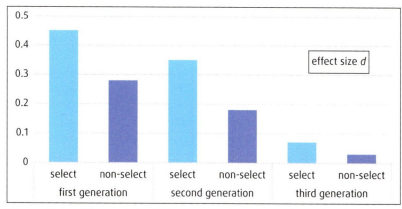

Figure 6.2 Effects of the Holocaust on first-, second-, and third-generation survivors in select and non-select samples. First-generation Holocaust survivors' traumatic stress did transmit to the second generation only in the presence of other risks and did not seem to be transmitted to the third generation.
Source: Authors.

Survival of the fittest?

The point may be raised that survivors of the Holocaust are perhaps not representative of the population of individuals who were exposed to the Holocaust. We have speculated that generally speaking, survivors must not have been genetically biased to develop intense post-traumatic stress reactions, or else they would not have survived the Holocaust, as these responses would have made them very vulnerable during the genocide (see also Schwartz et al., 1994). This genetic protection may have been transmitted to the next generation, in turn protecting children and grandchildren of survivors from developing symptoms when confronted with their parents' or grandparents' trauma. Some evidence for the exceptional resilience of Holocaust survivors emerges from our population-based retrospective cohort study including the entire population of immigrants from Poland to Israel ($N = 55{,}220$), who were between 4 and 20 years old when World War II started in 1939. We distinguished two groups: Holocaust survivors, immigrating to Israel between 1945 and 1950, and the group that immigrated to Israel before 1939 (comparison group; not exposed to the Holocaust).

We expected that psychosocial trauma, malnutrition, lack of hygienic and sanitary facilities, and medical and health services in the Holocaust survivor group would lead to a shorter life expectancy. However, we found that survivors were likely to live 6.5 months *longer* than comparisons (Sagi-Schwartz et al., 2013). We could think of two explanations for this unexpected finding. First, the genetic, temperamental, psychological, or physical characteristics that enabled them to survive the Holocaust may also predispose them to reach an older age. Second, so-called post-traumatic growth might be an alternative or complementary explanation (Calhoun et al., 2011; Van der Hal-Van Raalte et al., 2008). The idea of post-traumatic growth is that survivors find greater meaning and satisfaction in their later lives following the atrocities they experienced, which helps them reach old age. Of course, third factors such as differences in social support promoting survivors' longevity may also play a role, but such variables could not be examined in this study. One of our other studies showed, however, that quality of the care arrangements after the liberation at the end of World War II was predictive of the well-being of child survivors in old age (Van der Hal-Van Raalte et al., 2007).

Conclusions

Considering recent developments on the world stage, insights into intergenerational transmission of war-related trauma and specific resilience factors revealed by studies on the Holocaust are crucial. Our meta-analyses revealed profound post-traumatic stress effects on the first generation, accompanied by relatively mild effects in other domains of life. As parents, they seem to have managed to protect their children from being affected by the Holocaust, resulting in a second generation that only under conditions of severe stress showed increased vulnerability. The third generation was not significantly affected by their grandparents' trauma. The meta-analytic results mirror the findings of our carefully designed three-generation study of Holocaust survivors and matched controls with grandmothers, mothers, and children, conducted in Israel (Sagi-Schwartz et al., 2003), that found Holocaust survivors (now grandmothers) suffering from traumatic stress and lack of resolution of trauma, but not impaired in their general adaptation. Also, the traumatic effects did not transmit across second and third generations.

The remarkable resilience on the part of the survivors may be related to their pre-war experiences of supportive family life, the post-trauma support and care arrangements, and genetic or personal characteristics. In one study, a list of qualities was found to be predictive of post-war adaptation in Holocaust survivors. This list included optimism, intelligence, assertiveness, tenacity, courage, flexibility, group consciousness, distancing ability, assimilation of the knowledge that they survived, and finding meaning in one's life (Helmreich, 1992). These qualities are both genetically and environmentally influenced. For survivors of more recent and future war-related and genocidal catastrophes, care and support should aim at fostering such qualities to increase survivors' chances of post-war adaptation and – in spite of traumatic experiences – living fulfilling lives.

References

Barel, E., Van IJzendoorn, M. H., Sagi-Schwartz, A., & Bakermans-Kranenburg, M. J. (2010). Surviving the Holocaust: A meta-analysis of the long-term sequelae of genocide. *Psychological Bulletin, 136*, 677–698. https://doi.org/10.1037/a0020339

Barocas, H. A., & Barocas, C. B. (1973). Manifestations of concentration camp effects on the second-generation. *American Journal of Psychiatry, 130*, 820–821. https://doi.org/10.1176/ajp.130.7.820

Barocas, H. A., & Barocas, C. B. (1980). Separation–individuation conflicts in children of Holocaust survivors. *Journal of Contemporary Psychotherapy, 11,* 6–14. https://doi.org/10.1007/bf00946270

Ben-Zur, H., & Zimmerman, M. (2005). Aging Holocaust survivors' well-being and adjustment: Associations with ambivalence over emotional expression. *Psychology and Aging, 20,* 710–713. https://doi.org/10.1037/0882-7974.20.4.710

Bowlby, J. (1988). *A Secure Base: Clinical Applications of Attachment Theory.* Routledge. https://doi.org/10.1192/s0007125000224197

Calhoun L. G., Cann A., & Tedeschi R. G. (2011) The posttraumatic growth model: Socio-cultural considerations. In T. Weiss & R. Berger (Eds), *Posttraumatic Growth and Culturally Competent Practice: Lessons Learned from around the Globe* (pp. 1–14). Wiley. https://doi.org/10.1002/9781118270028.ch14

Danieli, Y. E. (1998). *International Handbook of Multigenerational Legacies of Trauma.* Plenum. https://doi.org/10.1007/978-1-4757-5567-1

Eaton, W. W., Sigal, J. J., & Weinfeld, M. (1982). Impairment in Holocaust survivors after 33 years: Data from an unbiased community sample. *American Journal of Psychiatry, 139,* 773–777. https://doi.org/10.1176/ajp.139.6.773

Eitinger, L., & Major, E. F. (1993). Stress of the Holocaust. In L. Goldberger & S. Breznitz (Eds.), *Handbook of Stress: Theoretical and Clinical Aspects* (2nd ed., pp. 617–640). Free Press. https://doi.org/10.1192/s0007125000202249

Elon, A. (2002). *The Pity of It All: A History of the Jews in Germany, 1743–1933.* Picador. https://doi.org/10.2307/20033385

Helmreich, W. (1992). *Against All Odds: Holocaust Survivors and the Successful Lives They Made in America.* Simon & Schuster. https://doi.org/10.1086/ahr/98.5.1701-a

Kahana, B., Harel, Z., & Kahana, E. (1988). Predictors of psychological well-being among survivors of the Holocaust. In J. Wilson, Z. Harel, & B. Kahana (Eds.), *Human Adaptation to Extreme Stress: From the Holocaust to Vietnam* (pp. 171–192). Plenum Press. https://doi.org/10.1007/978-1-4899-0786-8

Keilson, H. (1979). *Sequentielle traumatisierung bei Kindern. Deskriptiv-klinische und abelledive-statistische follow-up Untersuchung zum Schicksal der juedischen Kriegswaisen in den Niederlanden.* Enke. https://doi.org/10.1007/978-3-642-51871-3_8

Leon, G. R., Butcher, J. N., Kleinman, M., Goldberg, A., & Almagor, M. (1981). Survivors of the Holocaust and their children: Current status and adjustment. *Journal of Personality and Social Psychology, 41,* 503–516. https://doi.org/10.1037/0022-3514.41.3.503

Mazor, A., Gampel, Y., Enright, R. D., & Orenstein, R. (1990). Holocaust survivors: Coping with post-traumatic memories in childhood and 40 years later. *Journal of Traumatic Stress, 3,* 1–14. https://doi.org/10.1007/BF00975132

Niederland, W. G. (1968). The problem of the survivor: The psychiatric evaluations of emotional problems in survivors of Nazi persecution. In H. Krystal (Ed.), *Massive Psychic Trauma* (pp. 8–22). International University Press. https://doi.org/10.1001/archpsyc.1970.01740250096021

Rutter, M. (1992). Psychological resilience and protective mechanisms. In J. Rolf, A. S. Masten, D. Cicchetti, K. H. Nuechterlein, & S. Weintraub (Eds.), *Risk and Protective Factors in the Development of Psychopathology* (pp. 181–214). Cambridge University Press. https://doi.org/10.1017/cbo9780511752872

Sagi, A., Van IJzendoorn, M. H., Joels, T., & Scharf, M. (2002). Disorganized reasoning in Holocaust survivors. *American Journal of Orthopsychiatry, 72,* 194–203. https://doi.org/10.1037/0002-9432.72.2.194

Sagi-Schwartz, A., Bakermans-Kranenburg, M. J., Linn, S., & Van IJzendoorn, M. H. (2013). Against all odds: Genocidal trauma is associated with longer life-expectancy of the survivors. *PLoS One, 8*(7), e69179. https://doi.org/10.1371/journal.pone.0069179

Sagi-Schwartz, A., Van IJzendoorn, M. H., & Bakermans-Kranenburg, M. J. (2008). Does intergenerational transmission of trauma skip a generation? No meta-analytic evidence for tertiary traumatization with third generation of Holocaust survivors. *Attachment & Human Development, 10,* 105–121. https://doi.org/10.1080/14616730802113661

Sagi-Schwartz, A., Van IJzendoorn, M. H., Grossmann, K. E., Joels, T., Grossmann, K., Scharf, M., Koren-Karie, N., & Alkalay, S. (2003). Attachment and traumatic stress in female Holocaust child survivors and their daughters. *American Journal of Psychiatry, 160,* 1086–1092. https://doi.org/10.1176/appi.ajp.160.6.1086

Schwartz, S., Dohrenwend, B. P., & Levav, I. (1994). Nongenetic familial transmission of psychiatric disorders? Evidence from children of Holocaust survivors. *Journal of Health and Social Behavior, 35*, 385–402. https://doi.org/10.2307/2137216

Segev, T. (1992). *The Seventh Million*. Keter.

Shanan, J., & Shahar, O. (1983). Cognitive and personality functioning of Jewish Holocaust survivors during the midlife transition (46–65) in Israel. *Archiv für Psychologie, 135*, 275–294. https://doi.org/10.1080/00207411.1988.11449113

Shmotkin, D., & Lomranz, J. (1998). Subjective well-being among Holocaust survivors: An examination of overlooked differentiations. *Journal of Personality and Social Psychology, 75*, 141–155. https://doi.org/10.1037/0022-3514.75.1.141

Sigal, J. J. (1998). Long-term effects of the Holocaust: Empirical evidence for resilience in the first, second, and third generation. *Psychoanalytic Review, 85*, 579–585. https://doi.org/10.1017/s0954579407070290

Van der Hal-Van Raalte, E. A. M., Bakermans–Kranenburg, M. J., & Van IJzendoorn, M. H. (2007). Quality of care after early childhood trauma and well-being in later life: Child Holocaust survivors reaching old age. *American Journal of Orthopsychiatry, 77*, 514–522. https://doi.org/10.1037/0002-9432.77.4.514

Van der Hal-Van Raalte, E. A. M., Van IJzendoorn, M. H., & Bakermans–Kranenburg, M. J. (2008). Sense of coherence moderates late effects of early childhood Holocaust exposure. *Journal of Clinical Psychology, 64*, 1352–1367. https://doi.org/10.1002/jclp.20528

Van IJzendoorn, M. H., Bakermans-Kranenburg, M. J., & Sagi-Schwartz, A. (2003). Are children of Holocaust survivors less well-adapted? A meta-analytic investigation of secondary traumatization. *Journal of Traumatic Stress, 16*, 459–469. https://doi.org/10.1023/A:1025706427300

Yehuda, R., Golier, J. A., Harvey, P. D., Stavitsky, K., Kaufman, S., Grossman, R. A., & Tischler, L. (2005). Relationship between cortisol and age-related memory impairments in Holocaust survivors with PTSD. *Psychoneuroendocrinology, 30*, 678–687. https://doi.org/10.1016/j.psyneuen.2005.02.007

Yehuda, R., Halligan, S. L., Grossman, R., Golier, J. A., & Wong, C. (2002). The cortisol and glucocorticoid receptor response to low dose dexamethasone administration in aging combat veterans and Holocaust survivors with and without posttraumatic stress disorder. *Biological Psychiatry, 52*, 393–403. https://doi.org/10.1016/S006-3223(02)01357-4

Yehuda, R., Schmeidler, J., Siever, L. J., Binder-Brynes, K., & Elkin, A. (1997). Individual differences in posttraumatic stress disorder symptom profile in Holocaust survivors in concentration camps or in hiding. *Journal of Traumatic Stress, 10*, 453–463. https://doi.org/10.1023/A:1024845422065

7
Jumping from 'is' to 'ought'?

Naturalistic fallacy

What 'is' the case cannot be automatically translated into what 'ought' to be done even when 'is' is a replicated finding. Hume's law of ethics states that one cannot jump from 'is' to 'ought' in a logically valid way because any sound argument for a normative conclusion must (perhaps implicitly) contain a normative premise. Jumping from 'is' to 'ought' without such a premise is committing a 'naturalistic fallacy'. For example, the bridge between the evidence base for our video-feedback intervention (VIPP-SD, see Chapter 4) and the desirability of promoting secure attachments in families cannot be taken for granted but must be constructed. Assessing the desirability from the perspective of the parents of both parental sensitive responsiveness and child attachment security is one way to construct such a bridge.

But is empirical consensus sufficient? We do not pretend to have found a solution for the conundrum of the naturalistic fallacy. Inspired by John Rawls' contractualism, we wonder what minimal parenting styles and attachment relationships people would agree upon if they were without any knowledge of their future position in the family and in the wider, global society. From this perspective, we speculate, for example, that (international) adoption is justifiable as a last option to get an institutionalised child out of structural neglect and into a safe family environment (see Chapter 14). In the case of court decisions about out-of-home placement of children, we suggest that 'good-enough', non-maltreating parenting is sufficient to retain children in their original homes as it would protect vulnerable children from being unsafe even if they are at increased risk of insecure attachments (see Chapter 12).

Replicated evidence is not sufficient

Against the background of the replication crisis, we propose that only scientific results which have been successfully replicated multiple times and for which meta-analytic evidence is available may responsibly be translated into recommendations for policy or practice. Yet, multiple replications are a necessary but not sufficient condition for practical applications. Take as an example advice to parents on how to handle their crying infant. If we only had replicated meta-analytic evidence that early parental sensitive responsiveness predicted later increased frequency of infant crying, we still would not know whether this association was genuinely causal, and whether a change in parental behaviour would be followed by a desirable change in infant crying. And even when causality could be demonstrated, we should take into account that lowering the level of parental sensitive responsiveness might have some unexpected consequences or collateral damage and breaches the basic ethical rule of 'non nocere' or avoid damage. For example, an iatrogenic effect in the long term might consist in harmful disappointment of the children's expectation of parental availability in times of (di-)stress as a core component of secure attachments (Bosmans et al., 2020; Hubbard & Van IJzendoorn, 1991).

Our recent meta-analysis of 25 randomised controlled trials (RCTs) conducted on the Video-feedback Intervention to promote Positive Parenting and Sensitive Discipline (VIPP-SD) that we developed over the past 30 years (Juffer et al., 2017; Bakermans-Kranenburg et al., 2019) demonstrates the positive effect of sensitive parental responses for children's attachment development. We showed that the VIPP-SD intervention is effective in enhancing parental sensitive responsiveness and sensitive limit setting (combined effect size $d = 0.33$). The VIPP-SD intervention also promoted a secure child–parent attachment relationship, with a robust effect size of $d = 0.48$. Larger effect sizes for parenting predicted stronger effects for secure attachments, suggesting once more a causal relation ($r = 0.48$) (Van IJzendoorn et al., 2023; see Chapter 4). Effect sizes of VIPP-SD might even be stronger in susceptible sub-groups as predicted by the differential susceptibility theory (see Bakermans-Kranenburg & Van IJzendoorn, 2015, for elaborations on this theory of the hidden efficacy of interventions).

Even though we have some firm meta-analytic evidence for a causal role of parental sensitive behaviour in the development of attachment security, however, one link between science and practice is still missing. What 'is' the case cannot be automatically translated into what 'ought' to be done. Hume's law of ethics states that one cannot jump from 'is' to 'ought' in a logically valid way because any sound argument for a normative conclusion must contain a (perhaps implicit) normative premise (Richards, 2000). Jumping from 'is' to 'ought' without such a premise is sometimes called committing a 'naturalistic fallacy' (Wilson, Dietrich, & Clark 2003; Kohlberg, 1971). The step from the effectiveness of VIPP-SD ('is') to the desirability of promoting secure attachments in families ('ought') cannot be taken for granted. It requires, for example, assessing the desirability of both parental sensitive responsiveness and limit setting as well as child attachment security from the perspective of the parents. This is what we studied with the Q-sort method in a range of countries and cultures (see also Chapter 11). We found that a large majority of parents considered both sensitive parenting and secure attachment as highly desirable. The 751 mothers from 26 cultural groups sorted the Maternal Behavior Q-Sort for their ideal image of how a parent should interact with their children. Their combined Q-sort correlated $r = 0.68$ with the expert sort of ideally sensitive parenting (Mesman, Van IJzendoorn et al., 2016). In a similar vein, a study with the Attachment Q-Sort showed high convergence between attachment experts and mothers in six different countries (Posada et al., 1995; 2013).

This empirical consensus would be appreciated by Bowlby, who argued pragmatically: 'how do we know what is bad? I know it is bad to leave my rent unpaid because I agreed, when making the contract, to regard it so. In other words, external morality is a matter of social agreement. If two people agree to regard a thing as bad within those limits it is bad. If they agree to regard it as good then it is good' (Bowlby in Chapter 7 'Guilt and family contracts', published in Duschinsky & White, 2020, p. 144). It is debatable, however, whether Hume would find this satisfactory, because a genuine normative statement would still be absent in this reasoning. Philosopher G.E. Moore would also be troubled by evidence consisting of such an empirical consensus (Richards, 2000). Applying his 'Open Question' to the ethical desirability of sensitive parenting or secure attachment, Moore might still have had his doubts about the answer to this question: 'Is a securely attached person a good person?' or 'Is a sensitive parent a good person?' He might still wonder whether secure attachment would be a morally good property in itself. And Moore indeed might be right because, to our disappointment, in 40 years of searching for the predictive relation between parenting, attachment, and moral choices, e.g., costly donating, we have not been able to find any robust and replicable association (Van IJzendoorn & Bakermans-Kranenburg, 2021; see Chapter 12). Securely attached individuals seem more inclined to choose their moral options depending on social context such as nudges instead of an inner compass – just like insecurely attached individuals (Bakermans-Kranenburg & Van IJzendoorn, 2019).

The ABC of attachment

Bowlby was acutely aware of the value-laden connotations of attachment terminology. Mary Ainsworth wanted to use for attachment classifications concepts like 'prematurely independent', 'secure', and 'disturbed', but Bowlby insisted on avoiding such normative terms. This led to the use of the prosaic labels A, B, and C (John Bowlby, 1967, letter to Mary Ainsworth on April 19, cited by Duschinsky, 2020). The use of the concept of 'contract' by John Bowlby may be seen as some kind of contractualism and maybe points to John Rawls' (1999) theory of justice and the central role of the 'original position' in that theory. If people would not have any knowledge of their position in the family or in the wider, global society and had to decide on a contract for living in such a community, they would agree on some general, even universal ethical rules to guide their interactions and relationships and to protect the most vulnerable individuals from a life without self- and social respect (Van IJzendoorn, 1980).

Applying this idea to the question of justifiability of (international) adoption, we argued that Rawls' maximin rule, that is, maximalisation of minimum requirements for a minimally satisfactory life of the most vulnerable members of a society, would prevail (Van IJzendoorn & Juffer, 2006). From the perspective of an original position, we argued that international adoption is therefore justifiable as a last option to get an institutionalised child out of structural neglect and into a safe family environment (see Chapter 14). In the case of parenting and attachment, individuals in the original position might argue that 'good-enough', non-maltreating parenting is sufficient as it would protect vulnerable children from feeling unsafe and unable to explore their environment. Whether '(a) secure attachment to parents for a child ought to be seen as a basic human right' (Steele, 2019) is doubtful as it may not be a necessary condition to live a minimally satisfactory life. It is helpful to be reminded of the distinction between safety and security (see Van IJzendoorn & Bakermans-Kranenburg, 2021). Bowlby distinguished between safety and security in an unpublished manuscript by tracing the etymology of 'safe' to the Latin word 'salvus', that is, the absence of injury, and 'secure' as originating from 'se cura', that is, being without a care (see Duschinsky,

2020). The primary function of attachment figures and attachment relationships is to provide safety, increasing the child's chances for survival and reproductive fitness. In the optimal scenario, attachment relationships and figures also provide security. In an insecure attachment relationship, the caregiver may still provide safety, even in the absence of security.

Evolutionary jump from is to ought?

Theories of inclusive fitness, life history, and cross-cultural models suggest that it is not universally possible to evaluate a specific parenting style or attachment type as optimal in all socio-economic or cultural contexts. Instead, these theories approach parenting and attachment from a 'value-free' perspective of adaptation to a specific niche (Hinde, 1982; Hochberg & Belsky, 2013). In life-history theory, the term 'adaptive' refers to reproductive fitness and does not imply that a trait is socially desirable or beneficial for well-being per se (Ellis & Del Giudice, 2019). In some environments, harsh parenting and insecure attachment may improve children's inclusive fitness, for example, by increasing their vigilance against threats.

To avoid the counterintuitive implication that parenting interventions should promote insensitive parenting, additional ethical considerations are necessary. Simply stating that secure attachment is a basic right of children (Steele, 2019) is a jump from 'is' to 'ought' with unintended risky consequences, such as a legitimisation of transferring 40% of the children (namely, those who are insecurely attached) to another family, which in some contexts (e.g., families with poverty stress leading to less sensitive parenting) might be even more than 40%.

However, inclusive fitness theory, life-history theory, and cross-cultural models also fail to explicitly consider the ethical implications of supporting parents to be harsh to their children or empowering them to change their harsh environments based on the reasoning that insecure attachments and harsh parenting may be adaptive in niches characterised by unpredictability. For example, Ellis and colleagues have proposed the 'hidden talents' model, which posits that children who survive and adapt to harsh and dangerous environments should not be viewed as 'delayed' or as developing in an atypical way. Instead, their hidden talents should be used 'to promote success in normative contexts' (see Ellis et al., 2020, Figure 1). Applied questions such as what 'normative contexts' mean for these children and which alternative approaches could be

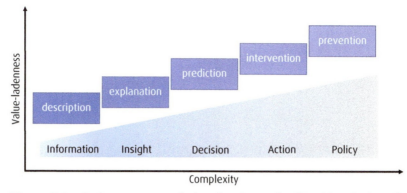

Figure 7.1 Stairways to translational action and policy. Translation of replicated findings to practice and policy is increasingly complex and more value-laden.
Source: Authors.

used to empower parents to change their children's harsh environments remain unanswered. As we move closer to policy and practice, intervention and prevention, ethical issues and choices become more pressing (see Figure 7.1).

Avoiding such choices, the concept of adaptation in the service of fitness only shifts ethical issues to the justifiability of the social context (e.g., a fast reproductive strategy as an adaptation to poverty). Addressing the ethical challenges inherent in the concept of 'good-enough' parenting and child development may be best achieved through open communication about minimal ethical standards for a just society (Habermas, 1984/1987; How, 2001; Rawls, 1999). Bowlby's, Ainsworth's, and Main's foci on the evolutionary expected and natural adaptive value of parental sensitivity and child security imply 'a fundamental compatibility between man and society' (Stayton et al., 1971, p. 1059), but they ignore the need for open discourse on socio-ethical standards – a neglect of the ethical dimension not much different from life-history theory.

The idea that insecure attachments may be 'conditional strategies' (Main, 1990) and second-best options in difficult child-rearing environments highlights the 'ontological' or 'natural' status of secure attachments, rather than the potential ethical superiority of this 'default option'. This still requires ethical arguments to avoid jumping from is to ought (Kohlberg, 1971) and falling in the ravine. To her credit, Main did not promote herself as an authority on what parents should do, emphasising that her suggestions might not be interpreted as authoritative for practitioners (Duschinsky, 2020). In contrast to John Bowlby, most members of the first and second generation of empirical attachment researchers have also avoided going public (except in rare cases of consensus statements, e.g., Forslund et al., 2021). It is hoped that Mary Main's caution in translating preliminary, shaky results to practice is inherited by the coming generations of attachment researchers.

References

Bakermans-Kranenburg, M. J., & Van IJzendoorn, M. H. (2015). The hidden efficacy of interventions: Gene x Environment experiments from a differential susceptibility perspective. *Annual Review of Psychology, 66*, 381–409. https://doi.org/10.1146/annurev-psych-010814-015407

Bakermans-Kranenburg, M. J., & Van IJzendoorn, M. H. (2021). Dimensions, determinants, and development of prosocial behaviour: A differential susceptibility hypothesis on attachment and moral character. In E. Harcourt (Ed.), *Attachment and Character: Attachment Theory, Ethics, and the Developmental Psychology of Vice and Virtue* (pp. 44–70). Oxford University Press. https://doi.org/10.1093/oso/9780192898128.001.0001

Bakermans-Kranenburg, M. J., Juffer, F., & Van IJzendoorn, M. H. (2019). Reflections on the mirror: On video-feedback to promote positive parenting and infant mental health. In Ch.H. Zeanah (Ed.), *Handbook of Infant Mental Health* (4th ed., pp. 527–542). Guilford Press.

Bosmans, G., Bakermans-Kranenburg, M. J., Vervliet, B., Verhees, M. W. F. T., & Van IJzendoorn, M. H. (2020). A learning theory of attachment: Unraveling the black box of attachment development. *Neuroscience & Biobehavioral Reviews, 113*, 287–298. https://doi.org/10.1016/j.neubiorev.2020.03.014

Bowlby, J. (2020). Guilt and family contracts. In R. Duschinsky & K. White (Eds.), *Trauma and Loss: Key Texts from the John Bowlby Archive* (pp. 141–164) Routledge. https://doi.org/10.4324/9780429329234-8

Duschinsky, R. (2020). *Cornerstones of Attachment Research in the Twenty First Century*. Oxford University Press. https://doi.org/10.1093/med-psych/9780198842064.001.0001

Duschinsky, R., & White, K. (2020). *Trauma and Loss: Key Texts from the John Bowlby Archive*. Routledge.

How, A. R. (2001). Habermas, history and social evolution: Moral learning and the trial of Louis XVI. *Sociology, 35*(1), 177–194. https://doi.org/10.1177/0038038501035001011

Juffer, F., Bakermans-Kranenburg, M. J., & Van IJzendoorn, M. H. (2017). Pairing attachment theory and social learning theory in video-feedback intervention to promote positive parenting. *Current Opinion in Psychology, 15*, 189–94. https://doi.org/10.1016/j.copsyc.2017.03.012

Ellis, B. J., & Del Giudice, M. (2019). Developmental adaptation to stress: An evolutionary perspective. *Annual Review of Psychology, 70*(1), 111–139. https://doi.org/10.1146/annurev-psych-122216-011732

Ellis, B. J., Abrams, L. S., Masten, A. S., Sternberg, R. J., Tottenham, N., & Frankenhuis, W. E. (2020). Hidden talents in harsh environments. *Development and Psychopathology, 34*, 95–113. https://doi.org/10.1017/S0954579420000887

Forslund, T., Granqvist, P., Van IJzendoorn, M. H., et al. (2021). Attachment goes to court: Child protection and custody issues. *Attachment and Human Development, 24*, 1–52. https://doi.org/10.1080/14616734.2020.1840762

Habermas, J. (1984/1987). *The Theory of Communicative Action* (Volumes 1 and 2). Beacon Press. https://doi.org/10.1515/9780773581692-008

Hochberg, Z., & Belsky, J. (2013). Evo-devo of human adolescence: Beyond disease models of early puberty. *BMC Medicine, 11*, 113. https://doi.org/0.1186/1741-7015-11-113

Hubbard, F. O., & Van IJzendoorn, M. H. (1991). Maternal unresponsiveness and infant crying across the first nine months: A naturalistic longitudinal study. *Infant Behavior and Development, 14*(3), 299–312. https://doi.org/10.1016/0163-6383(91)90024-M

Hinde, R. A. (1982). Attachment: Some conceptual and biological issues. In C. Murray Parkes & J. Stevenson-Hinde (Eds.), *The Place of Attachment in Human Behavior* (pp. 60–76). Basic Books. https://doi.org/10.1192/s0007125000119051

Kohlberg, L. (1971). From is to ought: How to commit the naturalistic fallacy and get away with it in the study of moral development. In T. Mischel (Ed.), *Cognitive Development and Psychology* (pp. 151–235). Academic Press. https://doi.org/10.1017/s0012217300036957

Main, M. (1990). Cross-cultural studies of attachment organization: Recent studies, changing methodologies, and the concept of conditional strategies. *Human Development, 33*(1), 48–61. https:// doi.org/10.1159/000276502

Mesman, J., Van IJzendoorn, M., Behrens, K., Alicia Carbonell, O., Carcamo, R., Cohen-Paraira, I., de la Harpe, C., Ekmekci, H., Emmen, R., Heidar, J., Kondo-Ikemura, K., Mels, C., Mooya, H., Murtisari, S., Noblega, M., Ortiz, J. A., Sagi-Schwartz, A., Sichimba, F., Soares, I., Steele, H., Steele, M., Pape, M., Van Ginkel, J., Van der Veer, R., Wang, L., Selcuk, B., Yavuz, M., & Zreik, G. (2016). Is the ideal mother a sensitive mother? Beliefs about early childhood parenting in mothers across the globe. *International Journal of Behavioral Development, 40*(5), 385–397. https://doi.org/10.1177/0165025415594030

Posada, G. (2013). Is the secure base phenomenon evident here, there, and anywhere? A cross-cultural study of child behavior and experts' definitions. *Child Development, 84*(6), 1896–1905. https://doi.org/10.1111/cdev.12108

Posada, G., Gao, Y., Wu, F., Posada, R., Tascon, M., Schöelmerich, A., Sagi, A., Kondo-Ikemura, K., Haaland, W., & Synnevaag, B. (1995). The secure-base phenomenon across cultures: Children's behavior, mothers' preferences, and experts' concepts. *Monographs of the Society for Research in Child Development, 60*(2/3), 27–48. www.jstor.org/stable/1166169

Richards, J. R. (2000). *Human Nature after Darwin: A Philosophical Introduction*. Routledge. https://doi.org/10.4324/9780203991909-5

Rawls, J. (1999). *A Theory of Justice* (Rev. edition). Harvard University Press. https://doi.org/ 10.4159/9780674042582

Steele, H. (2019). Commentary: Money can't buy you love, but lack of love costs families and society plenty – A comment on Bachmann et al. *Journal of Child Psychology and Psychiatry, 60*(12), 1351–1352. https://doi.org/10.1111/jcpp.13111

Stayton, D. J., Hogan, R., & Ainsworth, M. D. (1971). Infant obedience and maternal: The origins of socialization reconsidered. *Child Development, 42*(4), 1057–1069. https://doi.org/10. 2307/ 1127792

Van IJzendoorn, M. H. (l980). *Moralität und politisches Bewusstsein. Eine Untersuchung zur politischen Sozialisation*. [Morality and political attitudes. A study in political socialization]. Beltz Verlag.

Van IJzendoorn, M. H., & Bakermans-Kranenburg, M. J. (2021). Replication crisis lost in translation? On translational caution and premature applications of attachment theory. *Attachment & Human Development, 23*, 422–437. https://doi.org/10.1080/14616734.2021.1918453

Van IJzendoorn, M., Schuengel, C., Wang, Q., & Bakermans-Kranenburg, M. (2023). Improving parenting, child attachment, and externalizing behaviors: Meta-analysis of the first 25 randomized controlled trials on the effects of Video-feedback Intervention to promote Positive Parenting and Sensitive Discipline. *Development and Psychopathology, 35*(1), 241–256. https://doi.org/10.1017/S0954579421001462

Van IJzendoorn, M. H., & Juffer, F. (2006). The Emanuel Miller Memorial Lecture 2006: Adoption as intervention: Meta-analytic evidence for massive catch-up and plasticity in physical, socio-emotional, and cognitive development. *Journal of Child Psychology and Psychiatry, 47*, 1228–1245. https://doi.org/10.1111/j.1469-7610.2006.01675.x

Wilson, D. S., Dietrich, E., & Clark, A. B. (2003). On the inappropriate use of the naturalistic fallacy in evolutionary psychology. *Biology & Philosophy, 18*, 669–681. https://doi.org/10.1023/A:1026380825208

8
Dubious effect size standards and cost-effectiveness criteria

Inflated effect size standards

Disseminating a treatment or intervention in a large population via training of professionals and influencing policymakers requires not only the highest level of replicated causal evidence (see Chapter 4) and agreement about the ethics of the intervention goals (Chapter 7) but also a balance between the programme's effect size and its costs. The two criteria of effect size and costs are central to Kraft's (2020) schema for evaluating cost-effectiveness of educational intervention programmes. When, for example, we would like to evaluate the cost-effectiveness of our VIPP-SD intervention according to this schema, we have to first estimate whether its effects are small, medium, or large. According to conventional Cohen's d criteria, its effectiveness for both parenting and child attachment security is medium. Yet, already at the introduction of these criteria Cohen (1988) warned that we should weigh effect sizes in the context of a specific research and translational domain. Without consideration of context, effect sizes are incorrectly interpreted when estimating the translational value of interventions (Cuijpers et al., 2014; Kraft, 2020).

For the domain of home-visiting parenting support programmes like the VIPP-SD, sobering effectiveness figures have been found. For example, HomVEE, the Home Visiting Evidence of Effectiveness that is sponsored by the U.S. Department of Health and Human Services (HHS) and produces yearly reviews of parenting interventions, reported a meta-analytic effect size of $d = 0.10$ for parenting interventions (Sama-Miller et al., 2020), which is similar to the combined effect size for positive parenting in four widely used home-visiting programmes examined by another team (Michalopoulos et al., 2019). Perhaps even more sobering

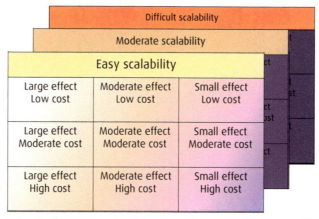

Figure 8.1 Evaluating societal impact of interventions according to their (replicated) effects, costs in comparison to care-as-usual, and scalability to larger populations (according to Kraft, 2020).

is the $d = 0.40$ improvement of academic achievement across a whole school year in fifth grade (Kraft, 2020), which was reason for Kraft to propose considering effect sizes (d) lower than 0.05 as small, 0.05–0.20 as medium, and 0.20 or more as large in the field of educational interventions (Kraft, 2020). Cross-tabulating these effectiveness criteria with cost per child (low < $500; $500 < moderate < $4000; high > $4000) produces a schema with nine cost-effectiveness ratios (Kraft, 2020, p. 250); see Figure 8.1. Scalability is an additional factor that might be taken into account (see below).

In our economic evaluation of the pre-registered pragmatic randomised trial with VIPP-SD for toddlers at risk for conduct problems in the United Kingdom (Healthy Start, Happy Start; led by Paul Ramchandani and Christine O'Farrelly, see O'Farrelly et al., 2021a) we estimated the all-in cost per family compared to usual care to be £1,450 (per financial year 2017–2018; O'Farrelly et al., 2021b). Home-visiting programmes such as VIPP-SD are relatively expensive because of the personalised coaching and travelling time on the side of the intervener, which is one of the reasons for developing an online or hybrid version of VIPP-SD with Eloise Stevens and other colleagues. The COVID-19 pandemic and lockdowns precluding home visits added to the urgency to speed up the development of an online or virtual version of VIPP-SD (Van IJzendoorn et al., 2023). However, compared to a popular group-based parenting intervention programme with pre-schoolers in the UK, Incredible Years,

VIPP-SD is less expensive, as the estimated costs of Incredible Years amount to £1,612–£2,418 per individual. Based on intervention effectiveness and costs, VIPP-SD would be projected at the crossroads of large effect sizes and moderate costs in the Kraft schema and get the green light for dissemination.

Cost-effectiveness not considered before implementation?

Unfortunately, the cost-effectiveness of interventions is not always considered before implementation. An example of a red light for an already implemented programme can be found in the large-scale Preventive Intervention Team project (PIT; Swaab, 2012) that has been implemented in the Dutch cities of Amsterdam and Leiden. The PIT does meet almost no translational criteria. According to the analysis of Spanjaard (2019), no detailed protocol for PIT is available, even several years after the start of the implementation. The theoretical foundation of the programme is an eclectic neuropsychological model of social information processing, social perspective taking, applying social scripts, and self-regulation. School-aged children at risk for conduct problems and antisocial behaviour are screened for problems with these four components, and a tailored intervention offered (Spanjaard, 2019).

In one of the few scientific publications on the PIT model and dataset, Van Zonneveld et al. (2017) found no differences at baseline in social attention and cognitive empathy of the PIT participants with typically developing children. Physiological measures of affective empathy (heart rate, skin conductance level, and response to brief pain stimuli) did show lower levels for the PIT group, with partial eta squared ranging from 0.03 to 0.07. These effect sizes are statistically significant but not practically relevant for screening or diagnostic purposes because separate and combined they fail basic sensitivity and specificity criteria (see Chapter 12).

Furthermore, the PIT intervention has not been tested in a randomised controlled trial, not even in a quasi-experimental comparison, because no attempt was made to create equivalent groups, for example, with propensity score matching (Purnama Sari et al., 2022). On the contrary, the two groups differed more than 20 IQ points as average IQ of the PIT group was 83 versus 104 in the control group. Last but not least, the PIT is estimated to cost €18,000 per family and ranked highest on costs per unit in Spanjaard's (2019, p. 18) list of eight interventions focusing on prevention of antisocial behaviour. Incredible Years and VIPP-SD would rank in the lower middle part of the distribution. The PIT therefore is a waste of efforts by all parties involved, especially for the families who run the risk of becoming disappointed because they do not experience any progress in solving their issues. Unintended harm and collateral damage of interventions are important costs to be included in the balance with benefits, and *no nocere* is one of the four essential criteria in biomedical ethics (Gillon, 1994).

Besides effect size and cost-effectiveness, a third dimension relevant to decision about implementing intervention programmes is scalability (Kraft, 2020); see Figure 8.1. If a parent training programme would be embedded in regular care for young parents (in well-baby clinics or by home-visiting nurses), even small meta-analytic effects would have high impact population wide. Societal costs of insecure compared to secure attachments in adolescents with conduct problems have been estimated at £3,456 per individual (Bachmann et al., 2019). The benefits of secure attachments might increase after adolescence and further accumulate across the lifespan (as predicted by Nobel Prize–winning economist James Heckman, 2006). Effective early interventions may have substantial returns, not only in saved money but also, and perhaps more importantly, in attachment security between the children and their parents.

Quality Adjusted Life-Years

A cost-utility analysis with Quality Adjusted Life-Years or QALYs is a highly ambitious health economics project that aims to make the investment in any intervention comparable to all kinds of mental and physical health interventions and treatments (see Chapter 2 for a preliminary discussion). It is somewhat overzealous to search for a theory of everything with an amazingly simplistic approach that suffers from questionable psychometrics of the questionnaire method (see Chapter 2) but already has real-life consequences. If the QALY standard would be valid, a cognitive behaviour therapy for depression in adults can be compared with an intervention to support families with infants at risk for internalising problems in terms of returns on investment. For policymakers and clinicians this facilitates cost-effective budgetary decision making. A seemingly objective yardstick or common currency for interventions and treatments might save tons of money. But we argue that health economics still has a long way to go before the cost-utility approach can be validly applied to developmental mental health interventions.

We illustrate our sceptical position with an analysis of the EQ-5D that is often used in health economics, but other measures may struggle with similar issues. In the EQ-5D approach, healthy, rational individuals are asked to choose a specific number of years of full health in five domains over years with 'some' or 'a lot' of problems in one or more of those domains. The domains are physical mobility, looking after yourself, doing usual activities, having pain or discomfort, and feeling anxious or depressed. The scores provide a set of Time Trade-Off (TTO) weights for the health states represented by the five domains. Healthy instead of clinical individuals provide these QALY norms because ill people are suggested to 'overestimate' the impact of their condition. Thus, in a TTO study several thousands of non-clinical adults chose how many life years with handicaps they would trade for healthy years, thereby providing the weights for QALY score computation through the trade-off of imagined healthy life years versus life years with more or less severe handicaps (see Van IJzendoorn & Bakermans-Kranenburg, 2020, for computational examples).

Before and after treatment or intervention, individuals score whether they have no, some, or a lot of problems in the five domains. Their change in scores (or the difference between a treatment and a control group) are multiplied by the weights assigned by the healthy norm group, resulting in a QALY score as index for the effectiveness of the intervention. The TTO approach to determining QALYs is, however, based on an impossible choice between different states of health. For example, a 25-year-old individual who has not experienced any health problems may not be the best person to compare two different types of health issues. Without having experienced both the impact of physical pain and the impact of a depression with suicidal thoughts, these conditions are incomparable. According to the TTO weights, however, 'a lot' of problems with depression or anxiety (.236) are given a lower weight than 'a lot' of problems with pain or discomfort (.386). Moreover, older individuals may place a higher value on mobility and self-care than younger individuals, but given their shorter life expectancy they may also be less willing to exchange healthy years for years with impaired health (Szende, Janssen, & Cabases, 2014).

It has been suggested that in cases where children are unable to answer the five questions used in the QALY approach, a proxy such as a parent could complete the questionnaire on behalf of the child. For children, the EuroQol 5 Dimensions for Youth scale (EQ-5D-Y) is used. The healthy child according to the EQ-5D-Y does not have problems in the five domains, rephrased for children as 'Walking about', 'Washing or dressing themselves', 'Doing their usual activities', 'Pain or discomfort', 'Worried, sad or unhappy'. A brief parent- or self-report questionnaire with one question on each of the five domains is completed. The individual scoring pattern is compared to a set of calibrated TTO weights for the various health states represented by the EQ-5D-Y, and a QALY score is computed. This approach has several limitations. First, research on attachment has shown that some parents may be insensitive to their children's negative emotions and dismiss them, perhaps because they trigger their own childhood distress experiences (Bowlby, 1969). Additionally, poverty has been shown to negatively impact parents' sensitivity to their children's emotions (Bakermans-Kranenburg et al., 2004, see Chapter 11), as they may be more focused on survival and coping with adversities. Parents and children may even have different interests in terms of health and happiness for the child. For example, the parent's interest may be uninterrupted sleep, whereas the child's interest may be night-time feeding. This concurs with evidence that parents and children differ rather strongly in their evaluation of child mental health needs (De Los Reyes et al., 2015). From an evolutionary perspective, Trivers (1974) argued that parents should distribute scarce resources among their offspring, while each child tries to maximise their own chances of survival and parental care, potentially at the expense of their siblings. These factors contribute to the biased nature of using a proxy to establish QALY norms for children.

The use of adult weights in the calculation of QALYs for children and adolescents is also problematic from a developmental perspective. Human development is a dynamic, transactional process that changes the meaning of a good life, of 'health and happiness', over time. In infancy, the main caregivers play a significant role in protecting the child, meeting their basic needs, and regulating their stress. The well-being of parent and child are closely connected. In adolescence, peer relationships become more important and 'health and happiness' must be redefined to account for challenges such as social rejection or aggression (Vrijhoff et al., 2016). Additionally, utility is assumed to be a static numerator, but the long-term effects of treatment, interventions, or social policies for developing youth with changing needs are often unknown. The time frame used in the TTO approach, 10 years, may not be appropriate for children, as a decade in a child's life is not equivalent to a decade in the life of a 40-year-old adult (see also Rowen et al., 2020). To accurately evaluate and compare the cost-effectiveness of (preventive) interventions in childhood and adolescence (see Chapter 4), these developmental differences cannot be left out of the equation.

Weaknesses of the QALY health economics approach are thus numerous. Why is only one of the five domains focusing on mental health (and then only of the internalising type), which makes it more difficult for mental health interventions to be financially competitive with physical health treatments? How are socio-economic status differences, cultural origin, and minority status disparities accounted for? What is a society willing to pay for a QALY when, as an example, current estimates of the Dutch willingness to pay per QALY range from €13,000 to €110,000 (Stadhouders et al., 2019)? We argue that the QALY approach is suffering from a neo-liberal emphasis on individuals' striving for maximisation of their own personal health and happiness. The health economics analyses of interventions in the area of child and adolescent development are based on untenable assumptions and wrong standards in terms of age and domains of health and happiness.

The lack of focus on the externalising domain ignores the social nature of the human species (Gintis & Helbing, 2015). Externalising problems have a negative impact not only on the individual but also on their social network and the larger society. Many evidence-based parent-child interventions, such as VIPP-SD (Juffer, Bakermans-Kranenburg & Van IJzendoorn, 2017, see Chapter 4), ABC (Bernard et al., 2012), and Incredible Years (Gardner, Leijten, Melendez-Torres et al., 2019; O'Neil, McGilloway, Donnelly et al., 2013), aim to reduce or prevent externalising behaviour problems such as aggression, conduct problems, and oppositional behaviour. With the EQ-5D they cannot claim QALY gains in this domain. The QALY approach fails to consider the importance of prosocial behaviour or regulating aggressive impulses in defining optimal (mental) health. In general, health economics focuses on intervention effects on the individual's health and happiness. The potential negative effects of externalising behaviour on parents or siblings in their family (Mortimer & Segal, 2006) and on peers in day-care or school settings (Belsky, 2009) are ignored.

Evaluation committees for interventions to support families and children

The Netherlands Youth Institute (NJi) evaluates interventions aiming at a broad range of social, mental, and physical health problems of children and adolescents from age 0 to 17 years emerging in families or schools. NJi informs government, municipalities, insurance companies, and others about (non-)effective interventions. The evaluation criteria of NJi can be summarised as interventions that are protocolised, rooted in validated theory, and used in at least two randomised controlled trials showing effectiveness, one of which should have been successfully conducted in the Netherlands. Incredible Years and VIPP-SD are among the effective interventions evaluated with the NJi criteria applied by a committee of senior researchers. The PIT discussed above has not yet been submitted to NJi (as of 12 October 2022), and effectiveness studies are still missing – 10 years after the translation to practice.

The USA team that evaluates the evidence base for 'early childhood home visiting service delivery models' is the abovementioned HomVEE (Sama-Miller et al., 2020). Eligible papers target studies on pregnant women or families with children whose ages range from birth up through age 5. Home visiting is an essential component of interventions selected for evaluation. Criteria for an evidence-based label include at least one of the following: one high- or moderate-quality study showing statistically significant effects in two outcome domains, and at least two high- or moderate-quality studies finding one statistically significant effect in the same domain. Surprisingly, HomVEE does not only rely on randomised controlled trials but also gives credit to quasi-experimental studies that cannot establish causality. HomVEE counts statistical significance instead of effect sizes and does not rely on meta-analytic evidence for effectiveness. Last, they only select interventions with families served in a developed-world context (Sama-Miller et al., 2020, p. 19). The term 'developed-world context' is used for studies in countries that had high incomes in the year the manuscript on intervention effects was published, according to the World Bank Indicators list (World Bank 2020). Randomised trials in countries like Turkey or Colombia are ignored, indicating ethnocentrism of the approach in a country in which many families have to raise their children below the official poverty line, in dire circumstances.

Unfortunately, NJi, HomVEE, and similar evaluators of interventions fail to consider sound meta-analytic evidence, demonstrated absence of iatrogenic side effects, ethical justification of intervention goals and means by the targeted population (see Chapter 7), responsibly determined positive cost-effectiveness or cost-utility ratings, and scalability. The application of these criteria requires quite a bit of extra investments by researchers and evaluation committees. But a more careful evaluation with this extended catalogue of criteria might in the long run save money and prevent substantial waste of human capital of researchers, implementers, and targeted families or schools struggling with mental or physical health issues of the children and adolescents in their care. In the meantime, few family (preventive) support interventions measure up to the required standards and even the work of the evaluating committees falls short of the demands of science and society for responsible translation. Paraphrasing John Ioannidis' provocative statement, we submit that most translations of interventions to policy or (clinical) practice are irresponsible. The replication crisis seems to be lost in translation.

References

Bachmann, C. J., Beecham, J., O'Connor, T. G., Scott, A., Briskman, J., & Scott, S. (2019). The cost of love: Financial consequences of insecure attachment in antisocial youth. *Journal of Child Psychology and Psychiatry, 60*, 1343–1351.

Bakermans-Kranenburg, M. J., Van IJzendoorn, M. H., & Kroonenberg, P. M. (2004). Differences in attachment security between African-American and white children: Ethnicity or socioeconomic status? *Infant Behavior & Development, 27*, 417–433. https://doi.org/10.1016/j.infbeh.2004.11.002

Belsky, J. (2009). Classroom composition, childcare history and social development: Are childcare effects disappearing or spreading? *Social Development, 18*, 230–238. https://doi.org/10.1111/j.1467-9507.2008.00511.x

Bernard, K., Dozier, M., Bick, J., Lewis-Morrarty, E., Lindhiem, O., & Carlson, E. (2012). Enhancing attachment organization among maltreated children: Results of a randomized clinical trial. *Child Development, 83*(2), 623–636. https://doi.org/10.1111/j.1467-8624.2011.01712.x

Bowlby, J. (1969/1982). *Attachment and Loss: Attachment*. Vintage.

Cohen, J. (1988). *Statistical Power Analysis for the Behavioral Sciences* (2nd ed.). Lawrence Erlbaum Associates, Publishers.

Cuijpers, P., Turner, E. H., Koole, S. L., Dijke, A. V., & Smit, F. (2014). What is the threshold for a clinically relevant effect? The case of major depressive disorders. *Depression & Anxiety, 31*(5), 374–378. https://doi.org/10.1002/da.22249

De Los Reyes, A., Augenstein, T. M., Wang, M., Thomas, S. A., Drabick, D. A. G., Burgers, D. E., & Rabinowitz, J. (2015). The validity of the multi-informant approach to assessing child and adolescent mental health. *Psychological Bulletin, 141*(4), 858–900. https://doi.org/10.1037/a0038498

Gardner, F., Leijten, P., Melendez-Torres, G. J., Landau, S., Harris, V., Mann, J., ... Scott, S. (2019). The earlier the better? Individual participant data and traditional meta-analysis of age effects of parenting interventions. *Child Development, 90*, 7–19.

Gillon R. (1994). Medical ethics: Four principles plus attention to scope. *BMJ (Clinical research ed.), 309*(6948), 184–188. https://doi.org/10.1136/bmj.309.6948.184

Gintis, H., & Helbing, D. (2015). Homo socialis: An analytical core for sociological theory. *Review of Behavioral Economics, 2*, 1–59.

Heckman, J. J. (2006). Skill formation and the economics of investing in disadvantaged children. *Science, 312*(5782), 1900–1902. https://doi.org/10.1126/science.1128898

Juffer, F., Bakermans-Kranenburg, M. J., & Van IJzendoorn, M. H. (2017). Pairing attachment theory and social learning theory in video-feedback intervention to promote positive parenting. *Current Opinion in Psychology, 15*, 189–194. https://doi.org/10.1016/j.copsyc.2017.03.012

Kraft, M. A. (2020). Interpreting effect sizes of education interventions. *Educational Researcher, 49*(4), 241–253. https://journals.sagepub.com/doi/full/10.3102/0013189X20912798

Michalopoulos, C., Faucetta, K., Hill, C. J., Portilla, X. A., Burrell, L., Lee, H., & Knox, V. (2019). *Impacts on Family Outcomes of Evidence-based Early Childhood Home Visiting: Results from the Mother and Infant Home Visiting Program Evaluation*. Office of Planning, Research, and Evaluation, Administration for Children and Families, U.S. Department of Health and Human Services, Washington, DC, OPRE Report 2019-07.

Mortimer, D., & Segal, L. (2006). Economic evaluation of interventions for problem drinking and alcohol dependence: Do within-family external effects make a difference? *Alcohol and Alcoholism, 41*, 92–98. https://doi.org/10.1093/alcalc/agh224

O'Farrelly, C., Barker, B., Watt, H., Babalis, D., Bakermans-Kranenburg, M., Byford, S., Ganguli, P., Grimås, E., Iles, J., Mattock, H., McGinley, J., Phillips, C., Ryan, R., Scott, S., Smith, J., Stein, A., Stevens, E., Van IJzendoorn, M., Warwick, J., & Ramchandani, P. (2021a). A video-feedback parenting intervention to prevent enduring behavior problems in at-risk children aged 12–36 months: The Healthy Start, Happy Start RCT. *Health Technology Assessment, 25*(29). https://doi.org/10.3310/hta25290.

O'Farrelly, C., Watt, H., Babalis, D., Bakermans-Kranenburg, M. J., & Ramchandani, P. G. (2021b). A brief home-based parenting intervention to reduce behavior problems in young children: A pragmatic randomized clinical trial. *JAMA Pediatrics, 175*(5), 567–576. https://doi.org/10.1001/jamapediatrics.2020.6834

O'Neil, D., McGilloway, S., Donnelly, M., Bywater, T., & Kelly, P. (2013). A cost effectiveness analysis of the Incredible Years parenting programme in reducing childhood health inequalities. *European Journal of Health Economics, 14*, 85–94.

Purnama Sari, N., Van IJzendoorn, M. H., Jansen, P., Bakermans-Kranenburg, M., & Riem, M. M. E. (2022). Higher levels of harsh parenting during the COVID-19 lockdown in the Netherlands. *Child Maltreatment, 27*(2). https://doi.org/10.1177/10775595211024748

Rowen, D., Rivero-Arias, O., Devlin, N., & Ratcliffe, J. (2020). Review of valuation methods of preference-based measures of health for economic evaluation in child and adolescent populations: Where are we now and where are we going? *PharmacoEconomics, 38*, 325–340. https://doi.org/10.1007/s40273-019-00873-7

Sama-Miller, E., Lugo-Gil, J., Harding, J., Akers, L., & Coughlin, R. (2020). *Home Visiting Evidence of Effectiveness (HomVEE) Systematic Review: Handbook of Procedures and Evidence Standards, Version 2*. OPRE Report # 2020-151, Washington, DC: Office of Planning, Research, and Evaluation, Administration for Children and Families, U.S. Department of Health and Human Services.

Stadhouders, N., Koolman, X., Van Dijk, C., Jeurissen, P., & Adang, E. (2019). The marginal benefits of healthcare spending in the Netherlands: Estimating cost-effectiveness thresholds using a translog production function. *Health Economics, 28*, 1331–1344. https://doi.org/10.1002/hec.3946

Spanjaard, H. (2019). *Interventies voor vroegtijdige voorkoming van ernstige criminaliteit* [Interventions for early prevention of serious criminality]. Spanjaard Development & Training.

Swaab, H. (2012). Preventief Interventie Team (PIT). *Sociale leerbaarheid* [Social learning]. Gemeente Amsterdam.

Szende, A., Janssen, B., & Cabases, J. (Eds.). (2014). *Self-Reported Population Health: An International Perspective based on EQ-5D*. Springer.

Trivers, R. L. (1974). Parent-offspring conflict. *American Journal of Zoological Research, 14*, 249–264. https://doi.org/10.1093/icb/14.1.249

Van IJzendoorn, M. H., & Bakermans-Kranenburg, M. J. (2020). Problematic cost–utility analysis of interventions for behavior problems in children and adolescents. *New Directions for Child and Adolescent Development*, 89–102. https://doi.org/10.1002/cad.20360

Van IJzendoorn, M. H., Stevens, E., & Bakermans-Kranenburg, M. J. (2023). Development of the virtual-VIPP and a systematic review of online support for families during the COVID-19 pandemic. *Attachment & Human Development, 25*(2), 223–239. https://doi.org/10.1080/14616734.2023.2179575

Vrijhof, C. I., Van den Bulk, B. G., Overgaauw, S., Lelieveld, G.-J., Engels, R. C. M. E., & Van IJzendoorn, M. H. (2016). The Prosocial Cyberball Game: Compensating for social exclusion and its associations with empathic concern and bullying in adolescents. *Journal of Adolescence, 52*, 27–36. https://doi.org/10.1016/j.adolescence.2016.07.005

World Bank. (2020). *Word Bank Indicators. Historical Classification for 2009/2020*. https://datahelpdesk.worldbank.org/knowledgebase/articles/906519

Part 3
Busting myths is translation

In the third section we present an alternative approach to translation. Application of scientific research to practice is often interpreted in a technical way. Assuming pre-established goals, replicated effectiveness of a family support intervention is taken as sufficient ground for rolling the intervention out in the larger community. In Jurgen Habermas' theory of *'Erkenntnisinteressen'* on knowledge and human interests (1968) this is a typical example of knowledge acquisition and translation from the perspective of a *technical interest* in explaining the natural and social world. The implicit aim is to control the environment and induce changes to achieve undisputed goals, though this often serves to perpetuate socioeconomic disparities.

According to Habermas' critical epistemology, a technical interest in knowledge acquisition should be combined with a *'practical-hermeneutical interest'* in understanding the social world in order to engage in open communication with others about the values implied in the goals and their relation to the technical means, and their significance for daily life. In addition to these two knowledge interests, the *'emancipatory interest'* is concerned with striving for freedom from unduly large socioeconomic and health disparities, injustices, and power structures to create a more just global society. In contrast to the usual social engineering approach of translation, falsification of fake findings is valorisation of developmental science at the level of busting social prejudices and ideologies with scientific means. Core propositions of attachment theory and research can, for example, be used to refute established but baseless ideas about the influence of genes, brain, and hormones on child development.

9
It's all in the genome?

The genomic era

A pervasive myth about the role of genetics has been most concisely phrased by Robert Plomin with his slogan, 'Parents matter but they don't make a difference' in his book *Blueprint: How DNA makes us who we are* (Plomin, 2018). He argues that DNA accounts for about half of the variance in psychological traits, with the other half explained by chance experiences without long-term effects or by errors of measurement (Judith Harris presents a similar view in her 1998 book entitled *The nurture assumption*). More specifically, he elaborates that 'Parents matter, schools matter and life experiences matter, but they don't make a difference in shaping who we are. DNA is the only thing that makes a substantial systematic difference.' It would not really make a difference whether parents leave their infants crying or not throughout the night or whether they stimulate their children to attend a vocational or grammar school; children's future would be imprinted in their DNA. We reject this bold statement and give three scientific reasons to do so: measurement and design issues, the amount of variance explained in genetic studies, and the effectiveness of interventions. Next, we argue for a more nuanced perspective.

Let us first review the basis for such strong conclusions as made by Robert Plomin and Judith Harris. Twin studies have often been used to quantify heritability, because the difference in similarity between monozygotic (or identical) and dizygotic (or fraternal) twins is informative on how influential an individual's structural DNA is. Monozygotic twins are genetically identical, while dizygotic twins are genetically full siblings, sharing on average 50% of their structural DNA. In general, both types of twins share the same home environment (see Figure 9.1).

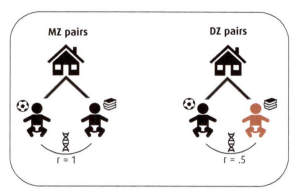

Figure 9.1 The basic twin design with monozygotic and dizygotic twin pairs to estimate the heritability of psychological traits.
Source: Authors.

When for a specific trait, e.g., height, monozygotic twins are much more similar than dizygotic twins, it is concluded that genetic similarity matters, and that heritability substantially influences heights. But for, e.g., religiosity, monozygotic twins are about as similar to each other as dizygotic twins. This implies that genetic similarity is not important for this trait and shared or unique environmental factors influence religiosity. In 2015, a meta-analysis of twin studies conducted between 1958 and 2012 was published (Polderman et al., 2015). Polderman and colleagues retrieved twin studies in which complex human traits were measured and variation was partitioned into genetic and environmental influences. The conclusions were based on 2,748 publications and in total several millions of twins. Across all traits, the average heritability was 49%. Although the heritability estimates for physical traits were higher than those for traits related to social behaviour, the latter was still substantial, namely 32%. Such data warrant Robert Plomin's slogan: they demonstrate that DNA determines who we are and will be, or don't they? We argue they don't. We note some issues with twin studies and review evidence not supporting an overwhelming influence of genetics or pointing to a more complex interplay between nature and nurture.

Counter-arguments against the genomic myth

Twin studies suffer from some methodological issues that may lead to inflated heritability estimates. First, most studies on psychological traits use questionnaires. In the case of children, their parents complete the questionnaires. In the majority of cases, parents know whether their twins are monozygotic or dizygotic, and expectations about greater similarity of monozygotic than dizygotic twins may influence their perception of their twin children. For older children, we found that answering tendencies or response biases are heritable as well (see Chapter 2), leading to the prediction that questionnaires on whatever trait will necessarily be completed in a more similar way by monozygotic twins than by dizygotic twins. If this is true, then traits or behaviours that are measured by independent observers will show lower heritability estimates than traits or behaviours measured with self-report or parent-report questionnaires. Indeed, studies on observed parenting or observed attachment found lower heritability estimates and more influence of the shared and unshared environment (e.g., Bokhorst et al., 2003; for reviews see Bakermans-Kranenburg & Van IJzendoorn, 2016 and Mileva-Seitz et al., 2016). Admittedly, studies with observational measures rated by trained observers have smaller sample sizes than studies relying on questionnaires, resulting in large confidence intervals around the point estimates for genetic and environmental influences. But the consistently lower estimates for heritability in observational studies compared to questionnaire studies indicate that measurement issues do play a role in estimating the influence of genetics.

Second, the amount of variance molecular genetic studies explain is usually very small and in contrast with the substantial heritability estimates reported above. While twin studies suggest that half of the variance in a trait is accounted for by variation in our DNA, large-scale genome-wide association studies (GWAS) typically find that many genetic variants together explain not more than 5–10% of the variance in a specific trait, and often less than 1–2%. This is called 'missing heritability', the intractable gap between the heritability estimates of twin studies and molecular genetic studies. Part of this gap may be explained by, again, measurement issues. While DNA is measured with great precision, the assessment of complex phenotypes is often unprecise and sometimes even sloppy, such as a single item asking about individual's happiness: 'In general, how happy are you?' (Ward et al., 2022). Twin studies had found heritability estimates for self-reported happiness ranging from 22% to 41% (Bartels, 2015). The GWAS identified three significant loci that together explained 0.8% of the variance in happiness (Ward et al., 2022). This example illustrates that for happiness, and so far for all human traits, the answer to the question of *whodunnit* (the central question of GWAS) is lagging substantially behind the amount of variance attributed to genetic influences in twin studies.

Moreover, the vast majority of behavioural genetic studies have been conducted in western, industrialised countries. In the Polderman et al. (2015) study, twin subjects came from only 39 different countries, and the largest proportion of studies (34%) was conducted in the USA. Continents like South America (0.5%), Africa (0.2%), and Asia (5%) were heavily under-represented. The same is true of GWASs, which mostly include homogeneously WEIRD (Henrich et al., 2010) populations with homogeneous genotypes functioning in homogeneous environments. Such homogeneity of environments underestimates environmental effects and produces inflated heritability estimates (Uchiyama, Spicer, & Muthukrishna, 2022). This restriction in environmental variation severely limits generalisability of behavioural genetic findings to populations from cultures and countries not included in the heritability evidence base.

Third, interventions demonstrate that environmental context does make a difference for developmental outcomes. Interventions are experimental manipulations of the environment, and they may be especially influential in early life. Experiments manipulating the caregiving environment of young rhesus monkeys showed the long-term effects of being raised with peers instead of their biological mothers. Peer-reared monkeys showed normal physical and motor development but were shy, socially incompetent, and highly aggressive during puberty. Moreover, they differed in brain structure and function from their mother-reared peers and had, for instance, a greater tolerance for alcohol as predicted from a faster central nervous system serotonin turnover rate (Suomi, 2016). In chimpanzees who could not remain with their biological mothers because of severe abuse or neglect, we showed that an intervention with 4 hours of dyadic interaction with a human caregiver per day made a difference of 17 IQ points at 9 months of age (Van IJzendoorn et al., 2009).

Unfortunately, 4 hours of dyadic interaction is usually far beyond what human infants in institutionalised care can expect to have, and the devastating effects on their development are well documented (see Chapter 5). The intervention that comes closest to 4 hours of dyadic interaction in the case of human infants is placement in family care, with adoptive or foster parents. Indeed, the amazing effects of adoption and foster care on the physical and mental development of previously institutionalised children document the influence of environmental factors, even on traits with high heritability estimates (Van IJzendoorn et al., 2020a).

But not only all-encompassing interventions like being moved from institutionalised care to family-based care bring about changes in child development. Successful parenting interventions, resulting in more sensitive parenting, predict improvement in children's attachment behaviour and reduction of behaviour problems (Van IJzendoorn et al., 2023, see Chapter 4). Parenting sensitivity in early childhood has been found to be related to larger total brain volume ($r = 0.15$) and grey matter volume ($r = 0.16$) at 8 years in the Generation R birth cohort (Kok et al., 2015). Insensitive parenting accelerates the development of the amygdala-medial prefrontal cortex circuit (Thijssen et al., 2017), in line with Life History Theories that predict that organisms follow slow or accelerated trajectories of development, depending on environmental experiences. Cues to greater scarcity, harshness, and unpredictability in the environment promote faster life history strategies (Belsky & Shalev, 2016; Callaghan & Tottenham, 2016; Ellis & Del Giudice, 2019), and parental insensitivity is such a cue to environmental scarcity affecting developmental pace and outcomes.

Child influences on parenting

The arguments presented above are meant to counter the idea that our DNA would be of surpassing influence in an almost deterministic way, but they do not mean to convey the idea that genetics do not play a role in the development of individual differences or do not warrant attention. Genetics can influence the environment (gene-environment correlation) or affect the influence of environmental factors (gene-environment interaction). Genetics can also help reveal causal associations between environmental predictors and developmental outcomes. As an example of the influence of child genetics on parenting, we found in a child-based twin design study including 236 families with 4- to 5-year-old twins that individually observed parental limit-setting was more similar to each of the twin siblings in families with monozygotic twins than in families with dizygotic twins. Apparently, greater similarity in the twins' behaviour elicited more similar parental responses, at least for parental limit-setting, not for observed parental sensitivity (Euser et al., 2020).

If child behaviour can elicit specific parenting behaviours, as we found in this twin study, it makes sense to wonder whether genetics of the child might also play a role in the prediction of the most unsupportive type of parenting behaviour, child maltreatment. Child maltreatment is rather prevalent across the globe. Estimates of the prevalence diverge depending on the measures used, with lower rates for informant reports than for self-reports (Stoltenborgh et al., 2015). Self-reported prevalence of physical abuse and physical neglect amounts to about 20%. Emotional abuse and neglect are more difficult to assess but seem more prevalent, with estimates of around

30%. The most important predictor of perpetrating child maltreatment is having experienced maltreatment in childhood. In our umbrella synthesis on child maltreatment antecedents, we found a combined effect size across a large number of studies covered by recent meta-analyses of Cohen's $d = 0.47$. This is almost half a standard deviation and roughly comparable with a correlation of around $r = 0.22$. Intergenerational transmission of maltreatment seems to be the most powerful determinant of the perpetuation of abuse across generations (Madigan et al., 2019; Van IJzendoorn et al., 2020b). This may point to heritability of maltreatment, e.g., when parental proneness to aggression is genetically transmitted to child tendencies to oppositional behaviours or conduct disorder.

Using an extended family design with grandparents, parents, uncles and aunts, and grandchildren, we found considerable heritability estimates of overall experienced child maltreatment (38%), with a somewhat lower percentage (30%) for neglect and a higher percentage (62%) for severe physical abuse (Pittner et al., 2020). For perpetration of physical abuse and emotional neglect genetic factors did not significantly contribute to the model. For perpetrated emotional abuse, however, heritability was found (33%). Because these studies are based on differences in genetic relatedness between siblings, parents and children, uncles and aunts, and grandparents and grandchildren, only crude estimates of heritability can be produced. Moreover, some of the assumptions about similarity of environmental influences (e.g., between siblings from the same family) are questionable.

A more direct approach uses molecular genetics, relating the DNA structure to variance in maltreatment experiences. In a GWAS including more than 185,000 individuals we found a SNP heritability of less than 10% (Warrier et al., 2021). In total, 14 independent genetic variants were associated with childhood maltreatment. Using within-family polygenic score analyses, the pattern of results was best explained by gene-environment correlation mechanisms: we found some direct evidence for active and reactive rGE, and passive rGE may also play a role. These gene-environment correlation mechanisms point again to the crucial role of the environment in addition to a genetic effect.

Genetic differential susceptibility

Not all individuals are affected by environmental influences to the same extent. There is evidence to suggest that individuals differ in the extent to which environmental stressors and adversity affect them negatively, as well as in the degree to which environmental resources and supports positively impact them. Additionally, the same characteristics that make people vulnerable to adversity may also make them more likely to benefit from support. This idea is known as the 'differential susceptibility hypothesis', which posits that in positive environments, people who are more susceptible to adversity may do better than those who are less susceptible to both negative and positive environments (Bakermans-Kranenburg & Van IJzendoorn, 2015; Belsky, 1997; 2005; Ellis et al., 2011; Van IJzendoorn & Belsky, 2017). A crucial difference between the differential susceptibility model and the traditional diathesis-stress model is that the latter proposes that individuals with a vulnerable constitution and poor developmental experiences (e.g., insensitive parenting, stressful life experiences) deviate from the developmental pathway of their peers, but that these individuals do not benefit disproportionally from contextual support (see Figure 9.2).

What distinguishes susceptible individuals ('orchids') from those that are less susceptible ('dandelions', Boyce, 2016)? We were the first

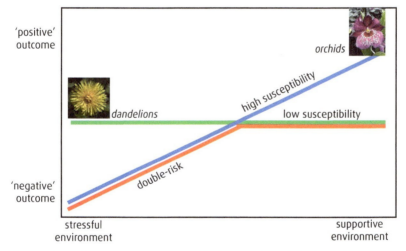

Figure 9.2 Differential susceptibility to the environment for better *and* for worse. The dichotomy between susceptible (orchid-like) and non-susceptible (dandelion-like) individuals might in reality be a continuum. Graphic: Authors. Dandelion CC BY SA-3.0 Mr Checker/Wikimedia Commons, https://commons.wikimedia.org/wiki/File:Taraxacum_officinale_2.jpg; Orchid CC BY-SA 4.0 Emőke Dénes/Wikimedia Commons, https://commons.wikimedia.org/wiki/File:Miltonia_cultivars_-_kew_1.jpg

to show that genetic characteristics (related to the dopaminergic system) could be susceptibility factors: Children with a specific variant of the dopamine D4 receptor gene showed at age 3 years more externalising behaviour than their peers when they had experienced less sensitive parental care in their first year of life, but less externalising behaviour after highly sensitive care (Bakermans-Kranenburg et al., 2011). This *for better and for worse* pattern was replicated in other studies and meta-analytically confirmed (Bakermans-Kranenburg et al., 2011). To counter some of the problems with correlational G × E studies, we also meta-analysed 22 randomised G × E experiments (Bakermans-Kranenburg & Van IJzendoorn, 2015; Van IJzendoorn et al., 2011). We found that intervention effects were much stronger in the *a priori* chosen susceptible genotypes ($r = 0.33$) than in the non-susceptible genotypes ($r = 0.08$). Extending the candidate-gene approach to a polygenetic score (PGS) for susceptibility, Keers et al. (2016) conducted a GWAS with a monozygotic twin sample to capture genetic variants associated to intra-pair differences in internalising symptoms. These phenotypic differences in genetically identical twins sharing the same family environment point to genetic susceptibility to potentially subtle non-shared environmental factors. The PGS for susceptibility predicted differential response to psychological treatments for child anxiety disorders. Although so far replications of this study are scarce (but see Shaw et al., 2019), the polygenetic approach may be a promising way to further examine genetic differential susceptibility.

Genetics can reveal causal associations

Genetics can also help reveal causal associations between environmental predictors and developmental outcomes. The statistical approach of Mendelian randomisation is a method that uses genetic variation as a proxy for non-genetic factors to make inferences about cause-and-effect relationships (see Hamaker et al., 2020; Pearl & MacKenzie, 2018). This approach is based on the idea that genetic variants are randomly assigned at conception and are not influenced by subsequent environmental exposures or reverse causality. By comparing the association between a genetic variant (usually a GWAS-based PGS) and an outcome of interest, inference can be made about the causal effect of the exposure on the outcome while avoiding many of the biases that can occur with correlational studies. Mendelian randomisation is not a definitive proof of causality but rather a way to provide evidence in favour of or against causality. The assumption of Mendelian randomisation that genetic variants only affect the outcome through its effect on the exposure should be carefully evaluated and, if not met, any conclusion should be interpreted with caution.

Using Mendelian randomisation, the causal influence of maltreatment experiences in childhood on later mental health, in particular depression, could be shown. Bidirectional causal effects on ADHD and schizophrenia were found, but surprisingly, no causal influence of maltreatment on later physical health (cardiovascular or inflammatory issues, Warrier et al., 2021). An essential next step in research on parenting and child development is the determination of a PGS for sensitive parenting, to be used in Mendelian randomisation studies on the uni- or bidirectional (causal) associations between parenting and child development.

Mendelian randomisation might also be used to examine the causal role of DNA methylation in genetic and environmental influences on the development of behaviour problems. In attachment research methylation is often considered to mediate the influence of insecure or disorganised attachment on later development (e.g., Jones-Mason et al., 2016; Van IJzendoorn, Caspers, Bakermans-Kranenburg et al., 2010). Because methylation modulates the expression of genes, and methylation patterns are malleable by environmental input, methylation has been considered to undermine the causal effects of 'fixed' genotypes on child development. In a way, genes seemed to have become part of the environment.

In our first study on methylation, we concluded that 'Methylation may serve as the interface between adverse environment and the developing organism' (Van IJzendoorn et al., 2010). Unfortunately, this suggestion might not be tenable in view of some of our recent large-scale epigenome-wide studies (EWASs). One of those EWASs failed to find associations between parenting and methylation variations at candidate genes such as the oxytocin receptor gene. Methylation patterns around these usual suspects previously dominating the field with rather small studies were not replicated (Dall'Aglio et al., 2020). Furthermore, our EWASs also documented widespread non-linear change of methylation patterns over time (Mulder et al., 2021), and a rather substantial molecular genetic determination of levels of methylation (explaining 15–17% of the variance, Min et al., 2021). We also failed to replicate associations between methylation patterns and complex phenotypes such as prosocial behaviour; robust associations across different studies remain elusive (Luo et al., 2021). Last but not least, some Mendelian randomisation evidence for reverse causation from complex phenotypic traits to levels of methylation (Min et al., 2021) makes a mediating role of methylation in the association between environmental risks and subsequent mental or physical health issues less plausible.

Conclusion

Our DNA provides the clay, the raw material. Genes do not dictate our behaviour; they carry the instructions for the expression of proteins, which are the building blocks for cellular structures and perform a wide variety of functions in the body. In Polderman et al. (2015) meta-analysis, the lowest reported heritability for a specific trait was for gene expression, with an estimated heritability of 5%. The physical and social environment, the experiences and interactions in our daily lives shape development from the cradle to the grave. Parents matter *and* do make a difference.

References

Bakermans-Kranenburg, M. J., & Van IJzendoorn, M. H. (2011). Differential susceptibility to rearing environment depending on dopamine-related genes: New evidence and a meta-analysis. *Development and Psychopathology, 23*, 39–52. https://doi.org/10.1017/S0954579410000635

Bakermans-Kranenburg, M. J., & Van IJzendoorn, M. H. (2015). The hidden efficacy of interventions: Gene x Environment experiments from a differential susceptibility perspective. *Annual Review of Psychology, 66*, 381–409. https://doi.org/10.1146/annurev-psych-010814-015407

Bakermans-Kranenburg, M. J., & Van IJzendoorn, M. H. (2016). Attachment, parenting, and genetics. In J. Cassidy & P. R. Shaver (Eds.), *Handbook of Attachment* (3rd ed., pp. 155–179). Guilford.

Bartels, M. (2015). Genetics of wellbeing and its components satisfaction with life, happiness, and quality of life: A review and meta-analysis of heritability studies. *Behavior Genetics, 45*, 137–156. https://doi.org/10.1007/s10519-015-9713-y

Belsky, J. (1997). Theory testing, effect-size evaluation, and differential susceptibility to rearing influence: The case of mothering and attachment. *Child Development, 68*, 598–600. https://doi.org/10.1111/j.1467-8624.1997.tb04221.x

Belsky, J. (2005). Differential susceptibility to rearing influences: An evolutionary hypothesis and some evidence. In B. Ellis & D. Bjorklund (Eds.), *Origins of the Social Mind: Evolutionary Psychology and Child Development* (pp. 139–163). Guilford Press. https://doi.org/10.1002/icd.567

Belsky, J., & Shalev, I. (2016). Contextual adversity, telomere erosion, pubertal development, and health: Two models of accelerated aging, or one? *Development and Psychopathology, 28*, 1367–1383. https://doi.org/10.1017/S0954579416000900

Belsky, J., Bakermans-Kranenburg, M. J., & Van IJzendoorn, M. H. (2007). For better and for worse: Differential susceptibility to environmental influences. *Current Directions in Psychological Science, 16*, 300–304. https://doi.org/10.1111/j.1467-8721.2007.00525.x.

Belsky, J., & Van IJzendoorn, M. H. (2017). Genetic differential susceptibility to the effects of parenting. *Current Opinion in Psychology, 15*, 125–130. https://doi.org/10.1016/j.copsyc.2017.02.021

Bokhorst, C. L., Bakermans-Kranenburg, M. J., Fearon, P., Van IJzendoorn, M. H., Fonagy, P., & Schuengel, C. (2003). The importance of shared environment in mother-infant attachment security: A behavioral genetic study. *Child Development, 74*, 1769–1782. Doi:10.1046/j.1467-8624.2003.00637.x

Boyce, W. T. (2016). Differential susceptibility of the developing brain to contextual adversity and stress. *Neuropsychopharmacology, 41*, 142–162. http://dx.doi.org/10.1038/npp.2015.294

Callaghan, B. L., & Tottenham, N. (2016). The stress acceleration hypothesis: Effects of early-life adversity on emotion circuits and behavior. *Current Opinion in Behavioral Sciences, 7*, 76–81. https://doi.org/10.1016/j.cobeha.2015.11.018

Dall' Aglio, L., Rijlaarsdam, J., Mulder, R., Neumann, A., Felix, J., Kok, R., Bakermans-Kranenburg, M. J., Van IJzendoorn, M. H., Tiemeier, H., & Cecil, C. (2020). Epigenome-wide associations between observed maternal sensitivity and offspring DNA methylation: A population-based prospective study in children. *Psychological Medicine*, 1–11. https://doi.org/10.1017/S00332 91720004353

Ellis, B. J., Boyce, W. T., Belsky, J., Bakermans-Kranenburg, M. J., & Van IJzendoorn, M. H. (2011). Differential susceptibility to the environment: An evolutionary-neurodevelopmental theory. *Development and Psychopathology, 23*, 7–28. https://doi.org/10.1017/S0954579410000611

Ellis, B. J., & Del Giudice, M. (2019). Developmental adaptation to stress: An evolutionary perspective. *Annual Review of Psychology, 70*, 111–139. https://doi.org/10.1146/annurev-psych-122 216-011732

Euser, S., Bosdriesz, J. R., Vrijhof, C. I., Van den Bulk, B. G., Van Hees, D., De Vet, S. M., Van IJzendoorn, M. H., & Bakermans-Kranenburg, M. J. (2020). How heritable are parental sensitivity and limit-setting? A longitudinal child-based twin study on observed parenting. *Child Development, 91*, 2255–2269. https://doi.org/10.1111/cdev.13365

Harris, J. R. (1998). *The Nurture Assumption: Why Children Turn Out the Way They Do*. The Free Press. https://doi.org/10.1136/bmj.320.7245.1347

Hamaker, E. L., Mulder, J. D., & Van IJzendoorn, M. H. (2020). Description, prediction and causation: Methodological challenges of studying child and adolescent development. *Developmental Cognitive Neuroscience, 46*, 100867, ISSN 1878–9293. https://doi.org/ 10.1016/j.dcn.2020.100867

Henrich, J., Heine, S. J., & Norenzayan, A. (2010). The weirdest people in the world? *The Behavioral and Brain Sciences, 33*(2–3), 61–135. https://doi.org/10.1017/S0140525X0999152X

Jones-Mason, K., Allen, I. E., Bush, N., & Hamilton, S. (2016). Epigenetic marks as the link between environment and development: Examination of the associations between attachment, socioeconomic status, and methylation of the SLC6A4 gene. *Brain and Behavior, 6*(7), e00480. https://doi.org/10.1002/brb3.480

Keers, R., Coleman, J. R. I., Lester, K. J., et al. (2016). A genome-wide test of the differential susceptibility hypothesis reveals a genetic predictor of differential response to psychological treatments for child anxiety disorders. *Psychotherapy and Psychosomatics, 85*, 146–158. https:// doi.org/10.1159/000444023.

Kok, R., Thijssen, S., Bakermans-Kranenburg, M. J., Jaddoe, V. W. V., Verhulst, F. C., White, T., Van IJzendoorn, M. H., & Tiemeier, H. (2015). Normal variation in early parental sensitivity predicts child structural brain development. *Journal of the American Academy of Child & Adolescent Psychiatry, 54*, 824–831. https://doi.org/10.1016/j.jaac.2015.07.009

Luo, M., Meehan, A. J., Walton, E., Röder, S., Herberth, G., Zenclussen, A. C., Cosín-Tomas, M., Sunyer, J., Mulder, R. H., Cortes Hidalgo, A. P., Bakermans-Kranenburg, M. J., Felix, J. F., Relton, C., Suderman, M., Pappa, I., Kok, R., Tiemeier, H., Van IJzendoorn, M. H., Barker, E. D., & Cecil, C. A. M. (2021). Neonatal DNA methylation and childhood low prosocial behavior: An epigenome-wide association meta-analysis. *American Journal of Medical Genetics Part B: Neuropsychiatric Genetics, 186B*, 228–241. https://doi.org/10.1002/ajmg.b.32862

Madigan, S., Cyr, C., Eirich, R., Fearon, R. P., Ly, A., Rash, C., Poole, J. C., & Alink, L. R. (2019). Testing the cycle of maltreatment hypothesis: Meta-analytic evidence of the intergenerational transmission of child maltreatment. *Development & Psychopathology, 31*(1), 23–51. https:// doi.org/10.1017/s0954579418001700

Min, J. L., Hemani, G., Hannon, E., et al. (2021). Genomic and phenotypic insights from an atlas of genetic effects on DNA methylation. *Nature Genetics, 53*(9), 1311–1321. https://doi.org/ 10.1038/s41588-021-00923-x.

Mulder, R. H., Neumann, A., Cecil, C. A. M., Walton, E., Houtepen, L. C., Simpkin, A. J., Rijlaarsdam, J., Heijmans, B. T., Gaunt, T. R., Felix, J. F., Jaddoe, V. W. V., Bakermans-Kranenburg, M. J., Tiemeier, H., Relton, C. L., Van IJzendoorn, M. H., & Suderman, M. (2021). Epigenome-wide change and variation in DNA methylation in childhood: Trajectories from birth to late adolescence. *Human Molecular Genetics, 30*, 119–134. https://doi.org/10.1093/hmg/ddaa280

Mileva-Seitz, V. R., Bakermans-Kranenburg, M. J., & Van IJzendoorn, M. H. (2016). Genetic mechanisms of parenting. *Hormones and Behavior, 77*, 211–23. https://doi.org/10.1016/ j.yhbeh.2015.06.003

Pittner, K., Bakermans-Kranenburg, M. J., Alink, L. R. A., Buisman, R. S. M., Van den Berg, L. J. M., Compier-de Block, L. H. C. G. C., Voorthuis, A., Elzinga, B. M., Lindenberg, J., Tollenaar, M. S., Linting, M., Diego, V. P., & Van IJzendoorn, M. H. (2020). Estimating the heritability of experiencing child maltreatment in an extended family design. *Child Maltreatment, 25*(3), 289–299. https://doi.org/10.1177/1077559519888587

Pearl, J., & MacKenzie, D. (2018). *The Book of Why: The New Science of Cause and Effect*. Basic Books. https://doi.org/10.1126/science.aau9731

Plomin, R. (2018). *Blueprint: How DNA Makes Us Who We Are.* Penguin Books. https://doi.org/10.1042/bio20200084

Polderman, T. J. C., Benyamin, B., de Leeuw, C. A., Sullivan, P. F., Van Bochoven, A., Visscher, P. M., & Posthuma, D. (2015). Meta-analysis of the heritability of human traits based on fifty years of twin studies. *Nature Genetics, 47*, 702–709. https://doi.org/10.1038/ng.3285

Shaw, D. S., Galán, C. A., Lemery-Chalfant, K., Dishion, T. J., Elam, K. K., Wilson, M. N., & Gardner, F. (2019). Trajectories and predictors of children's early-starting conduct problems: Child, family, genetic, and intervention effects. *Development & Psychopathology, 31*(5), 1911–1921. doi: 10.1017/S0954579419000828

Stoltenborgh, M., Bakermans-Kranenburg, M. J., Alink, L. R. A., & Van IJzendoorn, M. H. (2015). The prevalence of child maltreatment across the globe: Review of a series of meta-analyses. *Child Abuse Review, 24*, 37–50. https://doi.org/10.1002/car.2353

Suomi, S. J. (2016). Attachment in rhesus monkeys. In J. Cassidy & P. R. Shaver (Eds.), *The Handbook of Attachment: Theory, Research, and Clinical Applications* (3rd ed., pp. 133–154). The Guilford Press.

Thijssen, S., Wildeboer, A., Van IJzendoorn, M. H., Muetzel, R. L., Langeslag, S. J. E., Jaddoe, V. W. V., Verhulst, F. C., Tiemeier, H., Bakermans-Kranenburg, M. J., & White, T. (2017). The honest truth about deception: Demographic, cognitive, and neural correlates of child repeated deceptive behavior. *Journal of Experimental Child Psychology, 162*, 225–241. https://doi.org/10.1016/j.jecp.2017.05.009

Uchiyama, R., Spicer, R., & Muthukrishna, M. (2022). Cultural evolution of genetic heritability. *Behavioral and Brain Sciences, 45*, e152. https://doi.org/10.1017/S0140525X21000893

Van IJzendoorn, M. H., Bakermans-Kranenburg, M. J., Belsky, J., Beach, S., Brody, G., Dodge, K. A., Greenberg, M., Posner, M., & Scott, S. (2011). Gene-by-environment experiments: A new approach to finding the missing heritability. *Nature Reviews Genetics, 12*, 881–881. https://doi.org/10.1038/nrg2764-c1

Van IJzendoorn, M. H., Bakermans-Kranenburg, M. J., & Ebstein, R. P. (2011). Methylation matters in child development: Toward developmental behavioral epigenetics. *Child Development Perspectives, 4*, 305–310. https://doi.org/10.1111/j.1750-8606.2011.00202.x

Van IJzendoorn, M. H., Caspers, K., Bakermans-Kranenburg, M. J., Beach, S. R. H., & Philibert, R. (2010). Methylation matters: Interaction between methylation density and 5HTT genotype predicts unresolved loss or trauma. *Biological Psychiatry, 68*, 405–407. https://doi.org/10.1016/j.biopsych.2010.05.008

Van IJzendoorn, M. H., Bakermans-Kranenburg, M. J., Duschinsky, R., Goldman, P. S., Fox, N. A., Gunnar, M. R., Johnson, D. E., Nelson, C. A., Reijman, S., Skinner, G. C. M., Zeanah, C. H., & Sonuga-Barke, E. J. S. (2020a). Institutionalisation and deinstitutionalisation of children I: A systematic and integrative review of evidence regarding effects on development. *The Lancet Psychiatry, 7*, 703–720. https://doi.org/10.1016/S2215-0366(19)30399-2

Van IJzendoorn, M. H., Bakermans-Kranenburg, M. J., Coughlan, B., & Reijman, S. (2020b). Child maltreatment antecedents and interventions: Umbrella synthesis and differential susceptibility perspective on risk and resilience. *Journal of Child Psychology and Psychiatry, 61*, 272–290. https://doi.org/10.1111/jcpp.13147

Van IJzendoorn, M. H., Bard, K. A., Bakermans-Kranenburg, M. J., & Ivan, K. (2009). Enhancement of attachment and cognitive development of young nursery-reared chimpanzees in responsive versus standard care. *Developmental Psychobiology, 51*, 173–185. https://doi.org/10.1002/dev.20356

Van IJzendoorn, M., Schuengel, C., Wang, Q., & Bakermans-Kranenburg, M. (2023). Improving parenting, child attachment, and externalizing behaviors: Meta-analysis of the first 25 randomized controlled trials on the effects of Video-feedback Intervention to promote Positive Parenting and Sensitive Discipline. *Development and Psychopathology, 35*(1), 241–256. doi:10.1017/S0954579421001462

Ward, J., Lyall, L., Cullen, B., Strawbridge, R. J., Zhu, X., Stanciu, I., Aman, A., Niedwiedz, C. L., Anderson, J., Bailey, M. E. S., Lyall, D. M., & Pell, J. (2022). The genetics of happiness: Consistent effects across the lifespan and ancestries in multiple cohorts. *European Neuropsychopharmacology, 63*, e282. https://doi.org/10.1016/j.euroneuro.2022.07.501

Warrier, V., Siu Fung Kwong, A., Luo, M., Dalvie, S., Croft, J., Sallis, H. M., Baldwin, J., Munafo, M. R., Nievergelt, C. M., Grant, A. J., Burgess, S., Moore, T. M., Barzilay, R., McIntosh, A., Van IJzendoorn, M. H., & Cecil, C. M. (2021). Gene-environment correlations and causal effects of childhood maltreatment on physical and mental health: A genetically informed approach. *The Lancet Psychiatry, 8*(5), 373–386. https://doi.org/10.1016/S2215-0366(20)30569-1

10
Attachment and parenting in the brain and hormones?

Transactional relations between hormones, brain, and behaviour

We are our brains is the title of the 2010 bestseller from Dutch brain researcher Dick Swaab, arguing that we don't just have brains, but that we are our brains. He argues that everything we think, do, or refrain from doing is determined by our brain. And he is not the only one who takes this radical position. The neurosurgeon and author Henry Marsh (2017) writes that everything he is, is just the electrochemical activity of billions of brain cells. Are the brains the first cause of human behaviour, or is perhaps – a more nuanced position – brain functioning as a result of hormonal levels the starting point of what we do, think, and feel? For example, Swain and Ho (2017) suggested that oxytocin (OT) would be, together with cortisol, a key regulator of parental brain function. They proposed that the 'parental brain' regulating parenting includes the amygdala, nucleus accumbens, insula, and anterior cingulate, and that parental brain mechanisms affect child development. We argue here that the available evidence does not allow for such directional conclusions. In the absence of replicated results from studies with designs allowing for causal conclusions, only bidirectional associations as proposed in Figure 10.1 can be taken for granted.

In many models of parenting and attachment, OT figures as a popular hormone, the supposed motor of sensitive parenting behaviour and secure attachment relationships (Feldman, 2017; Swain & Ho, 2017). In spite of the relevance of other hormones for social interaction, parenting, and attachment (e.g., prolactin, vasopressin, testosterone, oestradiol; Bakermans-Kranenburg et al., 2022), we will therefore focus on OT.

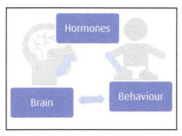

Figure 10.1 The relations between neural activation in the brain, hormonal levels, and behavioural adaptations to environmental demands might be bidirectional.
Source: Authors.

The name of the hormone is derived from the Greek ὀξύς τόκος, meaning *speedy birth*, and indeed parturition is accompanied by a strong increase of oxytocin, as is, to a lesser extent, breastfeeding. Whereas mammalian mothering in non-human animals is hormone dependent, with crucial roles for OT and prolactin in the onset of maternal behaviour, human parenting is not determined by hormone levels. Yet, correlational studies point to links between OT levels and parenting and many other (pro-)social behaviours.

Hormones and behaviour

Our first study on oxytocin related polymorphisms of the oxytocin receptor gene OXTR to observed parenting behaviour. In hindsight, it was a naïve idea to expect an association between a candidate gene and behaviour as complex as parenting, but we found an association between the OXTR rs53576 minor allele and lower levels of observed parenting sensitivity (Bakermans-Kranenburg & Van IJzendoorn, 2008). The paper was accompanied by an enthusiastic recommendation of the editor. However, the meta-analysis of associations between two OXTR SNPs and social behaviour that we conducted 5 years later (Bakermans-Kranenburg & Van IJzendoorn, 2014) revealed our early study as an illustration of a 'winner's curse' (see Chapter 1) that could not be replicated.

We then focused on the neuropeptide OT itself. It is represented in Figure 10.2, with each oxygen molecule replaced by a heart (the 'love' hormone). OT is primarily synthesised in the hypothalamus, a small region

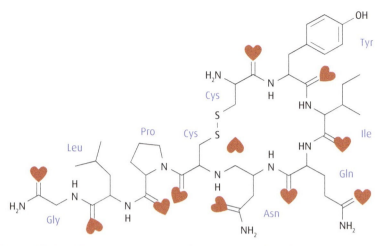

Figure 10.2 The oxytocin molecule (oxygen replaced by hearts). Oxytocin is a nonapeptide hormone with a specific amino acid sequence acting as a neurotransmitter in the brain. Despite the hearts the term 'love hormone' is a misnomer.
Source: Authors.

located at the base of the brain. It is then transported to and released by the posterior pituitary, from which it is released into the bloodstream as a hormone influencing various bodily functions. Additionally, neurons in the paraventricular nuclei project to various limbic, mid-brain, and hindbrain structures, such as the hippocampus, amygdala, and nucleus accumbens, which contain a high density of OT receptors.

In two early double-blind randomised designs we found nasal administration of OT related to more sensitive structuring behaviour in fathers observed at their homes while playing with their toddlers (Naber et al., 2010; 2013). This experimental finding seemed to complement correlational results from Ruth Felman's lab, showing that fathers who displayed more active sensitive behaviour with their infants had an increase in OT levels after the parent-child interaction (Feldman et al., 2010). At the same time, this combination of findings, while supporting an association between OT and parenting behaviour, refutes a specific directionality of the association. Over the years, numerous correlational studies examining the link between parental OT levels and parenting behaviour have been conducted. Results are ambiguous: sometimes significant associations are found, either for mothers or for fathers, and sometimes associations are absent or even negative. In our own studies in fathers with young infants, we found sensitive parenting unrelated to basal OT levels (and vasopressin, testosterone, and cortisol levels) and hormone reactivity in response to parent-child interaction (Lotz et al., 2022). In a recent review, Grumi et al. (2021) noted that all studies reporting significant associations between fathering and OT levels came from one lab (Ruth Feldman's lab in Israel), with other studies not replicating these findings.

One explanation for diverging findings may be found in variation in sampling methods and materials (see Bakermans-Kranenburg et al., 2022; see also Chapter 3 on 'utosti'); blood versus saliva, once versus repeated, baseline at home versus baseline after arrival at the research facilities, with or without children, and with or without guidelines about food, drink, and sports in the hours before the assessment. These issues are not unique to OT, as they are known from the literature on cortisol, where serious doubts about measurement issues have been raised (Leng & Leng, 2020). In women, additional intra- and interindividual variation in OT levels due to hormonal contraceptives and phases in the cycle should be taken into account. With this abundance of interfering covariates, replicable findings are not easily obtained.

Another source of variation in results is the analysis of OT levels from either blood or saliva. A crucial difference in the procedure is whether or not extraction is done. Because OT is present in very low concentrations in biological fluids, an extraction process is often used to concentrate and purify the hormone from the sample prior to analysis. Different extraction methods are used, depending on the type of sample and the desired level of sensitivity. In saliva samples, a common method is to use solid-phase extraction to selectively adsorb the OT molecules onto a solid support. This allows for the removal of other proteins, salts, and lipids present in the sample. Unextracted samples may overestimate OT levels and be less accurate (Leng & Leng, 2020).

Lastly, diverging associations between OT levels and social behaviour in a more general sense may be due to the fact that OT is not the cuddly prosocial hormone that it is often believed to be, increasing trust and cooperation while reducing stress and aggression. The function of OT is to 'tend and defend' (Bakermans-Kranenburg & Van IJzendoorn, 2017; Taylor et al., 2000), which implies that it is expected to promote trust and care in the 'in-group' and aggression to the 'out-group'. This is what we found meta-analytically (Van IJzendoorn & Bakermans-Kranenburg, 2012): a nasal spray of OT increased trust to the in-group, but decreased trust to the out-group. It is not difficult to imagine that individuals differ in whom they consider as members of their in-group versus their out-group. Clinical groups may, following from their mental health issues or from negative (childhood) experiences, perceive more of their social environment as out-group rather than in-group. Moreover, early childhood experiences may affect methylation of the oxytocin receptor gene and the density of OT receptors in the brain. Indeed, we found that positive effects on social functioning in clinical groups were minimal or absent (Van IJzendoorn & Bakermans-Kranenburg, 2012), a finding that was confirmed in a later updated and more comprehensive meta-analysis together with Bruce Ellis and Sue Carter (Ellis et al., 2021).

For example, using within-subject designs, we found that postnatally depressed mothers were not more sensitive with their infants after nasal sniffs of OT, and although they were more likely to rate an infant cry as more urgent, they were also more likely to indicate they would choose a harsh caregiving strategy in response (Mah et al., 2017). In a non-clinical group of childless women, experiences with harsh parental discipline during childhood moderated the effect of OT sniffs on using excessive force on a hand-grip dynamometer while listening to infant cry sounds. Women without harsh discipline experiences used less excessive force in the OT condition, but for women who were disciplined harshly no difference between the oxytocin and placebo condition emerged (Bakermans-Kranenburg et al., 2012).

Thus, clinical conditions and early caregiving experiences constitute an important moderator of the stress-reducing and trust-enhancing effects of OT. OT sniffs may increase trust and cooperation in healthy individuals with supportive backgrounds but not generate this effect in individuals who – as a consequence of their mental health condition or unfavourable early childhood experiences – may have a bias towards negative interpretation of social cues or have undergone (epigenetic) alterations in their oxytocinergic system (Ellis et al., 2021).

Mind over matter

Our first imaging studies examined the effects of OT administration on processing infant crying and laughter sounds, conducted in collaboration with Madelon Riem. In our non-clinical female sample, we found that OT reduced activation in the amygdala and increased activation in the insula and inferior frontal gyrus pars triangularis while listening to infant crying (Riem et al., 2011). The findings were later partly but not completely replicated in fathers with a first-born infant (Witte et al., 2022). Reduced activation in the neural circuitry for anxiety and aversion and increased activation in regions involved in empathy may promote responsiveness to infant crying. OT also reduced activation in the amygdala during exposure to infant laughter. Moreover, it enhanced functional connectivity between the amygdala and the orbitofrontal cortex, the anterior cingulate, the hippocampus, the precuneus, the supramarginal gyri, and the middle temporal gyrus, thus enhancing the incentive salience of infant laughter (Riem et al., 2012a). Yet, these studies had not enough power to test for moderation by childhood experiences.

One of the most interesting findings awaiting replication is the effect of OT on responses to infant crying-in-context (Riem et al., 2014). We measured neural activity in response to infant crying at fundamental frequencies (pitch) of 500 and 700 Hz. Infants who are in pain cry at higher pitches than infants who are hungry (Soltis, 2004), and infants with neurological issues tend to cry at higher pitches than healthy infants. Higher-pitched cry sounds are usually perceived as more urgent. In our study, we presented the cry sounds preceded by information about the context of the sound. The information provided the reason why the infant was crying: sickness ('This infant is sick') or boredom ('This infant is bored'). Both types of information, *sick* and *bored*, were combined with crying sounds at both 500 and 700 Hz.

Results showed that OT administration increased brain activity in the insula and inferior frontal gyrus in response to crying that was labelled as coming from a sick infant but decreased activation in these areas when hearing crying of a bored infant. Additionally, OT reduced amygdala activation to 500 Hz crying but increased activation to 700 Hz crying. These findings suggest not only that OT increased attention to higher-pitched infant cries but also that labelling the same crying as sick or bored alters neural activity in response to oxytocin. OT increased empathic reactions to sick infants' crying but lowered the perceived urgency of crying of a bored infant's crying, whatever the pitch of the crying (*'mind over matter'*). This pattern of results seems to indicate that OT promotes flexible parenting responses to crying infants.

Having said that, the field is hampered by a lack of meta-analytic research on the effects of hormone administration on parenting-related functional brain measures (Chapter 3). Individual studies are usually small and underpowered. Although methods are available for combining the results of individual studies (Radua et al., 2012) as we have done in the development of a neural model of infant cry perception with Jurriaan Witteman et al. (2019), such combination of studies into the effects of hormone administration on the so-called *parental brain* is still a wish for the future.

Brain and behaviour

The brain-behaviour gap is not an easy one to bridge. Interindividual differences in brain structure or functioning are not very powerful in predicting parenting or attachment behaviours. In one study we found that insecure adult attachment was related to heightened amygdala activation when exposed to infant crying compared to individuals with secure attachment representations. Moreover, insecure individuals reported feeling more irritated during infant crying and they had more trouble modulating their force using a handgrip dynamometer than individuals with a secure attachment representation. Yet, amygdala activation did not mediate the association between insecure attachment and emotional or behavioural response to infant crying (Riem et al., 2012b), because it was not associated with irritation or using excessive force.

In another study we measured resting state functional connectivity between the amygdala and other brain regions in a group of first-time expectant and new fathers (total $N = 131$). No differences were found between expectant and new fathers, but in fathers with a firstborn baby of approximately 2.5 months old the time they spent with their child was positively related to amygdala connectivity with the supramarginal gyrus, postcentral gyrus, and superior parietal lobule (Horstman et al., 2022). These regions belong to the cognition/mentalising network and have been associated with empathy and social cognition. Thus, fathers' time investment in their child was related to connectivity networks in the parental brain. The correlational nature of the study does not allow for causal inference. Nevertheless, it is tempting to suggest that fathers' brains do adapt to their new role and behaviour, just like dancers show training-related functional connectivity differences (Burzynska et al., 2017).

Dick Swaab's position that we are our brains, that everything we think and do is determined by our brain, presents the image of a homunculus in our head directing our comings and goings. For parenting and attachment, the evidence for such determinism is elusive. Turning the direction of effects around, there is evidence for the lasting impression of childhood experiences on the brain. Based on a meta-analysis of all available evidence (49 studies including 2,720 participants), we found that cumulative maltreatment experiences predicted smaller hippocampal volume (Riem et al., 2015). As another example of environmental impact, the randomised Bucharest Early Intervention Project documented delays in grey matter development 7 years after the children had been removed from institutional care and placed in foster care (Sheridan et al., 2012). In a meta-analysis of 20 studies on brain development in institutionalised children (N = 2,042 children) we found smaller head circumferences (as a proxy for neural development) in institutionalised children, with a very large effect size d = 1.44. One could argue that selective placement of children with smaller brains in institutions might explain this effect, but we also found impressive recovery in head circumference after transition into family care (Van IJzendoorn et al., 2020; see also Chapter 5).

Less extreme experiences appear to leave their mark as well. In the Generation R study, a longitudinal cohort study in Rotterdam, Netherlands, we found parental sensitivity in early childhood related to larger total brain and grey matter volume, also when early head circumference, gender, age, and various other potential confounders were taken into account (Kok et al., 2015). Additionally, amygdala-medial prefrontal cortex (mPFC) connectivity was accelerated in 8- to 10-year-old children who experienced low parental sensitivity in early childhood (Thijssen et al., 2017). This suggests that lower-quality parenting may lead to the early development of brain structures responsible for managing emotions, allowing children in challenging caregiving situations to regulate themselves and be independent of parental regulation at a younger age. A study by Wang et al. (2019) found similar shifts in the relationship between early parental sensitivity and an anterior hippocampal functional network in preschool children. These findings align with life history theory, which suggests that children from disadvantaged and stressful backgrounds will have accelerated brain development so that they can function earlier without the support of their caregivers (Bolhuis et al., 2022; Ellis & Del Giudice, 2019).

Associations between children's attachment classification and brain morphology are scarce. In Generation R we found that infants with a smaller gangliothalamic ovoid, as measured with cranial ultrasound at 6 weeks, had a higher risk of disorganised attachment at 14 months (N = 629). In turn, disorganised attachment was related to larger hippocampal volumes at age 10 years (N = 551; Cortes Hidalgo et al., 2019). Disorganised attachment in infancy was unrelated to amygdala volume at age 10, failing to replicate a result found in a small study on adults by Lyons-Ruth and colleagues (2016). Localisation of attachment in the right hemisphere as Schore (2017) assumed in his *regulation theory of attachment* is premature and in contrast with some of our meta-analytic evidence documenting the bi-hemispheric control of emotional prosody in a large set of lesion studies (Witteman et al., 2011) or ventral to dorsal emotion regulation (Morawetz et al., 2020). More replications and larger studies are needed for conclusions based on meta-analytic results, which might help build a genuinely new neurobiological theory of attachment. One such new approach focuses on biobehavioural synchrony, testing the idea that in a secure relationship the dyad displays neural synchrony (Feldman, 2017; Long et al., 2020). However, in hyperscanning, that is, collecting and processing imaging data of two communicating partners (see, e.g., Nguyen et al., 2021), unsystematic errors ('noise') may be multiplied, and this issue has received too little attention.

Causal claims not yet warranted

Hormones, behaviour, and brain structure and functioning are associated. But the vast majority of studies in our field are correlational, and causal claims about the direction of effects need experimental evidence or other advanced designs (e.g., Mendelian Randomisation, see Chapter 9, and Hamaker et al., 2020). How about randomised controlled trials manipulating hormonal levels, behaviour, or the brain, testing for their effects on the other domains? In randomised controlled trials manipulating hormones we have demonstrated effects on parenting or parenting-related behaviours in men and women (e.g., Alyousefi-van Dijk et al., 2019; Mah et al., 2017; Naber et al., 2010, 2013; Witte et al., 2022) and on brain responses to infant signals (Riem et al., 2010, 2011, 2012, 2014; Thijssen et al., 2018; Witte et al., 2022).

So far, we have been able to establish few effects of behavioural interventions on hormone levels. We found that massage applied by a massage seat cover elevated salivary oxytocin levels in two exploratory studies (Riem et al., 2017), but using a soft baby carrier did not result in changes in fathers' OT and cortisol levels (Verhees et al., 2023). However, the soft baby carrier intervention had an effect on brain functioning: it increased amygdala reactivity to infant cry sounds. The effect was most pronounced in fathers with experiences of childhood abuse, who tend to show hypo-reactivity to infant signals (Riem et al., 2021).

Randomised controlled trials manipulating the brain may be the most difficult to imagine. Yet, transcutaneous vagus nerve (TVN) stimulation has been used in non-parenting contexts (e.g., Sellaro et al., 2015) and might be applied in a proof-of-concept study of parenting. Importantly, any such randomised controlled trial should meet the highest standards for design (pre-registration) and measurement (observed caregiving and child behaviour) and take childhood experiences into account. Awaiting the evidence, we refute the claim that attachment or parenting can be localised in a specific brain region and that in fact we would be our brains.

References

Bakermans-Kranenburg, M. J., & Van IJzendoorn, M. H. (2008). Oxytocin receptor (OXTR) and serotonin transporter (5-HTT) genes associated with observed parenting. *Social Cognitive and Affective Neuroscience, 3*, 128–134. https://doi.org/10.1093/scan/nsn004

Bakermans-Kranenburg, M. J., & Van IJzendoorn, M. H. (2017). Oxytocin and human sensitive and protective parenting. In R. Hurlemann (Ed.), *Behavioral Pharmacology of Neuropeptides: Oxytocin* (pp. 421–448). Springer. https://doi.org/10.1007/7854_2017_23

Bakermans-Kranenburg, M. J., Van IJzendoorn, M. H., Riem, M. M. E., Tops, M., & Alink, L. R. A. (2012). Oxytocin decreases handgrip force in reaction to infant crying in females without harsh parenting experiences. *Social Cognitive and Affective Neuroscience, 7*, 951–957. https://doi.org/10.1093/scan/nsr067

Bakermans-Kranenburg, M. J., Verhees, M. W., Lotz, A. M., Alyousefi-van Dijk, K., & Van IJzendoorn, M. H. (2022). Is paternal oxytocin an oxymoron? Oxytocin, vasopressin, testosterone, oestradiol and cortisol in emerging fatherhood. *Philosophical Transactions of the Royal Society B, 377*(1858), 20210060. https://doi.org/10.1098/rstb.2021.0060

Bolhuis, E., Belsky, J., Frankenhuis, W. E., Shalev, I., Hastings, W. J., Tollenaar, M. S., ..., Beijers, R. (2022). Attachment insecurity and the biological embedding of reproductive strategies: Investigating the role of cellular aging. *Biological Psychology, 175*. https://doi.org/10.1016/j.biopsycho.2022.108446

Burzynska, A. Z., Finc, K., Taylor, B. K., Knecht, A. M., Kramer, A. F. (2017). The dancing brain: Structural and functional signatures of expert dance training. *Frontiers in Human Neuroscience, 11*. https://doi.org/10.3389/fnhum.2017.00566

Cortes Hidalgo, A. P., Muetzel, R., Luijk, P. C. M., Bakermans-Kranenburg, M. J., El Marroun, H., Vernooij, M. W., Van IJzendoorn, M. H., White, T., & Tiemeier, H. (2019). Observed infant-parent attachment and brain morphology in middle childhood: A population-based study. *Developmental Cognitive Neuroscience, 40*, 100724. https://doi.org/10.1016/j.dcn.2019.100724.

Ellis, B. J., & Del Giudice, M. (2019). Developmental adaptation to stress: An evolutionary perspective. *Annual Review of Psychology, 70*, 111–139. https://doi.org/10.1146/annurev-psych-122216-011732

Ellis, B. J., Horn, A. J. Carter, C. S., Van IJzendoorn M. H., & Bakermans-Kranenburg, M. J. (2021). Developmental programming of oxytocin through variation in early-life stress: Four meta-analyses and a theoretical reinterpretation. *Clinical Psychology Review, 86*, 101985. https://doi.org/10.1016/j.cpr.2021.101985

Feldman, R. (2017). The neurobiology of human attachments. *Trends in Cognitive Sciences, 21*(2), 80–99. https://doi.org/10.1016/j.tics.2016.11.007.

Feldman R., Gordon I., Schneiderman I., Weissman O., & Zagoory-Sharon O. (2010). Natural variations in maternal and paternal care are associated with systematic changes in oxytocin following parent-infant contact. *Psychoneuroendocrinology, 35*, 1133–1141. https://doi.org/10.1016/j.psyneuen.2010.01.013.

Grumi, S., Saracino, A., Volling, B. L., & Provenzi, L. (2021). A systematic review of human paternal oxytocin: Insights into the methodology and what we know so far. *Developmental Psychobiology 63*, 1330–1344. https://doi.org/10.1002/dev.22116.

Horstman, L. I., Riem, M. M., Alyousefi-van Dijk, K., Lotz, A. M., & Bakermans-Kranenburg, M. J. (2022). Fathers' involvement in early childcare is associated with amygdala resting-state connectivity. *Social Cognitive and Affective Neuroscience, 17*, 198–205. https://doi.org/10.1093/scan/nsab086

Kok, R., Thijssen, S., Bakermans-Kranenburg, M. J., Jaddoe, V. W. V., Verhulst, F. C., White, T., Van IJzendoorn, M. H., & Tiemeier, H. (2015). Normal variation in early parental sensitivity predicts child structural brain development. *Journal of the American Academy of Child & Adolescent Psychiatry, 54*, 824–831. DOI: 10.1016/j.jaac.2015.07.009

Leng, G., & Leng, R. I. (2020). *The Matter of Facts: Skepticism, Persuasion, and Evidence in Science*. MIT Press. https://doi.org/10.7551/mitpress/12228.001.0001

Lyons-Ruth, K., Pechtel, P., Yoon, S. A., Anderson, C. M., & Teicher, M. H. (2016). Disorganized attachment in infancy predicts greater amygdala volume in adulthood. *Behavioural Brain Research, 308*, 83–93. https://doi.org/10.1016/j.bbr.2016.03.050

Mah, B. L., Van IJzendoorn, M. H., Out, D., Smith, R., & Bakermans, M. J. (2017). The effects of intranasal oxytocin administration on sensitive caregiving in mothers with postnatal depression. *Child Psychiatry and Human Development, 48*(2), 308–315. https://doi.org/10.1007/s10 578-016-0642-7

Marsch, H. (2017). *Admissions: Life as a Brain Surgeon*. Orion Publishing Co. https://doi.org/ 10.1097/aln.0000000000004311

Naber, F. B. A., Poslawsky, I. E., Van IJzendoorn, M. H., Van Engeland, H., & Bakermans-Kranenburg, M. J. (2013). Oxytocin enhances paternal sensitivity to a child with autism: A double-blind within-subject experiment with intranasally administered oxytocin. *Journal of Autism and Developmental Disorders, 43*, 224–229. https://doi.org/10.1007/s10803-012-1536-6

Naber, F. B. A., Van IJzendoorn, M. H., Deschamps, P., Van Engeland, H., Bakermans-Kranenburg, M. J. (2010). Intranasal oxytocin increases fathers' observed responsiveness during play with their children: A double-blind within-subject experiment. *Psychoneuroendocrinology, 35*, 1583–1586. DOI: 10.1016/j.psyneuen.2010.04.007

Nguyen, T., Hoehl, S., & Vrtička, P. (2021). A guide to parent-child fNIRS hyperscanning data analysis. *Sensors (Section Biosensors; Special issue on Brain Signals Acquisition and Processing), 21*, 4075. https://doi.org/10.3390/s21124075.

Long, M., Verbeke, W., Ein-Dor, T., & Vrtička, P. (2020). A functional neuro-anatomical model of human attachment (NAMA): Insights from first- and second-person social neuroscience. *Cortex, 126*, 281–321. https://doi.org/10.1016/j.cortex.2020.01.010.

Lotz, A. M., Buisman, R. S. M., Alyousefi-van Dijk, K., Witte, A. M., Bakermans-Kranenburg, M. J., & Verhees, M. W. F. T. (2022). Exploring the role of endocrine factors in paternal sensitive parenting. *Hormones and Behavior, 140*, 105118. https://doi.org/10.1016/j.yhbeh.2022.105118

Morawetz, C., Riedel, M. C., Salo, T., Berboth, S., Eickhof, S. B., Laird, A. R., & Kohn, N. (2020). Multiple large-scale neural networks underlying emotion regulation. *Neuroscience and Biobehavioral Reviews, 116*, 382–395. https://doi.org/10.1016/j.neubiorev.2020.07.001

Radua, J., & Mataix-Cols, D. (2009). Voxel-wise meta-analysis of grey matter changes in obsessive-compulsive disorder. *British Journal of Psychiatry, 195*, 393–402. https://doi.org/10.1192/ bjp.bp.108.055046.

Radua, J., Mataix-Cols, D., Phillips, M. L., El-Hage, W., Kronhaus, D. M., Cardoner, N., & Surguladze, S. (2012). A new meta-analytic method for neuroimaging studies that combines reported peak coordinates and statistical parametric maps. *European Psychiatry, 27*, 605–611. https://doi. org/10.1016/j.eurpsy.2011.04.001.

Riem, M. E., Alink, L. R. A., Out, D., Van IJzendoorn, M. H., Bakermans-Kranenburg, M. J. (2015). Beating the brain about abuse: Empirical and meta-analytic studies of the association between maltreatment and hippocampal volume across childhood and adolescence. *Development and Psychopathology, 27*, 507–520. https://doi.org/10.1017/S0954579415000127

Riem, M. R. J. E., Bakermans-Kranenburg, M. J., Pieper, S., Tops, M., Boksem, M. A. S., Vermeiren, R. R. J. M., Van IJzendoorn, M. H., Rombouts, S. A. R. B. (2011). Oxytocin modulates amygdala, insula and inferior frontal gyrus responses to infant crying: A randomized control trial. *Biological Psychiatry, 70*, 291–297. https://doi.org/10.1016/j.biopsych.2011.02.006

Riem, M. M. E., Bakermans-Kranenburg, M. J., Van IJzendoorn, M. H., Out, D., & Rombouts, S. A. R. B. (2012). Attachment in the brain: Adult attachment representations predict amygdala and behavioral responses to infant crying. *Attachment & Human Development, 14*, 533–551. http://dx.doi.org/10.1080/14616734.2012.727252

Riem, M. M. E., De Carli, P., Van IJzendoorn, M. H., et al. (2017). Emotional maltreatment is associated with atypical responding to stimulation of endogenous oxytocin release through mechanically-delivered massage in males. *Psychoneuroendocrinology, 85*, 115–122. https:// doi.org/10.1016/j.psyneuen.2017.08.017

Riem, M. M. E., Lotz, A. M., Horstman, L. I., Cima, M., Verhees, M., Alyousefi-van Dijk, K., Van IJzendoorn, M. H., Bakermans-Kranenburg, M. J. (2021). A soft baby carrier intervention enhances amygdala responses to infant crying in fathers: A randomized controlled trial. *Psychoneuroendocrinology, 132*, 105380. https://doi.org/10.1016/j.psyneuen.2021.105380

Riem, M. M. E, Van IJzendoorn, M. H., Tops, M., Boksem, M. A. S., Rombouts, S. A. R. B., & Bakermans-Kranenburg, M. J. (2012). No laughing matter: Intranasal oxytocin administration changes functional brain connectivity during exposure to infant laughter. *Neuropsychopharmacology, 37*, 1257–1266. DOI:10.1038/npp.2011.313

Riem, M. M. E., Voorthuis, A., Bakermans-Kranenburg, M. J., & Van IJzendoorn, M. H. (2014). Pity or peanuts? Oxytocin induces different neural responses to the same infant crying labelled as sick or bored. *Developmental Science, 17*, 248–256. https://doi.org/10.1111/desc12103.

Schore, A. N. (2017). Modern attachment theory. In S. N. Gold (Ed.), *APA Handbook of Trauma Psychology: Foundations in Knowledge* (pp. 389–406). American Psychological Association. https://doi.org/10.1037/0000019-020

Sellaro, R., Steenbergen, L., Verkuil, B., Van IJzendoorn, & M. H., Colzato, L. S. (2015). Transcutaneaous Vagus Nerve Stimulation (tVNS) does not increase prosocial behavior in Cyberball. *Frontiers in Psychology, 6*, 499. doi 10.3389/fpsyg.2015.00499

Sheridan, M. A., Fox, N. A., Zeanah, C. H., McLaughlin, K. A., & Nelson, C. A., 3rd (2012). Variation in neural development as a result of exposure to institutionalization early in childhood. *Proceedings of the National Academy of Sciences of the United States of America, 109*(32), 12927–12932. https://doi.org/10.1073/pnas.1200041109

Soltis J. (2004). The signal functions of early infant crying. *The Behavioral and Brain Sciences, 27*(4), 443–490.

Swain, J. E., & Ho, S.-H. S. (2017). Neuroendocrine mechanisms for parental sensitivity: Overview, recent advances and future directions. *Current Opinion in Psychology, 15*, 105–110. https://doi.org/10.1016/j.copsyc.2017.02.027

Taylor, S. E., Klein, L. C., Lewis, B. P., Gruenewald, T. L., Gurung, R. A. R., & Updegraff, J. A. (2000). Biobehavioral responses to stress in females: Tend-and-befriend, not fight-or-flight. *Psychological Review, 107*, 411–429. https://doi.org/10.1037/0033-295x.107.3.411

Thijssen, S., Muetzel, R. L., Bakermans-Kranenburg, M. J., Jaddoe, V. W. V., Tiemeier, H., Verhulst, F. C., White, T., & Van IJzendoorn, M. H. (2017). Insensitive parenting may accelerate the development of the amygdala-medial prefrontal cortex circuit. *Development & Psychopathology, 29*(2), 505–518.

Van IJzendoorn, M. H., & Bakermans-Kranenburg, M. J. (2012). A sniff of trust: Meta-analysis of the effects of intranasal oxytocin administration on face recognition, trust to in-group, and trust to out-group. *Psychoneuroendocrinology, 37*, 438–443. https://doi.org/10.1016/j.psyneuen.2011.07.008

Van IJzendoorn, M. H., Bakermans-Kranenburg, M. J., Duschinsky, R., Goldman, P. S., Fox, N. A., Gunnar, M. R., Johnson, D. E., Nelson, C. A., Reijman, S., Skinner, G. C. M., Zeanah, C. H., & Sonuga-Barke, E. J. S. (2020). Institutionalisation and deinstitutionalisation of children I: A systematic and integrative review of evidence regarding effects on development. *The Lancet Psychiatry, 7*, 703–720. https://doi.org/10.1016/S2215-0366(19)30399-2.

Verhees, M. W. F. T., Lotz, A. M., de Moor, M. H. M., Van IJzendoorn, M. H., Fidder, A. A. E. J., Buisman, R. S. M., & Bakermans-Kranenburg, M. J. (2023). Effects of a soft baby carrier on fathers' behavior and hormones: A randomized controlled trial. *Journal of Child and Family Studies*. https://doi.org/10.1007/s10826-023-02678-x

Wang, Q., Zhang, H., Wee, C. Y., Lee, A., Poh, J. S., Chong, Y. S., Tan, K. H., Gluckman, P. D., Yap, F., Fortier, M. V., Rifkin-Graboi, A., & Qiu, A. (2019). Maternal sensitivity predicts anterior hippocampal functional networks in early childhood. *Brain Structure & Function, 224*(5), 1885–1895. https://doi.org/10.1007/s00429-019-01882-0

Witte, A. M., Riem, M. M. E., Van der Knaap, N., de Moor, M. H. M., Van IJzendoorn, M. H., & Bakermans-Kranenburg, M. J. (2022). The effects of oxytocin and vasopressin administration on fathers' neural responses to infant crying: A randomized controlled within-subject study. *Psychoneuroendocrinology, 140*, 105731. https://doi.org/10.1016/j.psyneuen.2022.105731

Witteman, J., Van IJzendoorn, M. H., Rilling, J. K., Bos, P. A., Schiller, N. O., & Bakermans-Kranenburg, M. J. (2019). Towards a neural model of infant cry perception. *Neuroscience & Biobehavioral Reviews, 99*, 23–32. ISSN: 0149-7634, 1873-7528. https://doi.org/10.1016/j.neubiorev.2019.01.026

11
Is attachment culture specific?

Attachment is universal *and* culture specific

Is attachment a culture-specific or a universal characteristic of human development? Attachment, defined as the innate bias of newborns to become attached to protective conspecifics, seems universal across species, historical times, and cultures. Attachment behaviours have been observed in a variety of species, including non-human primates, dogs, and human infants. For example, in our study on 46 chimpanzee infants raised with standard care or enriched responsive care in the Great Ape Nursery at Yerkes we were able to classify their attachment patterns at 1 year of age in the Strange Situation Procedure in a reliable and valid manner. Standard care consisted of being raised by their peers, with humans providing necessary care and feeding. Responsive care included an additional 4 hours of dyadic interaction with human caregivers who were trained to promote chimpanzee social and emotional development (Van IJzendoorn et al., 2008).

This was the first time the Strange Situation Procedure was used with chimpanzees, with their human caretaker as attachment figure. The results showed that the chimpanzees exhibited similar patterns of distress, proximity seeking, and exploration as human infants in the procedure. That is, play and exploratory behaviours were decreased during the separation episodes and returned to baseline levels in the reunion episodes. During the separation episodes, many showed searching behaviour and remained close to the door through which the caretaker had left. The chimpanzees who received standard care showed an attachment classification distribution similar to human infants raised in orphanages in Greece or Romania (see Chapter 5). In contrast, the chimpanzees who received responsive care displayed fewer disorganised attachment behaviours, had more advanced cognitive development, and had less attachment to objects compared to those who received standard care.

These results suggest that responsive care can improve attachment development in chimpanzees and mitigate some of the negative effects of institutional standard care (Van IJzendoorn et al., 2008). As evident from Chapter 5, 4 hours of dyadic interaction per day in the enriched condition entails many more interactions with the developing chimpanzees than is provided even in the most well-equipped human orphanages.

In humans, attachment behaviours have been documented across cultures and throughout history. The so-called 'Amarna family' is an ancient Egyptian sculpture dating back more than 3,000 years which illustrates attachment in another culture and era. The sandstone stele depicts Akhenaten, Nefertiti, and their three eldest daughters, Meritaten, Meketaten, and Ankhesenpaaten. The royal family is portrayed as a close, loving, and affectionate group with the children seeking close proximity and contact comfort with their parents who respond in a lovely, playful manner to their children, with no visible difference in interactions of mother or father with their children. The statue is one of the first realistic pictures of persons and their clothes, and this realism is reason to believe the impression of close affectionate relationships between the family members transpiring from this beautiful piece of art (see Figure 11.1).

Figure 11.1 A stele showing Akhenaten, Nefertiti, and three of their daughters. 18th dynasty, reign of Akhenaten. Limestone, ca. 1340 BC. Gerbil/Wikimedia Commons, CC BY SA 3.0, https://nl.m.wikipedia.org/wiki/Bestand:Akhenaten,_Nefertiti_and_their_children.jpg

While attachment has been observed in various species and across different cultures, the expression and experience of attachment may vary based on cultural values and practices. In a study of 26 Dogon mothers and their 1-year-old infants in Mali, attachment classifications were assigned using the traditional Strange Situation Procedure (True, 1994; True et al., 2001). The Dogon are subsistence farmers, and mothers breastfeed their infants on demand and keep them in a sling close by almost all the time. This study supports the universality of attachment by demonstrating that in the Strange Situation Procedure attachment behaviours such as proximity seeking after a brief separation from their parent can be observed in almost all infants in a non-WEIRD African culture despite their different caregiving histories compared to their WEIRD peers (WEIRD stands for Western, Educated, Industrialised, Rich, and Democratic; Henrich et al., 2010). Careful modulation of a level of mild stress generated in a culture in which infants almost never separate from their caregivers is critically important. The infants' behaviours in the first few episodes of the Strange Situation Procedure serve as the dyad-specific baseline for rating their behaviour in the reunion episodes (Mesman, Sagi-Schwartz & Van IJzendoorn, 2016).

We proposed the following hypotheses to examine the universality of the attachment patterns across cultures (originally suggested by Van IJzendoorn, 1990):

1. The *universality* hypothesis suggests that all infants without severe neurophysiological impairments will form attachments to one or more specific caregivers when given the opportunity.
2. The *normativity* hypothesis posits that the majority of infants will develop secure attachments in environments that do not pose a significant threat to their health and survival. Normativity here means majority, that is, being the quantitative norm, which does not suggest any ethical implication.
3. The *sensitivity* hypothesis proposes that the security of an infant's attachment is related to the responsiveness of their caregivers, particularly in regard to promptly responding to the infant's attachment signals.
4. The *competence* hypothesis states that secure attachment is linked to adaptive child outcomes in various areas of development in environments without significant threats to health or survival.

In the Dogon study the distribution of attachment classifications supported the normativity hypothesis because the majority of infants were securely attached (True et al., 2001). Avoidant attachments were almost absent because the procedure may have been experienced as more stressful than in Western cultures, causing even avoidant infants to seek proximity after separation (True, 1994). Additionally, this study found that infant attachment security was related to caregiving patterns characterised by sensitivity, a lack of frightening or frightened behaviours, and fewer violations of communication coherence and cooperativeness. The over-representation of disorganised children was speculated to be due to the high levels of poverty, stress, and trauma due to high mortality in this culture. Specific cultural practices which potentially created excessive stress for infants not being used to even short separations from the parent also might have been important (True, 2021). True's impressively careful study supports the universality, normativity, and sensitivity hypotheses but also suggests that the Strange Situation Procedure should be administered in a culturally sensitive manner. An alternative approach would be to embed attachment assessments in a locally existing practice with a mild stress component such as the weigh-in procedure (True et al., 1994). The weigh-in procedure is meant to measure infant anthropometrics by an unknown, medically trained 'stranger' but does not require separation from the parent who usually watches the procedure from nearby.

Attachment distributions across the world

In the large meta-analysis of the first 20,000 Strange Situation Procedures (Madigan et al., 2023) administered in over 285 studies from more than 20 countries, we found the following 'global' distribution of SSP attachment: 51.6% secure, 14.7% avoidant, 10.2% resistant, and 23.5% disorganised attachments. We did not find differences in the distribution among mothers and fathers, and no child age or sex differences. The hypothesis of the universality of attachment certainly is not incompatible with the slightly higher rates of secure attachment on the African continent and in Asia that we found (see Figure 11.2). Moreover, in Asia a lower percentage of disorganised attachment was observed. Racially minoritised samples did not show different distributions of attachment classifications or ratings compared to White majority samples. In the meta-analysis only the contrast between all ethnically minoritised samples versus White samples could be reliably tested. However, within the heterogeneous set of ethnicities included in this comparison some important differences might have been overshadowed. For example, Huang et al. (2012) compared Asian-American to Hispanic-American child-mother dyads using a continuous attachment measure (the Toddler Attachment Sort-45; Waters & Deane, 1985) and found that the Asian-American group had higher levels of attachment security.

It is in this context important to take differences in socio-economic status into account when comparing ethnic distributions of attachment. Ethnic minority differences might easily be confounded with socio-economic status disparities. In one of the largest samples to date ($N = 1,144$ families), we examined whether security of attachment (measured with the Attachment Q-Sort; Waters & Deane, 1985) varied between White and Black children of the NICHD Early Childcare Research Network study. We found lower attachment security in Black compared to White children, as well as lower levels of parental sensitivity (Bakermans-Kranenburg et al., 2004). On closer inspection, however, in both White and Black families higher parental sensitivity was associated with higher attachment security, confirming one of the core assumptions of attachment theory (Verhage et al., 2016).

Furthermore, in this USA sample ethnicity was strongly associated with income as a proxy for socio-economic status, and income almost completely mediated the relation of ethnicity with attachment security. Poverty might lead to more parental stress, more fragmented care, and lower sensitivity in their interactions with the children. This in turn may lead to lower levels of attachment security (Verhage et al., 2016; Cyr et al., 2010). In the recent meta-analysis (Madigan et al., 2023) we found that percentages of secure attachments were lower in demographic risk

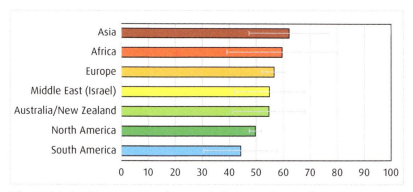

Figure 11.2 Percentages of secure infant-parent attachment relationships across the globe, derived from a meta-analysis of the first 20,000 Strange Situation Procedures. Adapted from Madigan et al. (2023).

samples (42%) than in non-risk samples (56%). We therefore caution that socio-economic status should always be considered a potential confounder when comparing ethnically minoritised families with their White counterparts.

Attachment to other caregivers

Humans are cooperative breeders, meaning that more than just the biological mother is involved in raising children. 'Alloparents' are indispensable (Hrdy, 2009) as 'it takes a village to raise a child' (Clinton, 1996). In WEIRD as well as non-WEIRD countries children are growing up in networks of attachment relationships, and there are at least two reasons for the universality of attachment networks. Human offspring need around 13 million calories to grow up to nutritional independence (Kaplan, 1994) which is way too much for any single caregiver to provide. Furthermore, in our evolutionary past the prevalence of mortality of mothers during childbirth was substantial and alloparents replaced the biological mother to care for the vulnerable newborn. From animal research Hrdy (2009) derives some determinants of paternal and alloparental involvement in caregiving, which is usually larger in species with twin births or more densely spaced sibling births (such as in the tamarin) and in (monogamous) species with more certainty of genetic relatedness of offspring (such as storks or titi monkeys, Bales et al., 2017). The human species is indeed characterised by rather rapid succession of births within a family, and fathers as well as extended family members can be fairly certain of genetic relatedness with the newborn. Against this evolutionary background, human babies are probably prepared to grow up in a modestly sized network of attachment figures that grows with the children's cognitive ability to deal with an expanding number of interacting individuals (Bakermans-Kranenburg, 2021).

Despite the universality of attachment networks, empirical studies on children's attachments with other caregivers than mothers have remained relatively scarce, although pioneering studies already were conducted in the 70s (e.g., Lamb, 1977). That is even true of infant-father attachments. In the meta-analysis of more than 20,000 Strange Situations only 12 studies collected infant-father attachment data (Madigan et al., 2023). The attachment distributions were similar to the infant-mother distributions. But the evidence base is growing, even in non-WEIRD cultures. Broesch et al. (2023) found, for example, in two subsistence populations, the Tsimane of lowland Bolivia and the Tannese of Vanuatu, that child-father attachment patterns were rather similar to samples from industrialised societies, with 52% of Tsimane dyads and 62% of Tannese dyads showing secure attachment. The insecure-ambivalent attachment seemed more frequent among Tsimane and Tannese dyads.

In an individual participant data (IPD) meta-analysis of 9 studies and 1,097 children with their mothers and fathers, Dagan et al. (2021) found an increased vulnerability to behavioural problems in children with insecure or disorganised attachment to both parents, and a buffering effect of having at least one secure attachment relationship regardless of parental gender. In some of the earliest studies on attachment networks with three attachment figures, mother, father, and professional caregiver, we found evidence for the presence of genuine attachment relationships of the infants with all three figures. The professional caregivers in the Dutch dual-earner families (Goossens & Van IJzendoorn, 1990) and Israeli kibbutzim (Sagi et al., 1985; 1995) served as attachment figures for the children in their care, as could be inferred from the low numbers of unclassifiable Strange Situations. The child-caregiver attachments were a unique reflection of the genetically unrelated caregivers' less or more sensitive interactions in the first year of life and did not necessarily mirror the attachments of the children with their parents (Van IJzendoorn et al., 1992).

With multiple caretakers involved, several developmental outcomes of combinations of secure and insecure attachments are possible (Van IJzendoorn et al., 1994). The first model is *monotropy*, in which only the biological mother is considered an important attachment figure, with the influence of other caretakers being minimal. The second model is *hierarchy*, in which the mother is the most important attachment figure, but other caretakers may serve as a secure base in the absence of the primary attachment figure. The third model is *independence*, in which a child may be attached to several different caretakers, but the attachment relationship would be functional only in those domains in which the dyad has been interacting over a long period of time. Each caretaker specialises in a certain domain, and only in that domain is the relationship effective as a secure base for the child. The fourth model is *integration*, in which secure attachment relationships can compensate for insecure attachments, with the optimal situation in the case of three attachment relationships being three secure relationships; with two secure relationships being better than one; and with the worst configuration being a network of only insecure relationships. Comparing the data from the Netherlands and Israel with these models, we found support for the integration model: in a multiple caretaker environment, the number of secure attachments appears to make a difference. Children seem to benefit most from having three secure relationships in terms of their socio-emotional and cognitive development. However, if the child had an insecure attachment to their mother but secure attachments to their father and professional caregiver, they fared better than if the insecure infant-mother attachment was not compensated by secure attachments to other caregivers.

The question of how many more than three attachment figures a network might contain cannot yet be answered on basis of empirical evidence. More than four decades ago, Smith (1980) estimated that in most cultures no more than ten caretakers interact frequently with the child, and he hypothesised that care shared between up to five caretakers would not lead to attachment problems. Meehan and Hawks (2013) suggest that among the Central African Aka hunter-gatherers children might have an average of six attachment figures. Even when their network of caregivers is larger, infants receive most personal attentive care from a small stable set of core caregivers (Chaudhary et al., 2023). Unfortunately, in the past 40 years no systematic research has been done on the number of attachment relationships that children can deal with. Doing such research should take into account the child's cognitive development and temperament. The limiting factor may not be the number of caregivers, but the developmental stage of the child and the number and duration of opportunities for the child to learn contingencies in social relationships with an attachment component (Bakermans-Kranenburg, 2021).

The universality of valuing attachment

The universality of attachment patterns across cultures would be questionable if parents from different cultures had vastly different ideas of what constitutes an ideal parent and an ideal pattern of attachment. Ideas about core concepts of attachment theory and measures might be WEIRD-culture-specific and in turn stimulate WEIRD-culture-specific attachment patterns. Two studies have examined parental concepts of sensitivity and security with the use of the Q-Sort method. This method requires participants to sort cards with behavioural descriptions into nine piles, ranking from not at all characteristic to highly characteristic of an ideal parent or ideal child. The distributions of these descriptions were compared with those of experts who also sorted the cards according to their thoughts about sensitivity and security. Posada and colleagues (1995) asked mothers from six different countries to sort cards with attachment-related child behaviours and found them strongly convergent with the profiles of experts' sorts of optimal secure child behaviour.

But among the six countries included in this study, only Colombia might be considered a non-WEIRD low-to-middle income country.

In a further Q-Sort study including 26 cultural groups from 15 countries around the world, we asked mothers to sort cards with descriptions of maternal interactive behaviours to reflect their ideas of the ideal mother. The similarity between the mothers' beliefs about the ideal mother and attachment experts' description of a sensitive mother was strong across all groups. Cultural background predicted hardly any variation in what was considered 'good' maternal behaviour, but socio-demographic factors made more difference. Mothers living in rural areas, with low family incomes and with more children, were less likely to describe the ideal mother with items that characterise highly sensitive parents as defined by attachment theory (Mesman, Van IJzendoorn et al., 2016). In this study more non-WEIRD countries were included than in Posada et al.'s (1995) pioneering study discussed above.

These Q-Sort studies indicate again that socio-economic status overshadows cultural variations in (valuing) attachment security or sensitive parenting. This finding reminds us of our study on attachment and sensitive parenting in Black and White families in the USA (Bakermans-Kranenburg et al., 2004). Poverty and stress can be in the way of (ideas about) sensitive parenting, but so far, the universality of attachment concepts and phenomena has not been refuted. The hypothesis of culture-specific parenting style and development of attachment was not confirmed in studies that explicitly examined the issue. We should, however, take this outcome as preliminary because attachment research has been mainly conducted in a small part of the world, although this part is growing. Countries such as India, with one of the largest populations worldwide, are conspicuously absent in the databases of attachment theory, and attachment research is only in its infancy in large countries like Indonesia, Brazil, and China. Yet, with the current state of research, categorically rejecting the claim to a universalistic interpretation of attachment development is arguably incorrect.

References

Bakermans-Kranenburg, M. J. (2021). The limits of the attachment network. *New Directions for Child and Adolescent Development, 2021*(180), 117–124. https://doi.org/10.1002/cad.20432

Bakermans-Kranenburg, M. J., Van IJzendoorn, M. H., & Kroonenberg, P. M. (2004). Differences in attachment security between African-American and white children: Ethnicity or socio-economic status? *Infant Behavior & Development, 27*, 417–433. doi:10.1016/j.infbeh.2004.11.002

Bales, K. L., Del Razo, R. A., Conklin, Q. A., Hartman, S., Mayer, H. S., Rogers, F. D., Simmons, T. C., Smith, L. K., Williams, A., Williams, D. R., Witczak, L. R., & Wright, E. C. (2017). Titi monkeys as a novel non-human primate model for the neurobiology of pair bonding. *The Yale Journal of Biology and Medicine, 90*(3), 373–387.

Broesch, T., von Rueden, C., Yurkowski, K., Quinn, H., Alami, S., Davis, H. E., Stupica, B., Tarry Nimau, J., & Bureau, J.-F. (2023). Fatherhood and child–father attachment in two small-scale societies. *Journal of Cross-Cultural Psychology.* https://doi.org/10.1177/00220221231176788

Chaudhary, N., Salali, G. D., & Swanepoel, A. (2023). Sensitive responsiveness and multiple caregiving networks among Mbendjele BaYaka hunter-gatherers: Potential implications for psychological development and well-being. *Developmental Psychology.* https://dx.doi.org/10.1037/dev0001601

Clinton, H. R. (1996). *It Takes a Village: And Other Lessons Children Teach Us*. Simon & Schuster. https://doi.org/10.2307/2967370

Cyr, C., Euser, E. M., Bakermans-Kranenburg, M. J., & Van IJzendoorn, M. H. (2010). Attachment security and disorganization in maltreating and high-risk families: A series of meta-analyses. *Development and Psychopathology, 22*(1), 87–108. https://doi.org/10.1017/S0954579409990289

Dagan, O., Schuengel, C., Verhage, M. L., Van IJzendoorn, M. H., Sagi-Schwartz, A., Madigan, S., Duschinsky, R., Roisman, G. I., Bernard, K., Bakermans-Kranenburg, M., Bureau, J.-F., Volling, B. L., Wong, M. S., Colonnesi, C., Brown, G. L., Eiden, R. D., Fearon, R. M. P., Oosterman, M., Aviezer, O., Cummings, E. M., & The Collaboration on Attachment to Multiple Parents and Outcomes Synthesis. (2021). Configurations of mother-child and father-child attachment as predictors of internalizing and externalizing behavioral problems: An individual participant data (IPD) meta-analysis. *New Directions for Child and Adolescent Development, 2021*(180), 67–94. https://doi.org/10.1002/cad.20450

Goossens, F. A., & Van IJzendoorn, M. H. (1990). Quality of infants' attachment to professional caregivers: Relation to infant-parent attachment and day-care characteristics. *Child Development, 61*, 832–837. https://doi.org/10.2307/1130967.

Henrich, J., Heine, S. J., & Norenzayan, A. (2010). The weirdest people in the world? *The Behavioral and Brain Sciences, 33*(2–3), 61–135. https://doi.org/10.1017/S0140525X0999152X

Hrdy, S. (2009). *Mothers and Others: The Evolutionary Origins of Mutual Understanding*. Belknap Press. https://doi.org/10.2307/j.ctt1c84czb

Huang, Z. J., Lewin, A., Mitchell, S. J., & Zhang, J. (2012). Variations in the relationship between maternal depression, maternal sensitivity, and child attachment by race/ethnicity and nativity: Findings from a nationally representative cohort study. *Maternal and Child Health Journal, 16*(1), 40–50. https://doi.org/10.1007/s10995-010-0716-2

Lamb, M. E. (1977). The development of mother-infant and father-infant attachments in the second year of life. *Developmental Psychology, 13*(6), 637–648. https://doi.org/10.1037/0012-1649.13.6.637

Madigan, S., Fearon, R. M. P., Van IJzendoorn, M. H. et al. (2023). A meta-analysis of the first 20,000 strange situation procedures. *Psychological Bulletin, 149*, 99–132. https://doi.org/10.1037/bul0000388

Meehan, C. L., & Hawks, S. (2013) Cooperative breeding and attachment among Aka foragers. In N. Quinn & J. M. Mageo (Eds.), *Attachment Reconsidered: Cultural Perspectives on a Western Theory* (pp. 85–114). Palgrave Macmillan. https://doi.org/10.1057/9781137386724

Mesman, J., Sagi-Schwartz, A., & Van IJzendoorn, M. H. (2016). Cross-cultural patterns of attachment: Universal and contextual dimensions. In J. Cassidy & P. R. Shaver (Eds.), *Handbook of Attachment: Theory, Research, and Clinical Applications* (3rd ed.). Guilford Press.

Mesman, J., Van IJzendoorn, M., Behrens, K., Alicia Carbonell, O., Carcamo, R., Cohen-Paraira, I., De la Harpe, C., Ekmekci, H., Emmen, R., Heidar, J., Kondo-Ikemura, K., Mels, C., Mooya, H., Murtisari, S., Noblega, M., Ortiz, J. A., Sagi-Schwartz, A., Sichimba, F., Soares, I., Steele, H., Steele, M., Pape, M., Van Ginkel, J., Van der Veer, R., Wang, L., Selcuk, B., Yavuz, M., & Zreik, G. (2016). Is the ideal mother a sensitive mother? Beliefs about early childhood parenting in mothers across the globe. *International Journal of Behavioral Development, 40*(5), 385–97. https://doi.org/10.1177/0165025415594030

Posada, G. (2013). Is the secure base phenomenon evident here, there, and anywhere? A cross-cultural study of child behavior and experts' definitions. *Child Development, 84*(6), 1896–1905. https://doi.org/10.1111/cdev.12108

Posada, G., Gao, Y., Wu, F., Posada, R., Tascon, M., Schöelmerich, A., Sagi, A., Kondo-Ikemura, K., Haaland, W., & Synnevaag, B. (1995). The secure-base phenomenon across cultures: Children's behavior, mothers' preferences, and experts' concepts. *Monographs of the Society for Research in Child Development, 60*(2/3), 27–48. www.jstor.org/stable/1166169

Sagi, A., Lamb, M. E., Lewkowicz, K. S., Shoham, R., Dvir, R., & Estes, D. (1985). Security of infant-mother, -father, and -metapelet attachments among kibbutz-reared Israeli children. In I. Bretherton & E. Waters (Eds.), *Growing Points in Attachment Theory and Research* (Monographs of the Society for Research in Child Development). Wiley. https://doi.org/10.2307/3333837

Sagi, A., Van IJzendoorn, M. H., Aviezer, O., Donnell, F., Koren-Karie, N., Joels, T., & Harel, Y. (1995). Attachments in a multiple caregiver and multiple infant environment: The case of the Israeli kibbutzim. In: E. Waters, B. E. Vaughn, G. Posada, & K. Kondo-Ikemura (Eds.), *Constructs, Cultures and Caregiving: New Growing Points of Attachment Theory*. Monographs of the Society for Research in Child Development, Serial No. 244, 60, Nos. 2–3, pp. 71–91. doi:10.1111/j.1540-5834.1995.tb00204.x

Sagi, A., Van IJzendoorn, M. H., Aviezer, O., Donnell, F., & Mayseless, O. (1994). Sleeping away from home in a kibbutz communal arrangement: It makes a difference for infant-mother attachment. *Child Development, 65*, 992–1004. https://doi.org/10.2307/1131299

Smith, P. K. (1980). Shared care of young children – alternative models to monotropism. *Merrill-Palmer Quarterly. Journal of Developmental Psychology, 26*, 371–389.

True, M. (2021) Multiple pathways to infant disorganization: Insights from an African dataset. In T. Forslund & R. Duschinsky (Eds.), *The Attachment Reader*. Blackwell.

True, M. M., Pisani, L., & Oumar, F. (2001). Infant–mother attachment among the Dogon of Mali. *Child Development, 72*(5), 1451–1466. https://doi.org/10.1111/1467-8624.00359

Van IJzendoorn, M. H. (1990). Developments in cross-cultural research on attachment: Some methodological notes. *Human Development, 33*, 3–10. doi:10.1159/000276498

Van IJzendoorn, M. H., Bard, K. A., Bakermans-Kranenburg, M. J., & Ivan, K. (2009). Enhancement of attachment and cognitive development of young nursery-reared chimpanzees in responsive versus standard care. *Developmental Psychobiology, 51*, 173–185. doi:10.1002/dev.20356

Van IJzendoorn, M. H., Sagi, A., & Lambermon, M. W. E. (1992). The multiple caregiver paradox. Some Dutch and Israeli data. In R. C. Pianta (Ed.), *Beyond the Parent: The Role of Other Adults in Children's Lives. New Directions for Child Development, 57*, 5–25. https://doi.org/10.1002/cd.23219925703

Verhage, M. L., Schuengel, C., Madigan, S., Fearon, R. M. P., Oosterman, M., Cassibba, R., Bakermans-Kranenburg, M. J., & Van IJzendoorn, M. H. (2016). Narrowing the transmission gap: A synthesis of three decades of research on intergenerational transmission of attachment. *Psychological Bulletin, 142*(4), 337–366. https://doi.org/10.1037/bul0000038

Verhage, M. L., Fearon, R. M. P., Schuengel, C., Van IJzendoorn, M. H., Bakermans-Kranenburg, M. J., Madigan, S., Roisman G. I., Oosterman, M., Behrens, K. Y., Wong, M. S., Mangelsdorf, S., Priddis, L. E., Brisch, K. H., & Collaboration on Attachment Transmission Synthesis. (2018). Constraints on the intergenerational transmission of attachment via individual participant data meta-analysis. *Child Development, 89*, 2023–2037. https://doi.org/10.1111/cdev.13085

Waters, E., & Deane, K. E. (1985). Defining and assessing individual differences in attachment relationships: Q-methodology and the organization of behavior in infancy and early childhood. *Monographs of the Society for Research in Child Development, 50*(1/2), 41–65. https://doi.org/10.2307/3333826

12
Parenting shapes prosocial child development?

Prosocial development in context

Some philosophers such as Thomas Paine and Jean-Jacques Rousseau have argued that human beings are inherently good at birth, and only in rough environments turn to aggression, dishonesty, and other antisocial behaviours. Others, including Augustine of Hippo, considered human beings as born with a natural inclination towards sin and evil, prevented from selfish and destructive behaviour only through socialisation and guidance. These are quite opposite views. What they have in common, however, is that independent of the belief whether we are born to be good or born to be disciplined, both perspectives stress the importance of environmental influences.

Because prosocial development is about social relationships with others and attachment has been shown to predict social competence (Groh et al., 2014), it is not far-fetched to expect that attachment relationships play a role in the development of moral reasoning and prosocial behaviour. Unfortunately, the picture that arises from empirical research does not align fluently with this hypothesis. In our own research, we often found it not supported. In contrast, contextual factors seemed to be the strongest predictors of prosocial and moral behaviour.

Moral reasoning and prosocial behaviour

In our research on moral development, we have always preferred observational measures over self-reports. The Piaget-Kohlberg tradition used moral dilemmas triggering participants' moral choices and reasoning in order to measure stages of moral development (Kohlberg, 1984). Moral reflection would shape moral attitudes and promote moral behaviour. After Marinus' doctoral dissertation based on moral dilemmas (Van IJzendoorn, 1980), we have hardly ever used moral dilemmas in our studies. One reason for our contrasting preference for observed moral behaviour is that our participants often were too young to reflect on moral dilemmas. A second reason is that, as in other areas of research (see Chapter 2), there may be a gap between moral reasoning and moral behaviour, and even between moral behaviour and self-reported moral behaviour (Van IJzendoorn, 1980).

A striking example is given by Schwitzgebel and Rust (2014). They examined the self-reported moral attitudes and moral behaviour of 198 ethics professors, 208 non-ethicist philosophers, and 167 professors in departments other than philosophy. Questions concerned moral issues such as organ and blood donation, donating to charities, keeping library books, responsiveness to student emails, and honesty in responding to surveys. Each of the participants also received three test email messages to examine their actual behaviour on 'responsiveness to student emails'. The vast majority (83%) considered non-responsiveness to student emails as morally bad, and about 50% of all three groups indicated that they responded to 100% of student emails. However, only 31% did respond to the student emails, and the association between self-reported and observed responsiveness was weak, $r = 0.14$ (explaining only 2% of the variance in observed responsiveness). Such findings illustrate that self-reported moral behaviour is a weak predictor of actual behaviour.

Assuming that we can measure moral development in children by observing their prosocial behaviour, it is important to define prosocial behaviour and indicate how it can be observed. The *Oxford Handbook of Prosocial Behavior* defines prosocial behaviour as 'any action that serves to benefit another person'. Studies of prosocial behaviour usually distinguish four broad dimensions of behaviour: helping, volunteerism, cooperation, and caregiving. We consider the first two as indicators of prosociality, but the latter two not, or only in specific conditions, as specified below.

Helping behaviour can be observed in children from a young age. In research settings children are, for example, exposed to an experimenter who reaches for an out-of-reach object or drops a box filled with paperclips. Comforting is also considered helping behaviour and can be triggered by an experimenter hurting her finger or knee in the child's presence.

Volunteerism, that is, participation in non-paid activities that benefit society but also include donating time or money, is usually not observed before adolescence. Yet, donating paradigms have been used in research with younger children, e.g., inviting them to share stickers with known or unknown peers or to donate (part of) the money that they received as compensation for their participation in research to a charity (see below). The clear advantage of donating paradigms in studies on prosocial behaviour is that donating money can be observed directly, while self-reported donating carries the risk of response biases (see Chapter 2).

Although *Cooperation* is often considered prosocial behaviour as well, we are of the opinion that it does not fit the definition. Cooperation involves a win-win situation where a wished-for goal can be reached by joining forces. It may benefit someone else, but this is not the primary aim and therefore fails to comply with the definition of prosocial behaviour ('any action that serves to benefit another person') if the term 'serve' implies that the aim of the prosocial action is to benefit another person.

Caregiving is a special case. Caregiving shown to one's own kin may be considered primarily an investment in the transmission of one's own genes. Should that be considered prosocial behaviour? Caring for one's own crying infant, or for one's sister's offspring contributes to one's own inclusive fitness (Simpson & Belsky, 2016; Trivers, 1974). Following from this line of reasoning, caregiving responses to unknown children would qualify as truly prosocial behaviour but parental sensitivity would not be considered prosocial behaviour. Thus, rather than labelling actions as prosocial when they serve to benefit another person, we advance that prosocial behaviour should serve to benefit another *unfamiliar* person. This is a critical difference, and essential for our thinking about the development and determinants of prosocial behaviour.

Species-wide development versus individual differences in prosociality

The development of prosocial behaviour can be studied from two perspectives. The first perspective is that of general development, the second perspective is that of individual differences in prosociality. The first perspective concerns questions such as: *When do children begin to show helping behaviour? Can they feel empathy for others' distress?* One-day-old newborns exposed to another infant's cry, a synthetic cry, and silence do cry most when they hear the infant's cry sound (Sagi & Hoffman, 1976). Although not qualifying for prosocial behaviour, such sympathetic or contagious distress might constitute a basis for the emergence of empathic concern. Helping behaviour is observed in children from a young age. Out of 24 infants in a group of 18-month-old infants, 22 showed helping behaviour such as handing out-of-reach objects or opening the door of a cabinet for a person when his hands were full (Warneken & Tomasello, 2006).

In studies with even younger children, infants' preferences for helping versus non-helping figures were observed. In the helper-hinderer paradigm children are shown a shape (the 'climber') who is at the bottom of a hill and repeatedly attempts to climb the hill, but without success. On the third attempt he either gets help from a 'helper' shape pushing from behind or is pushed down by a 'hinderer' shape (Hamlin, Wynn, & Bloom, 2007). When offered the choice between the wooden shapes of the helper and the hinderer, both 6- and 10-month-olds more often reached for the helper. Similar findings were reported for shapes helping and hindering opening a box (Hamlin & Wynn, 2011). However, others could not replicate this preference for helpers (Salvadori et al., 2015), which may be related to the very small sample sizes ($N < 20$) in the aforementioned studies (see Chapter 1).

In one of our own studies, we found that from before their second birthday children show concern for others who are in distress and can show comforting behaviour to help the other (Van der Mark et al., 2002), even though they lack some perspective taking and may offer the comfort they would prefer for themselves (e.g., offering their favourite cuddly toy). Such helping and comforting behaviour has been suggested to increase with age, as a result of children's advances in theory of mind (the ability to represent others' needs and mental states), and in emotional empathy (the capacity to share others' emotions and feelings).

A similar increase in prosociality has been reported for donating between ages 5 and 12 years, when children in five different countries were asked to share some of the stickers they received with another (unidentified) child of their school (Cowell et al., 2016). Similarly, age-related increases in donating were observed among children aged 5–12 years when the currency used was chocolate coins (Abramson et al., 2018). However, overall donation rates were higher when children had coins they couldn't use for themselves anyway. In our own research, we were disappointed to find that 7-year-olds who received money for their participation in our lab experiments donated hardly any money to UNICEF (Van IJzendoorn et al., 2010). One possible explanation is that donating to charities does not increase linearly. Grunberg et al. (1985) found that donating declined around the age of 7, which could be due to children becoming more aware of individual ownership. Another explanation could be the presence or absence of an experimenter, which does affect donating. We found repeatedly that the mere presence or subtle hint of an experimenter substantially enhanced the willingness to share or donate (Van IJzendoorn et al., 2010). This points to the significance of contextual factors.

The studies described so far concerned prosocial development from a species-wide perspective. Indeed, prosociality has been speculated to be an evolutionary-based universal competence. De Waal (2008) suggested that the origins of empathic concern and prosocial behaviour may have developed in the context of parental care, long before the human species evolved. Attachment behaviour was crucial for survival and reproduction. Long periods of offspring dependence necessitate mothers to identify and respond to their infants' distress signals, as good care increased the chances of survival. The neural circuits related to affiliative and caring behaviours, involving ancient subcortical circuits such as the brainstem, amygdala, hypothalamus, and basal ganglia, are highly conserved in mammals (Tucker, Luu, & Derryberry, 2005; Rilling & Mascaro, 2017; Witteman et al., 2019). Hrdy (2009) extended this evolutionary model, highlighting that what it takes to raise a human baby to nutritional independence is far more than what a foraging mother could provide alone, and thus, help from group members or 'alloparents' was required. Cooperative breeding was therefore necessary for survival and reproduction, and those individuals who contributed to cooperative breeding would be favoured by selection. As a result, prosocial behaviour, empathic concern, and sharing of resources would have their roots in the basic need for cooperative child rearing.

Yet, every study, independent of the measure used, shows variation in prosocial behaviour. Children differ in their tendency to help, comfort someone in distress, or donate to unknown others. In our field we are interested to understand this between-subject variance. Can differences in prosocial behaviour be due to variation in structural DNA and brain development, or are they related to early socialisation processes, parental sensitivity, and attachment quality? In the next sections, we will focus on efforts to explain individual differences in prosocial behaviour.

Genes for generosity?

An evolutionary explanation for prosocial behaviour means that prosocial competence is in our genetic heritance, but it does not imply that differences in prosociality are related to differences in structural DNA. Twin studies of prosocial behaviour, quantifying its heritability by comparing within-twin similarity of monozygotic and dizygotic twins, have been conducted since the 1980s. In adults, more than half of the variance in self-reported prosocial behaviours was accounted for by genetic factors, and only 2% of the variance was ascribed to shared environmental factors such as sharing the same family background (Rushton et al., 1986). For children the picture was different: no or low heritability was found for empathic concern and helping behaviour in the first 2 years. From 2 years onwards heritability seems on the increase (Bakermans-Kranenburg & Van IJzendoorn, 2021).

However, in our own work we failed to find such heritability for observed prosociality in older children. In one of our studies, we gave 7-year-old twins who had received ten coins of €0.20 for their participation in our research the opportunity to donate (part of) their money to UNICEF. While being alone in a room where they had been doing some tasks with the experimenter and received the money, they were shown a 2-minute promotional film of a child working in a stone pit who with the help of UNICEF might have a better life and go to school. At the end of the film a voice-over invited the children to donate, and a money box was placed in front of the screen. After 1 minute the experimenter returned and asked in a neutral, standardised way if the child would want to donate, giving another opportunity for donations (Van IJzendoorn et al., 2010). Spontaneous donating after the film was so minimal that the data did not allow for genetic modelling. After the experimenter's question, donations increased. The donations after the experimenter's prompt showed 45% of the variance explained by shared environmental influences and 55% by unique environmental influences. No role for genetic factors emerged.

Using Genome-Wide Complex Trait Analysis (GCTA), a method that predicts the phenotypic similarity among unrelated individuals from their genetic similarity, we found SNP heritability for parent-reported and self-reported prosocial behaviour in middle childhood of 21% in a sample of just over 3,000 children (Bakermans-Kranenburg & Van IJzendoorn, 2021). If replicated, the heritability of prosocial behaviour is not as evident as that of, for example, ADHD or externalising problems (Pappa et al., 2015). We also examined the epigenetics of (low) prosocial behaviour and tested whether methylation patterns were different for low versus typically prosocial children as assessed with the Strengths and Difficulties Questionnaire (SDQ). Methylation modulates the expression of genes. In four longitudinal birth cohorts from the Pregnancy And Childhood Epigenetics (PACE) Consortium we explored with Mannan Luo the relation between neonatal DNA methylation (DNAm) and prosocial development in more than 2,000 children. Three cohort-specific

CpGs were associated with chronic low prosocial behaviour in one cohort, but the results were not replicated in the other cohorts. No epigenome-wide significant CpGs or regions were found. In candidate gene follow-up analysis, none of the CpGs annotated to the usual suspect for altruism, oxytocin receptor gene (OXTR, see Chapter 10), reached gene-level Bonferroni significance (Luo et al., 2021). These 'null' findings stress the importance of multi-cohort replication approaches to reduce false positive discoveries and also show that the (epi-)genetic effects on prosociality are not strong. Currently we are only scratching the surface of the role of epigenetics in child development.

Brains for benefiting others?

Functional imaging studies and structural imaging studies are two relevant approaches to investigating the connection between the brain and prosocial behaviour. Functional imaging studies reveal the activity levels in specific brain regions during a particular task, while structural imaging studies provide insights into the relation between prosocial behaviour and brain morphology, such as cortical thickness and volume.

We tested the association between parent-reported prosocial behaviour and cortical thickness in 6- to 9-year-old children in the Generation R study, a population-based cohort study in Rotterdam, Netherlands (Thijssen et al., 2015). Prosocial behaviour was related to cortical thickness in regions related to theory of mind (superior frontal cortex, rostral middle frontal cortex, cuneus, and precuneus) and inhibitory control (superior frontal and rostral middle frontal cortex). In a partially overlapping sample, we tested associations with observed prosocial behaviour in the donating to UNICEF task detailed above when the children were 8 years old (Wildeboer et al., 2018). Donations were related to thickness in the lateral orbitofrontal cortex/pars orbitalis and pre-/postcentral cortex, with thicker cortex related to higher donations. Cortical thickness at age 8 years was related to parental sensitivity during early childhood (Kok et al., 2015), potentially suggesting that parental sensitivity might affect brain development which in turn would predict prosocial behaviour. This idea is too good to be true: the specific cortical areas in the two studies are not overlapping.

We also measured brain activity in the virtual four-player Prosocial Cyberball game, which offers participants the opportunity to toss the ball to an excluded player, thereby compensating for the exclusion by the other players (Riem et al., 2013). In the first round all players participate and toss the ball to each other (the fair game). In the next rounds one player (not the participant) no longer receives the ball from the other players (the unfair game). The participant can either join the excluders and toss no more balls to the excluded player or include the excluded player to the same extent as before or compensate by tossing more balls to the excluded player than before. This is non-costly prosocial behaviour to compensate for unfair treatment.

In the L-CID study the neural responses during the prosocial part of Cyberball were examined in 283 eight-year-old twin children (Van der Meulen et al., 2018). Across the whole sample the children tossed significantly more balls to the excluded player in the unfair compared to the fair condition. Prosocial helping compared to tossing to excluders was associated with activation in the precuneus. Furthermore, participants who showed less prosocial compensating recruited the bilateral insula more strongly when they tossed to the excluded player, maybe to suppress any initial prosocial inclination (Van der Meulen et al., 2018; Crone et al., 2020). However, following this sample longitudinally (at 8, 10, and 12 years) we did not find stability of prosocial Cyberball behaviour over time, which makes the insula less plausible as a stable neural signature of individual differences in prosociality in this age period (Dobbelaar et al., 2023). Structural features of the precuneus, however, showed high heritability in our L-CID twin study (Van der Meulen et al., 2020) and seem to predict parent-reported prosocial behaviour in Generation R (Thijssen et al., 2015) and parent-reported empathy in L-CID (Van der Meulen et al., 2020) (but see Chapter 2).

Parenting and attachment security as promoters of prosociality?

It is not difficult to come up with explanations of why parenting and attachment security would promote prosocial child behaviour (Van IJzendoorn, 1997). First, sensitive parenting models prosocial helping and caregiving behaviour to the child. Sensitive limit-setting with induction, that is, explaining why behaviour that is damaging to others is forbidden, trains the child in empathy and taking the perspective of others into account. Second, sensitive parenting helps the child cope with their own emotions, which protects them from being overwhelmed by others' distress or turning away from them. Third, securely attached children may be more open to their parents' and their teachers' directions and suggestions about (pro-)social interaction. Fourth, securely attached children have more positive social interactions with peers (Groh et al., 2014), which may provide a solid basis for concern for others, helping, sharing, and comforting behaviour when the situation arises.

Results of empirical studies testing the association between sensitive parenting and secure attachment on the one hand and prosocial child behaviour on the other hand have often not been as straightforward as might be expected. To our frustration, replicated results pointing to caregiver sensitivity or attachment security as predictors of prosocial development have been elusive. In our Leiden Longitudinal Empathy Study, with measures at 16 months, 22 months, and 7 years, no associations were found between attachment or parental sensitivity and empathic concern towards the mother or the experimenter who hurt their knee or finger (Van der Mark et al., 2002; Pannebakker et al., 2007). Moreover, observed empathy for mother was not related to empathy for the experimenter, countering the idea of empathy as a child characteristic independent of the target and the situation.

The work of others echoes these results: associations are sometimes found, but no consistent picture emerges, particularly not for observed parenting and (observed) altruistic prosocial behaviour (Wong et al., 2021). Of course, it could be that the scope of parenting behaviours has been too small, and other parenting dimensions such as modelling, scaffolding, or parental discipline may affect the development of child prosociality. Future studies may try to identify such relevant parenting dimensions. A complication of the link between parenting and child prosociality is, however, that the meta-analysis by Wong et al. (2021) also shows that type of prosocial child behaviour is a strong moderator; effect sizes are significantly different for nearly all types of prosocial behaviour. This meta-analytic finding confirms what we concluded based on our own studies, namely that prosociality is a multidimensional construct. Children who comfort an experimenter who hurt herself do not necessarily donate their money to UNICEF. Finding stability of prosocial behaviour across time and situations turns out to be very difficult, as is the identification of replicable predictors of prosocial behaviour.

A somewhat more optimistic picture arises from a meta-analysis on the association between secure infant-parent attachment and prosocial behaviour (Deneault et al., 2023). Attachment security and child prosociality were significantly associated ($r = 0.19$ for child-mother attachment and $r = 0.11$ for child-father attachment). Some studies used, however, parent-reported Attachment Q-Sorts which have dubious validity (Cadman et al., 2018; Van IJzendoorn et al., 2004, see also Chapter 2) and parent-reported prosocial behaviour, which may inflate the strength of the association. Another point for discussion is the inclusion of compliance as a dimension of prosocial behaviour in the meta-analysis. We are reluctant to consider compliance with caregiver requests as an index of prosocial behaviour. Although child compliance may benefit the caregiver, it is easy to imagine situations in which non-compliance (e.g., with oppressive regimes) is more prosocial than compliance. Having said that, compliance with parents' 'reasonable' requests does appear related to security (Kochanska et al., 2005; Londerville & Main, 1981) and attachment insecurity was related to active resistance to parental requests in our Generation R study (Kok et al., 2013). Note that when the Attachment Q-Sort is used, part of the association between attachment security and compliance may be explained by the high weights assigned to the items in the Attachment Q-Sort that concern compliance with parental requests.

Context characteristics make the difference

In passing, we noted that the 7-year-old twins donated hardly any money to UNICEF when left alone but donated various amounts of money when an experimenter suggested the possibility to do so (Van IJzendoorn et al., 2010). The proportion of children who donated increased from one-tenth to about two-thirds. A similar effect emerged when it was not an experimenter who gave the nudge, but a same-sex videotaped peer who modelled donating after the UNICEF commercial. Seeing a peer donate money increased donations by on average 27% (Wildeboer et al., 2018). Showing 8- to 13-year-old children an awe-eliciting clip from the film *Song of the Sea* led children to donate more to refugee children (Stamkou et al., 2023). Painting eyes on the wall results in more money in an honesty box next to a coffee machine (Bateson et al., 2006). Installing a security camera promotes helping behaviour (Van Rompay et al., 2009). In one of our own studies, 8-year-olds lying in the fMRI scanner could earn money by guessing correctly which of two dogs, presented on a screen, would get a bone on the next screen. When they pushed the button representing that they had correctly guessed which dog got the bone, they received €0.05. Children who reported improbably high levels of accuracy (one-tailed binomial test, $p < 0.05$; more than 13 correct guesses [72%] in 18 trials) were considered to have been lying about at least one of their guesses, and all other children were considered honest. After 18 trials, we suggested that with the fMRI scanner we could see whether they were being honest during the task. Eighteen more trials followed. The suggestion that they were monitored resulted in an increase of honest children from 26% in the first round to 66% in the second round (Thijssen et al., 2017).

We must conclude that it is more difficult to identify ways to raise children into altruistic, prosocial human beings than to identify ways to influence specific behaviour at a given time and place with contextual nudges. Parenting lays the ground for moral development of our species on the timescale of the evolution, but it does not predict individual differences in prosocial helping, comforting, or donating in any consistent way (or, alternatively, our measures of prosocial behaviour have serious deficits). The good news is that relatively tiny changes in the environment can change behaviour for the better (Thaler & Sunstein, 2021). It follows that for promoting prosocial behaviour we could better spend our money and efforts on environmental nudges than on parent support or educational programmes. Intervention aims should be adjusted, not aiming at individuals who act prosocially in most situations, but aiming at situations in which most individuals act prosocially.

References

Abramson, L., Daniel, E., & Knafo-Noam, L. (2018). The role of personal values in children's costly sharing and non-costly giving. *Journal of Experimental Child Psychology, 165,* 117–134. https://doi.org/10.1016/j.jecp.2017.03.007

Bakermans-Kranenburg, M. J., & Van IJzendoorn, M. H. (2021). Dimensions, determinants, and development of prosocial behaviour: A differential susceptibility hypothesis on attachment and moral character. In E. Harcourt (Ed.), *Attachment and Character: Attachment Theory, Ethics, and the Developmental Psychology of Vice and Virtue* (pp. 44–70). Oxford University Press. https://doi.org/10.1093/oso/9780192898128.001.0001

Bateson, M., Nettle, D., & Roberts, G. (2006). Cues of being watched enhance cooperation in a real-world setting. *Biology Letters, 2*(3), 412–14. http://doi.org/10.1098/rsbl.2006.0509

Cadman, T., Diamond, R., & Fearon, R. M. P. (2018). Reassessing the validity of the attachment Q-sort: An updated meta-analysis. *Infant & Child Development, 27,* e2034.

Cowell, J. M., Lee, K., Malcolm-Smith, S. Selcuk, B., Zhou, X., & Decety, J. (2016). The development of generosity and moral cognition across five cultures. *Developmental Science, 20*(4), e12403. http://doi.org/10.1111/desc.12403

Crone, E. A., Achterberg, M., Dobbelaar, S., Euser, S., Van den Bulk, B., Van der Meulen, M., Van Drunen, L., Wierenga, L., Bakermans-Kranenburg, M. J., & Van IJzendoorn, M. H. (2020). Neural and behavioral signatures of social evaluation and adaptation in childhood and adolescence: The Leiden Consortium on Individual Development (L-CID). *Developmental Cognitive Neuroscience, 45,* 100805. ISSN 1878-9293. https://doi.org/10.1016/j.dcn.2020.100805

De Waal, F. B. M. (2008). Putting the altruism back into altruism: The evolution of empathy. *Annual Review of Psychology, 59,* 279–300. https://doi.org/10.1146/annurev.psych.59.103 006.093625

Deneault, A.-A., Hammond, S. I., & Madigan, S. (2023). A meta-analysis of child–parent attachment in early childhood and prosociality. *Developmental Psychology, 59*(2), 236–255. https://doi.org/10.1037/dev0001484

Dobbelaar, S., Van Drunen, L., Van Duijvenvoorde, A. C. K., Van IJzendoorn, M. H., Crone, E. A., & Achterberg, M. (2023). Transitions in social responsivity from childhood to adolescence: Developmental patterns, neural correlates and associations with wellbeing. *Developmental Cognitive Neuroscience, 62,* 101264. https://doi.org/10.1016/j.dcn.2023.101264

Groh, A. M., Fearon, R. P., Bakermans-Kranenburg, M. J., Van IJzendoorn, M. H., Steele, R. D., & Roisman, G. I. (2014). The significance of attachment security for children's social competence with peers: A meta-analytic study. *Attachment & Human Development, 16,* 103–136. DOI.org/10.1080/14616734.2014.883636

Grunberg, N. E., Maycock, V. A., & Anthony, B. J. (1985). Material altruism in children. *Basic Applied Social Psychology, 6*(1), 1–11. https://doi.org/10.1207/s15324834basp0601_1

Hamlin J. K., & Wynn K. (2011). Young infants prefer prosocial to antisocial others. *Cognitive Development, 26*(1), 30–39. https://doi.org/10.1016/j.cogdev.2010.09.001

Hamlin, J., Wynn, J., & Bloom, K. (2007). Social evaluation by preverbal infants. *Nature, 450*(7169), 557–559. https://doi.org/10.1038/nature06288

Hrdy, S. (2009). *Mothers and Others: The Evolutionary Origins of Mutual Understanding.* Belknap Press. https://doi.org/10.2307/j.ctt1c84czb

Kochanska, G., Aksan, N., & Carlson, J. J. (2005). Temperament, relationships, and young children's receptive cooperation with their parents. *Developmental Psychology, 41*(4), 648–660. https://doi.org/10.1037/0012-1649.41.4.648

Kohlberg, L. (1984) *Essays on Moral Development, Volume 2: The Psychology of Moral Development.* Harper & Row.

Kok, R., Thijssen, S., Bakermans-Kranenburg, M. J., Jaddoe, V. W. V., Verhulst, F. C., White, T., Van IJzendoorn, M. H., & Tiemeier, H. (2015). Normal variation in early parental sensitivity predicts child structural brain development. *Journal of the American Academy of Child & Adolescent Psychiatry, 54,* 824–831. https://doi.org/10.1016/j.jaac.2015.07.009

Kok, R., Van IJzendoorn, M. H., Linting, M., Bakermans-Kranenburg, M. J., Tharner, A., Luijk, P. C. M., Székely, E., Jaddoe, V. W. V., Hofman, A., Verhulst, F. C., & Tiemeier, H. (2013). Attachment insecurity predicts child active resistance to parental requests in a compliance task. *Child: Care, Health and Development, 39,* 277–287. https://doi.org/10.1111/j.1365-2214.2012.01374.x

Londerville, S., & Main, M. (1981). Security of attachment, compliance, and maternal training methods in the second year of life. *Developmental Psychology, 17*(3), 289–299. https://doi.org/10.1037/0012-1649.17.3.289

Luo, M., Meehan, A. J., Walton, E., Röder, S., Herberth, G., Zenclussen, A. C., Cosín-Tomas, M., Sunyer, J., Mulder, R. H., Cortes Hidalgo, A. P., Bakermans-Kranenburg, M. J., Felix, J. F., Relton, C., Suderman, M., Pappa, I., Kok, R., Tiemeier, H., Van IJzendoorn, M. H., Barker, E. D., & Cecil, C. A. M. (2021). Neonatal DNA methylation and childhood low prosocial behavior: An epigenome-wide association meta-analysis. *American Journal of Medical Genetics Part B: Neuropsychiatric Genetics, 186B,* 228–241. https://doi.org/10.1002/ajmg.b.32862

Pannebakker, F. D. (2007). *Morality from Infancy to Middle Childhood.* Mostert and Onderen.

Pappa, I., Fedko, I. O., Mileva-Seitz, V. R., Hottenga, J.-J., Bakermans-Kranenburg, M. J., Bartels, M., ... Boomsma, D. I. (2015). Single nucleotide polymorphism heritability of behavior problems in childhood: Genome-wide complex trait analysis. *Journal of the American Academy of Child and Adolescent Psychiatry, 54*(9), 737–744. https://doi.org/10.1016/j.jaac.2015.06.004.

Riem, M. M. E., Bakermans-Kranenburg, M. J., Huffmeijer, R., & Van IJzendoorn, M. H. (2013). Does intranasal oxytocin promote prosocial behaviour to an excluded fellow player? A randomized controlled trial with Cyberball. *Psychoneuroendocrinology 38,* 1418–1425. https://doi.org/10.1016/j.psyneuen.2012.12.023

Rilling, J., & Mascaro, J. S. (2017). The neurobiology of fatherhood. *Current Opinion in Psychology, 15,* 26–32. https://doi.org/10.1016/j.copsyc.2017.02.013

Rushton, J. P., Littlefield, C. H., & Lumsden, C. J. (1986). Gene culture coevolution of complex social behaviour: Human altruism and mate choice. *Proceedings of the National Academy of Sciences of the United States of America, 83*(19), 7340–7343. https://doi.org/10.1073/pnas.83.19.7340

Sagi, A., & Hoffman, M. L. (1976). Empathic distress in the newborn. *Developmental Psychology, 12*(2), 175–176. https://doi.org/10.1037/0012-1649.12.2.175

Salvadori, E., Blazsekova, T., Volein, A., Karap, Z., Tatone, D., Mascaro, O., et al. 2015. Probing the strength of infants' preference for helpers over hinderers: Two replication attempts of Hamlin and Wynn (2011). *PLoS ONE, 10*(11), e0140570. https://doi.org/10.1371/journal.pone.0140570

Sellaro, R., Steenbergen, L., Verkuil, B., Van IJzendoorn, M. H., & Colzato, L. (2015). Transcutaneous Vagus Nerve Stimulation (tVNS) does not increase prosocial behavior in Cyberball. *Frontiers in Psychology, 6,* 499. https://doi.org/10.3389/fpsyg.2015.00499

Schwitzgebel, E., & Rust, J. (2014). The moral behavior of ethics professors: Relationships among self-reported behavior, expressed normative attitude, and directly observed behavior. *Philosophical Psychology, 27*(3), 293–327, DOI: 10.1080/09515089.2012.727135

Simpson, J., & Belsky, J. (2016). Attachment theory within a modern evolutionary framework. In J. Cassidy & P. R. Shaver (Eds.), *Handbook of Attachment: Theory, Research, and Clinical Applications* (3rd ed.). Guilford Press. https://doi.org/10.1017/s0021963001226754

Stamkou, E., Brummelman, E., Dunham, R., Nikolic, M., & Keltner, D. (2023). Awe sparks prosociality in children. *Psychological Science, 34*, 455–467. https://doi.org/10.1177/09567976221150616

Thaler, H., & Sunstein, C. S. (2021). *Nudge*. Penguin. https://doi.org/10.1017/err.2021.61

Thijssen, S., Wildeboer, A., Muetzel, R. L., Bakermans-Kranenburg, M. J., El Marroun, H., Hofman, A., Jaddoe, V. W. V., Van der Lugt, A., Verhulst, F. C., Tiemeier, H., Van IJzendoorn, M. H., & White, T. (2015). Cortical thickness and prosocial behaviour in school-age children: A population-based MRI study. *Social Neuroscience, 10*(6), 571–582. DOI: 10.1080/17470919.2015.1014063

Thijssen, S., Wildeboer, A, Van IJzendoorn, M. H., Muetzel, R., Langeslag, S. J. E., Jaddoe, V. W. V., Verhulst, F. C., Tiemeier, H., Bakermans-Kranenburg, M. J., & White, T. (2017). The honest truth about deception: Demographic, cognitive, and neural correlates of child repeated deceptive behaviour. *Journal of Experimental Child Psychology, 162*, 225–241. DOI: 10.1016/j.jecp.2017.05.009

Trivers, R. L. (1974) Parent-offspring conflict. *American Zoologist, 14*(1), 249–264. https://doi.org/10.1093/icb/14.1.249

Tucker, D. M., Luu, P., & Derryberry, D. (2005). Love hurts: The evolution of empathic concern through the encephalization of nociceptive capacity. *Development and Psychopathology, 17*, 699–713. https://doi.org/10.1017/S0954579405050339

Van der Mark, I. L., Van IJzendoorn, M. H., & Bakermans-Kranenburg, M. J. (2002). Development of empathy in girls during the second year of life: Associations with parenting, attachment, and temperament. *Social Development, 11*(4), 451–468. https://doi.org/10.1111/1467-9507.00210

Van der Meulen, M., Van IJzendoorn, M. H., & Crone, E. A. (2016). Neural correlates of prosocial behaviour: Compensating social exclusion in a four-player Cyberball game. *PLoS ONE, 11*(7), e0159045. https://doi.org/10.1371/journal.pone.0159045

Van der Meulen, M., Wierenga, L. M., Achterberg, M., Drenth, N., Van IJzendoorn, M. H., & Crone, E. A. (2020). Genetic and environmental influences on structure of the social brain in childhood. *Developmental Cognitive Neuroscience, 44*, 100782. https://doi.org/10.1016/j.dcn.2020.100782

Van der Meulen, M., Steinbeis, N., Achterberg, M., Van IJzendoorn, M. H., & Crone, E. A. (2018). Heritability of neural reactions to social exclusion and prosocial compensation in middle childhood. *Developmental Cognitive Neuroscience, 34*, 42–52. https://doi.org/https://doi.org/10.1016/j.dcn.2018.05.010

Van IJzendoorn, M. H. (1980). *Moralität und politisches Bewusstsein. Eine Untersuchung zur politischen Sozialisation. [Morality and political attitudes. A study in political socialization]*. Beltz Verlag.

Van IJzendoorn, M. H. (1997). Attachment, emergent morality and aggression: Toward a developmental socioemotional model of antisocial behaviour. *International Journal of Behavioural Development, 21*(4), 703–727. https://doi.org/10.1080/016502597384631

Van IJzendoorn, M. H., Vereijken, C. M. J. L., Bakermans-Kranenburg, M. J., & Riksen-Walraven, J. M. A. (2004). Is the Attachment Q-Sort a valid measure of attachment security in young children? *Child Development, 75*, 1188–1213. https://doi.org/10.1111/j.1467-8624.2004.00733.x

Van IJzendoorn, M. H., & Bakermans-Kranenburg, M. J. (2014). Prosocial development and situational morality: Neurobiological, parental, and contextual factors. In J. F. Leckman, C. Panter-Brick, & R. Salah (Eds.), *Pathways to Peace: The Transformative Power of Children and Families* (pp. 161–184). The MIT Press. https://doi.org/10.7551/mitpress/9780262027984.001.0001

Van IJzendoorn, M. H., Bakermans-Kranenburg, M. J., Pannebakker, F., & Out, D. (2010). In defense of situational morality: Genetic, dispositional and situational determinants of children's donating to charity. *Journal of Moral Education, 39*, 1–20. https://doi.org/10.1080/03057240903528535

Van Rompay, T. J. L., Vonk, D. J., & Fransen, M. L. (2009). The eye of the camera: Effects of security cameras on prosocial behavior. *Environment and Behavior, 41*(1), 60–74. https://doi.org/10.1177/0013916507309996

Warneken, F., & Tomasello, M. (2006) Altruistic helping in human infants and young chimpanzees. *Science, 311*(5765), 1301–1303. DOI: 10.1126/science.1121448

Wildeboer, A., Thijssen, S., Muetzel, R. L., Bakermans-Kranenburg, M. J., Tiemeier, H., White, T., & Van IJzendoorn, M. H. (2018). Neuroanatomical correlates of donating behavior in middle childhood. *Social Neuroscience, 13*(5), 541–552. https://doi.org/10.1080/17470919.2017.1361864

Witteman, J., Van IJzendoorn, M. H., Rilling, J. K., Bos, P. A., Schiller, N. O., & Bakermans-Kranenburg, M. J. (2019). Towards a neural model of infant cry perception. *Neuroscience & Biobehavioral Reviews, 99*, 23–32. https://doi.org/10.1016/j.neubiorev.2019.01.026

Witteman, J., Van IJzendoorn, M. H., Van de Velde, D., Van Heuven, V. J. J. P., Schiller, N. O. (2011). The nature of hemispheric specialization for linguistic and emotional prosodic perception: A meta-analysis of the lesion literature. *Neuropsychologia, 49*, 3722–3738. https://doi.org/10.1016/j.neuropsychologia.2011.09.028

Wong, T. K. Y., Konishi, C., & Kong, X. (2021) Parenting and prosocial behaviors: A meta-analysis. *Social Development, 30*, 343–373. https://doi.org/10.1111/sode.12481

13
Is assessing attachment of individual children in applied practice valid?

Attachment measures for individual diagnoses

When clinical or legal decisions about individual children and their parents need to be made, the principle of the best interests of the child is generally central and even solidified in the universal children's rights declaration. But it is not easy to determine what that interest is and how it is served best. The best interest of any child is to be born and grow up in a safe and secure relational network that provides all opportunities for developing into a respected, healthy, and happy social person. Most children, however, are not that lucky at conception and have to settle for less ambitious goals. Striving for 'good-enough' child-rearing conditions serving the interests of the child already seems a dot on the horizon at best (Bakermans-Kranenburg & Van IJzendoorn, 2022).

In disputes about how the child's best interests can be served, experts are called upon to examine the child's development and the quality of care provided by the biological parents or other caregivers. A misleading and potentially damaging translation of science to practice is the application of attachment measures in clinical and social work assessments or diagnostics and family court proceedings (Hammarlund et al., 2022). A common misunderstanding is the idea that attachment instruments that are valid at the group level can also be used to draw conclusions about individual children or caregivers (Beckwith et al., 2022; Forslund et al., 2022). Several attachment measures can be validly used in group-level research because they fulfil the essential psychometric criteria of reliability and validity (see, e.g., the Adult Attachment Interview, Bakermans-Kranenburg & Van IJzendoorn, 1993; Sagi et al., 1994). But the same measures cannot be validly applied in assessing the quality of an attachment relationship or attachment representation of children or parents to infer inferior caregiving behaviour or a child having been exposed to family violence or neglect (Granqvist et al., 2017). Neither can outcomes of attachment measures be validly used as input in divorce disputes about co-parenting arrangements in individual cases (Bakermans-Kranenburg & Van IJzendoorn, 2022; Van IJzendoorn et al., 2018; Forslund et al., 2022).

In attachment research on atypically developing children, one of the most important measures is the coding system for disorganised attachment applied to videotaped observations of child-parent interactions in a mildly stressful Strange Situation Procedure. The coding system describes child behaviours in presence of the parent or another caregiver with a focus on the reunion episodes after two brief separations of 3 minutes or less. From an observational perspective, disorganised attachment is coded on the basis of conflicted, confused, or apprehensive behaviour of the child towards the caregiver. Core criterion for disorganised attachment behaviour is its inexplicability in the context of a stressful setting with a caregiver present. Alternatively, the seemingly incomprehensible behaviour might only become explicable if the coder assumes that the child needs the caregiver but at the same time is afraid of the attachment figure. Disorganisation is inferred from sequential or simultaneous display of contradictory behaviour, freezing or stilling, and other often (momentary) interrupted movements (Main & Solomon, 1990).

Disorganised attachment has been linked to child maltreatment, with some studies finding that over 80% of maltreated children show disorganised attachment. This has led some researchers and many clinicians to believe that disorganisation is a valid proxy for the detection of maltreatment experiences. However, the meta-analytically established association between disorganised attachment and maltreatment is weaker than some studies have reported (Van IJzendoorn et al., 1999). In our recent meta-analysis combining ten studies we found that rates of disorganised attachment were about 60% in maltreated samples compared to 20% in non-maltreated samples (Madigan et al., 2023). Other adverse life experiences and cumulative risks, such as poverty, can also lead to disorganised attachment (Cyr et al., 2010), increasing the risk of falsely accusing parents struggling with poverty of maltreating their child when it shows disorganised behaviour in the SSP. Additionally, the average intercoder reliability of attachment assessments is barely adequate for research purposes (ICC = 0.64; Van IJzendoorn & Bakermans-Kranenburg, 2021) and falls short of the standard required for individual diagnosis (>0.80 according to Elliott et al., 2020; Guilford, 1946).

This means that while measures for disorganised attachment might be useful for studying inter-individual differences on a group level, they may produce false positives and negatives when used for individual diagnosis.

Furthermore, the principle of the best interest of the child is a central consideration when legal decisions about children need to be made. But how that interest is best served is by no means straightforward. Usually, many factors must be weighed that do not all point in the same direction. In complicated cases experts are called upon to examine the child's development and the quality of care provided by the biological parents or other caregivers. Too often they report about issues related to attachment while it is not clear at all what they actually mean with terms like 'insecure attachment' or 'attachment disorder' or how they infer these constructs. The way attachment is brought into play in such decisions is often not in accordance with the science that should lay the basis for it (Hammarlund et al., 2022).

For example, a reactive attachment disorder (RAD, DSM-V, American Psychological Association, 2013) is rather rare and is mainly seen in children who have lived in residential care or foster homes without personalised care at a young age. Children with a reactive attachment disorder may hardly seek support when they are upset, do not respond to parents' comforting behaviour, have difficulty forming social relationships, show little positive emotions, and can become unexpectedly angry, anxious, or sad in contact with adults. Differential diagnosis should exclude that the condition is caused by an autism-related or neurological disorder, although it can be present along with such disorders. But its roots should be found in extremely fragmented and neglecting care in early childhood (APA, 2013). In the past, it was thought that children with a reactive attachment disorder would be unable to become attached, but research on adoptees who have spent their early years in orphanages demonstrates that, even though they may arrive with RAD in their adoptive family, they do benefit from placement in a stable family context and are able to establish even secure attachment relationships with responsive new caregivers (Van IJzendoorn et al., 2020).

Unfortunately, it is not possible to draw conclusions about a child-caregiver attachment relationship from isolated behaviours such as excessive crying or not crying at all, leaving the caregiver, or seeking comfort on their lap. The amount a child cries is often more a matter of temperament and context than the type of attachment relationship. When observing attachment behaviour, we look at how children *organise* their behaviour at reunion after a short separation in an unfamiliar

Table 13.1 Assessing individual children for attachment insecurity or disorganisation should be evaluated according to the instrument's sensitivity and specificity which currently is insufficient for the existing attachment measures.

		Secure Attachment present	
		Yes	No
Classified as Secure	Yes	A True Positive (TP)	B False Positive (FP)
	No	C False Negative (FN)	D True Negative (TN)
Sensitivity and Specificity		Sensitivity TP/(TP+FN) = A/(A+C)	Specificity TN/(FP+TN) = D/(B+D)

environment with their caregiver, or how they behave during a few hours of observation at home with the family where attachment behaviour can be triggered by stressors such as unexpected loud noises, visitors, or frustrating moments when parents have to focus on other activities than responding to the child's needs. Such observations require intensive training and a reliability 'exam' with high agreement with an expert on at least 30 videotapes of children with their attachment figures.

But even then, observation by a certified coder is not sufficient to draw valid conclusions about an individual case. The instruments for measuring attachment are not suitable for individual diagnosis as they lack 'sensitivity' and 'specificity'. Sensitivity is the ability of an instrument to correctly classify an individual as 'securely attached' or the probability of a secure classification when the child is indeed securely attached. The ability of an instrument to correctly classify individuals as not secure when they are not securely attached is called the instrument's specificity. A valid diagnostic test should have high sensitivity and high specificity, meaning it can accurately detect both the presence and absence of a secure attachment relationship (see Table 13.1). With too low specificity and sensitivity too many children would be incorrectly classified. This implies that a diagnostic report mentioning a child's secure or insecure attachment to one of the parents should be taken with a grain of salt, even if the diagnosis has been done by a trained coder of attachment.

Importantly, no hard conclusions can be drawn at the individual level. Keep in mind that in non-clinical samples around 40% of children observed by experts might be classified as insecurely attached using the Strange Situation Procedure. This measure is considered the gold standard. Worldwide, across the general population, about 40% of children observed with the Strange Situation Procedure are found to be insecurely attached to one of the parents (see Introduction). Most of these children still develop fairly well. They are cared for in an adequate or at least good-enough manner, without neglectful, fragmented, or maltreating care. Developmental risks associated with insecure attachment at the group level can be compensated at the individual level by a child's resilience, other relationships in the attachment network (see Chapter 11), or favourable 'accidental' circumstances such as a caring friendship. The widely spread idea that group-level measures or findings can be translated to the individual level is a misconception in the larger area of mental health services (Van Os et al., 2019). In his book *The new mind readers*, Russ Poldrack showed that similar issues are associated with the use of MRI applications in practical settings and on the individual level, for example, in using fMRI as a lie detector. Such applications in real-life settings with high-stakes decisions, for example, in court procedures are ruled out by law, and on valid grounds (Poldrack, 2018).

In family court proceedings, assessments developed in the so-called Dynamic-Maturational Model of attachment (DMM, Spieker & Crittenden, 2018) are sometimes being used. Central in this theory is the development of relation-specific self-protective strategies for children who need comfort in situations of stress or danger. According to Spieker and Crittenden (2018), DMM theory and measures are ever-emergent and changing (p. 628). The implication is that researchers and clinicians who undergo training in DMM measures will have to retrain whenever such changes occur. This also means that any psychometric data indicating reliability, validity, sensitivity, and specificity soon become outdated and questionable. The DMM measures have already been multidimensional from the start and if they do continuously change, their credibility as sound and psychometrically robust measures is undermined. For example, the DMM circumplex classification system of adult attachment now includes 24 sub-categories of attachment (see Spieker & Crittenden, 2018), including 14 atypical sub-categories, somewhat loosely organised along 2 dimensions and placed in 5 main categories – a shower of colourful confetti (Bakermans-Kranenburg & Van IJzendoorn, 2009) hampering any test of its reliability and validity.

DMM attachment assessments, such as the Preschool Assessment of Attachment (PAA), are not reliable enough for diagnosis of individual cases in court procedures. Spieker and Crittenden (2010), who conducted the largest study to date using the PAA, found a 59% interrater reliability across the six main DMM attachment categories. This low reliability may be unacceptable even for research with large samples, and it is certainly not sufficient for court decisions involving individual cases, with high stakes, such as out-of-home placements for children. The interrater reliability of 59% leads to a low chance of a correct diagnostic decision when two trained diagnosticians evaluate an individual case. Jacob Bakermans demonstrated a maximum of only a 76% chance of correct classification for the child (Van IJzendoorn et al., 2018; see Figure 13.1). For individual children and their parents or caregivers, the 24% chance at best of a wrong diagnosis is unacceptably high. In the long run, court decisions based on expert diagnoses of attachment using DMM measures will be wrong in at least one of every four cases. This level of uncertainty is not acceptable and does not meet the standard of a justifiable decision in a life-course determining choice.

Intercoder reliability and chance of correct classification

Imagine that two raters have consensus in 59% of cases, and discuss the cases where they disagree. There are four possible outcomes:

a. Rater 1 is correct, Rater 2 is incorrect
b. Rater 1 is correct, Rater 2 is correct
c. Rater 1 is incorrect, Rater 2 is correct
d. Rater 1 is incorrect, Rater 2 is incorrect

The probability that one rater is right (pR) and convinces the other rater of being wrong when they discuss a disagreement (pC) should also be taken into account when computing the chance of a correct classification. The probabilities of the four possible outcomes can be calculated using products of pR and 1 − pR. Two scenarios show consensus: when both choose the correct classification (Scenario b), and when both choose the same incorrect classification (Scenario d). The probability of consensus in these scenarios can be expressed as

$$1 * pR * pR + 1/(N-1) * (1 - pR) * (1 - pR)$$

In this equation N is the number of attachment categories, assuming equal probabilities of all incorrect categories (the most optimistic scenario). When consensus is 59%, this implies that

$$1 * pR * pR + 1/(N-1) * (1 - pR) * (1 - pR) = 0.59$$

Assuming that pC = 0.50, that is, one rater convinces the other in 50% of the disagreements, the equation can be solved to find an upper boundary for a correct classification, which is 0.76. This means that there is a maximum of 76% chance of a correct diagnosis.

Figure 13.1 Intercoder reliability of attachment measures is too low and chance of incorrect classifications too high for individual assessments or diagnoses. For individual children and their parents or caregivers, the attachment assessment will be wrong in at least one of every four cases.
Source: Authors.

An alternative for the assessment of child attachment for diagnostic purposes might be to focus on parenting behaviour that may carry risks for the child to develop disorganised attachment. The AMBIANCE-Brief, a shortened version of the AMBIANCE (Madigan et al., 2020), was developed for professionals such as clinicians and social workers to assess disrupted caregiving. It consists of 45 behavioural items and is meant to be coded in real time on the basis of only 6 minutes of caregiver-child play. In a validation study on 69 adolescent mother-infant dyads, with the majority being single and poor, Cooke et al. (2020) found the AMBIANCE-Brief to be associated with infants' attachment disorganisation ($r > 0.30$). Considering the rather modest associations of disorganised attachment with maltreatment experiences on the one hand and later behaviour problems on the other hand (Groh et al., 2017) professionals might find the AMBIANCE-Brief easy to use but not very helpful in making decisions about support or treatment of child or family. We agree with Madigan et al. (2020) 'that this tool is not diagnostic in nature' and should not be used to make child placement decisions. Although it seems possible to train professionals to reliably code the AMBIANCE-Brief (Cooke et al., 2020), without further psychometric and diagnostic evidence the instrument cannot serve as screening tool for problematic parenting – unless maybe at the group level.

Unfortunately, attachment measures do not (yet) have the psychometric qualities for translation from group- to individual-level applications (Bakermans-Kranenburg & Van IJzendoorn, 2022). We analysed in some detail the psychometric issues with DMM measures. The same problems of lack of sensitivity and specificity on the individual level, however, exist for the more widely used attachment assessments like the Strange Situation Procedure, the Attachment Q-Sort, the Secure Base Script or the Adult Attachment Interview, the Brief Attachment Scale (Cadman, Fearon, & Belsky, 2018) or AMBIANCE-Brief (Madigan et al., 2020). Scientific research on individual diagnostics of attachment and atypical socio-emotional functioning of children and adolescents and their family environment is scarce and underfunded. Most promising seems a Parenting Capacity Assessment based on parents' response to evidence-based interventions (Harnett, 2007; Lindauer et al., 2010). This approach takes available family support and treatment as starting point for diagnosis of the openness for change in the parents as a predictor of the effect of a parenting intervention (Cyr et al., 2012; 2022; Van der Asdonk et al., 2019; 2020). This type of research has only recently started and showed some diverging results. Therefore, it does not yet allow for an evidence-based responsible translation to practice.

One might argue that even without demonstration of good reliability, sensitivity, and specificity, any more or less standardised instrument used as part of a suite of tests and observations should be preferred compared to a purely intuitive non-standardised clinical assessment. This argument, however, fails to acknowledge the large expertise of properly educated, experienced professionals in seeing patterns of risks and protective factors in complicated cases. And it fails to take account of the excessive weight that will be attached to apparently 'scientific' measures, yielding a compact and quantifiable or classifiable 'diagnosis'. For the families involved, the attachment assessment may lead to a self-fulfilling prophecy, exacerbating the psychological problems related to the assessment, as shown in the domains of school achievement and depression (Eble & Hu, 2022; Ohtani et al., 2023). In many countries child protection services are under-staffed and under-funded as well as have large turnover rates and poorly educated professionals. From an emancipatory perspective, they may feel less empowered by yet another 'promising' assessment tool or technique and might be better supported by a collaborative focus on improving their professional working conditions as well as the living conditions of the families in their care.

References

American Psychiatric Association. (2013). *Diagnostic and Statistical Manual of Mental Disorders* (5th ed.). https://doi.org/10.1176/appi.books.9780890425596

Bakermans-Kranenburg, M. J., & Van IJzendoorn, M. H. (1993). A psychometric study of the Adult Attachment Interview: Reliability and discriminant validity. *Developmental Psychology, 29*, 870–880. doi:10.1037//0012-1649.29.5.870

Bakermans-Kranenburg, M. J., & Van IJzendoorn, M. H. (2009). The first 10,000 Adult Attachment Interviews: Distributions of adult attachment representations in clinical and non-clinical groups. *Attachment & Human Development, 11*, 223–263. doi:10.1080/14616730902814762

Bakermans-Kranenburg, M. J., & Van IJzendoorn, M. H. (2022). Recht doen aan gehechtheid Misverstanden en inzichten omtrent gehechtheid bij juridische beslissingen over kinderen [Doing right in family court]. *Tijdschrift Relatierecht en Praktijk, 3*, 44–49.

Beckwith, H., Van IJzendoorn, M. H., Freeston, M., Woolgar, M., Stenner, P., & Duschinsky, R. (2022). A 'transmission gap' between research and practice? A Q-methodology study of perceptions of the application of attachment theory among clinicians working with children and among attachment researchers. *Attachment & Human Development*, DOI: 10.1080/14616734.2022.2144393

Cooke, J. E., Eirich, R., Racine, N., Lyons-Ruth, K., & Madigan, S. (2020). Validation of the AMBIANCE-brief: An observational screening instrument for disrupted caregiving. *Infant Mental Health Journal, 41*, 299–312. https://doi.org/10.1002/imhj.21851

Cadman T., Belsky J., & Fearon P. R. M. (2018). The Brief Attachment Scale (BAS-16): A short measure of infant attachment. *Child Care Health Development, 44*, 766–775. https://doi.org/10.1111/cch.12599

Crittenden, P. M. (2016). *Raising Parents: Attachment, Representation, and Treatment* (2nd ed.). Routledge. https://doi.org/10.4324/9781315726069

Cyr, C., Dubois-Comtois, K., Paquette, D., Lopez, L., & Bigras, M. (2022). An attachment-based parental capacity assessment to orient decision-making in child protection cases: A randomized control trial. *Child Maltreatment, 27,* 66–77. https://doi.org/10.1177/1077559520967995

Cyr, C., Dubois-Comtois, K., Geneviève, M., Poulin, C., Pascuzzo, K., Losier, V., ..., & Moss, E. (2012). Attachment theory in the assessment and promotion of parental competency in child protection cases. In A. Muela (Ed.), *Child Abuse and Neglect: A Multidimensional Approach* (pp. 63–86). Croatia: InTech. https://doi.org/10.5772/48771

Cyr, C., Euser, E. M., Bakermans-Kranenburg, M. J., & Van IJzendoorn, M. H. (2010). Attachment security and disorganization in maltreating and high-risk families: A series of meta-analyses. *Development & Psychopathology, 22,* 87–108. https://doi.org/10.1017/s0954579409990289

Eble, A., Hu, F. (2022). Gendered beliefs about mathematics ability transmit across generations through children's peers. *Nature Human Behavior, 6,* 868–879. https://doi.org/10.1038/s41562-022-01331-9

Elliott, M. L., Knodt, A. R., Ireland, D., Morris, M. L., Poulton, R., Ramrakha, S., Sison, M. L., Moffitt, T. E., Caspi, A., & Hariri, A. R. (2020). What is the test-retest reliability of common task-functional MRI measures? New empirical evidence and a meta-analysis. *Psychological Science, 31*(7), 792–806. https://doi.org/10.1177/0956797620916786

Forslund, T., Granqvist, P., Van IJzendoorn, M. H., Sagi-Schwartz, A., Glaser, D., Steele, M., Hammarlund, M., Schuengel, C., Bakermans-Kranenburg, M. J., Steele, H., Shaver, P. R., Lux, U., Simmonds, J., Jacobvitz, D., Groh, A. M., Bernard, K., Cyr, C., Hazen, N. L., Foster, S., Psouni, E., ..., & Duschinsky, R. (2021). Attachment goes to court: Child protection and custody issues. *Attachment & Human Development, 24,* 1–52. https://doi.org/10.1080/14616734.2020.1840762

Granqvist, P., Sroufe, L. A., Dozier, M., Hesse, E., Steele, M., Van IJzendoorn, M., Solomon, J., Schuengel, C., Fearon, P., Bakermans-Kranenburg, M., Steele, H., Cassidy, J., Carlson, E., Madigan, S., Jacobvitz, D., Foster, S., Behrens, K., Rifkin-Graboi, A., Gribneau, N., ... & Duschinsky, R. (2017). Disorganized attachment in infancy: A review of the phenomenon and its implications for clinicians and policy-makers. *Attachment & Human Development, 19,* 534–558. https://doi.org/10.1080/14616734.2017.1354040

Groh, A. M., Fearon, R. M. P., Van IJzendoorn, M. H., Bakermans-Kranenburg, M. J., & Roisman, G. I. (2017). Attachment in the early life course: Meta-analytic evidence for its role in socioemotional development. *Child Development Perspectives, 11*(1), 70–76.

Guilford, J. P. (1946). New standards for test evaluation. *Educational and Psychological Measurement, 6*(4), 427–438. https://doi.org/10.1177/001316444600600401

Hammarlund, M., Granqvist, P., Elfvik, S., Andram, C., & Forslund, T. (2022). Concepts travel faster than thought: An empirical study of the use of attachment classifications in child protection investigations. *Attachment & Human Development, 24*(6), 712–731. https://doi.org/10.1080/14616734.2022.2087699

Harnett, P. H. (2007). A procedure for assessing parents' capacity for change in child protection cases. *Children and Youth Services Review, 29*(9), 1179–1188. https//doi.org/10.1016/j.childyouth.2007.04.005

Lindauer, R. J. L., Bakermans-Kranenburg, M. J., Van IJzendoorn, M. H., & Schuengel, C. (2010). Thuiswonen of uithuisplaatsen: Betrouwbaarheid van de besluitvorming en innovatie van beslis- diagnostiek op basis van de capaciteit tot verbetering van ouderli- jke pedagogische vaardigheden middels een evidence-based inter- ventie [Out-of-home placement: Reliability of the decision process and innovation of diagnostic procedures on the basis of assessment of capacity for change in parenting through evidence-based intervention]. Unpublished manuscript. Amsterdam, Netherlands: de Bascule.

Madigan, S., Eirich, R., Racine, N., Borland-Kerr, C., Cooke, J. E., Devereux, C., Plamondon, A. R., Tarabulsy, G. M., Cyr, C., Haltigan, J. D., Bohr, Y., Bronfman, E., & Lyons-Ruth, K. (2020). Feasibility of training service providers on the AMBIANCE-Brief measure for use in community settings. *Infant Mental Health Journal, 42,* 438–451. https://doi.org/10.1002/imhj.21898

Madigan, S., Fearon, R. M. P., Van IJzendoorn, M. H. et al. (2023). A meta-analysis of the first 20,000 Strange Situation Procedures. *Psychological Bulletin, 149,* 99–132. https://doi.org/10.1037/bul0000388

Main, M., & Solomon, J. (1990). Procedures for identifying infants as disorganized/disoriented during the Ainsworth Strange Situation. In M. T. Greenberg, D. Cicchetti, & E. M. Cummings

(Eds.), *Attachment in the Preschool Years: Theory, Research, and Intervention* (pp. 121–160). The University of Chicago Press. https://doi.org/10.1097/00004583-199109000-00043

Ohtani, K., Tamura, A., Sakaki, M., Murayama, K., Ishikawa, S.-i., Ishii, R., Nakazato, N., Suzuki, T., & Tanaka, A. (2023). Parental perception matters: Reciprocal relations between adolescents' depressive symptoms and parental perceptions. *Journal of Counseling Psychology, 70*(1), 103–118. ISSN 1939-2168.

Poldrack, R. A. (2018). *The New Mind Readers: What Neuroimaging Can and Cannot Reveal about Our Thoughts*. Princeton University Press. https://doi.org/10.2307/j.ctvc77ds2

Sagi, A., Van IJzendoorn, M. H., Scharf, M., Koren-Karie, N., Joels, T., & Mayseless, O. (1994). Stability and discriminant validity of the Adult Attachment Interview: A psychometric study in young Israeli adults. *Developmental Psychology, 30*, 988–1000. https://doi.org/10.1037/0012-1649.30.5.771

Spieker, S., & Crittenden, P. M. (2010). Comparing two attachment classification methods applied to preschool strange situations. *Clinical Child Psychology and Psychiatry, 15*, 97–120. https://doi.org/10.1177/1359104509345878

Spieker, S. J., & Crittenden, P. M. (2018). Can attachment inform decision-making in child protection and forensic settings? *Infant Mental Health Journal, 39*(6), 625–641. https://doi.org/10.1002/imhj.21746

Van der Asdonk, S., de Haan, W. D., Van Berkel, S. R., Van IJzendoorn, M. H., Rippe, R. C. A., Schuengel, C., Kuiper, C., Lindauer, R. J. L., Overbeek, M., & Alink, L. R. A. (2020). Effectiveness of an attachment-based intervention for the assessment of parenting capacities in maltreating families: A randomized controlled trial. *Infant Mental Health Journal, 41*, 821–835. https://doi.org/10.1002/imhj.21874

Van der Asdonk, S., Van Berkel, S. R., de Haan, W. D., Van IJzendoorn, M. H., Schuengel, C., & Alink, L. R. A. (2019). Improving decision-making agreement in child protection cases by using information regarding parents' response to an intervention: A vignette study. *Children and Youth Services Review, 107*, 104501. http://10.1016/j.childyouth.2019.104501

Van IJzendoorn, M. H., Steele, M., & Granqvist, P. (2018). On exactitude in science: A map of the empire the size of the empire. *Infant Mental Health Journal, 39*, 652–655. https://doi.org/10.1002/imhj.21751

Van IJzendoorn, M. H., Schuengel, C., & Bakermans-Kranenburg, M. J. (1999). Disorganized attachment in early childhood: Meta-analysis of precursors, concomitants, and sequelae. *Development and Psychopathology, 11*, 225–249. doi:10.1017/S0954579499002035

Van IJzendoorn, M. H., Bakermans, J. J. W., Steele, M., & Granqvist, P. (2018). Diagnostic use of Crittenden's attachment measures in Family Court is not beyond a reasonable doubt. *Infant Mental Health Journal, 39*, 642–646. https://doi.org/10.1002/imhj.21747

Van IJzendoorn, M. H., & Bakermans-Kranenburg, M. J. (2021). Replication crisis lost in translation? On translational caution and premature applications of attachment theory. *Attachment & Human Development, 23*, 422–437. https://doi.org/10.1080/14616734.2021.1918453

Van IJzendoorn, M. H., Bakermans-Kranenburg, M. J., Duschinsky, R., Goldman, P. S., Fox, N. A., Gunnar, M. R., Johnson, D. E., Nelson, C. A., Reijman, S., Skinner, G. C. M., Zeanah, C. H., & Sonuga-Barke, E. J. S. (2020). Institutionalisation and deinstitutionalisation of children I: A systematic and integrative review of evidence regarding effects on development. *The Lancet Psychiatry, 7*, 703–720. https://doi.org/10.1016/S2215-0366(19)30399-2.

Van Os, J., Guloksuz S., Vijn T. W., Hafkenscheid A., & Delespaul P. (2019). The evidence-based group-level symptom-reduction model as the organizing principle for mental health care: Time for change? *World Psychiatry, 18*(1), 88–96. https://doi.org/10.1002/wps.20609.

14
SOS Children's Villages in the best interest of children?

'Tear down your institutions'

The damaging effects of growing up in institutions are well documented, both in meta-analytic work (Van IJzendoorn et al., 2020) and in *Romania's abandoned children*, the book about the impressive Bucharest Early Intervention Project (Nelson et al., 2014). Empirical evidence for the detrimental effects of structural neglect caused by any institutional child-rearing has accumulated since John Bowlby's *Maternal Care and Mental Health*, commissioned by the World Health Organization and published more than 70 years ago (Bowlby, 1951). But what about small orphanages such as the SOS Children's Villages (SOSCV)? Do they result in similar developmental damage as the more typical institutional settings? The reputation of the SOSCV is very positive, based on a persistent myth of children's protection in their best interest. For example, the Dutch Minister for Foreign Trade and Development Cooperation in 2019, Sigrid Kaag, questioned our call to abolish voluntourism of unprepared youngsters from WEIRD countries to orphanages, referring to the high quality of care in SOSCV (Sigrid Kaag, see Goldman et al., 2020). But small is not beautiful per se. Staff turnover seems unavoidable in a 24/7 care regime, and such caregiver instability is exacerbated by frequent separations from volunteers.

In our paper *'Tear down your institutions'. Empirical and evolutionary perspectives on institutional care in SOS Children's Villages,* we examined whether small-group care in institutional settings is the exception to the rule that institutional child-rearing is bad for child development or whether it does provide adequate care as SOSCV claims. SOSCV uses small-group housing with two caregivers and a limited number of children to try and mimic a family-like child-rearing environment. In a narrative and quantitative synthesis, we reviewed the scientific evidence on the associations between growing up in SOS villages and various child developmental outcomes (Van IJzendoorn & Bakermans-Kranenburg, 2021; 2022).

Hermann Gmeiner, founder of SOSCVI, called several decades ago for action to 'Tear down your institutions' (SOS Children's Villages International, 2018, p. 15). Indeed, there are good reasons for de-institutionalisation. It is empirically demonstrated and generally accepted that conventional institutions with large child-caregiver ratios are bad for the physical, cognitive, and socioemotional development of children (Van IJzendoorn et al., 2020; see Chapter 5). Institutional care is defined as group care of children around the clock (24/7) by professional caregivers who are not their (biological, foster, adoptive, kafalah, or kinship) parents. Crucial question is whether group care in small institutional settings is more adequate and might be used as a viable option on the continuum of care (Goldman et al., 2020; United Nations General Assembly, 2019). Herman Gmeiner and his associates of SOSCVI argue that their approach of family-like housing of small numbers of children with more or less permanent mother figures would facilitate development and be in the 'best interest of the abandoned or orphaned child' (SOS Children's Villages International, 2018). However, the ideal of the same mother figure taking care 24/7 of a small number of children in each of the houses in SOSCV has been replaced in recent years by teams of mothers and fathers per house (Nobis, 2023). In this chapter we review the publicly available scientific evidence on the associations between growing up in SOS villages and child development in various domains.

In a series of meta-analyses of more than 300 empirical studies including more than 100,000 children in more than 60 countries, we demonstrated that institutional care predicts large delays in physical and brain growth, in cognitive development, and in socioemotional development (Van IJzendoorn et al., 2020). Dose-response associations between duration of stay in the institution and severity of the delays provide support for a causal interpretation of the meta-analytic findings based on the correlational studies. Furthermore, the findings of the Bucharest Early Intervention Project (BEIP, Nelson et al., 2014), the unique randomised controlled trial comparing institutional with foster care that allows for causal conclusions, converged with the meta-analytic outcomes. This convergence solidifies the meta-analytic conclusions about the negative effects of institutionalisation and the accelerated catch-up growth after the child's transition to family-type care (see Chapter 5).

Against this background SOSCV may be seen as a special case of institutional care for abandoned children without parental care as they are claimed to be radically different from the classic type of institutional care. Founded in post-war Austria in 1949, it has become 'the world's largest non-governmental organisation focused on supporting children and young people without parental care, or at risk of losing it' (SOS Children's Villages International, 2018). SOSCV is active in 136 countries, operating more than 2,600 programmes involving more than a million children, young people, and families, and some 39,000 employees. Ideally, children in institutional care are housed in separate homes on a large compound with facilities such as (pre-)schools, medical centres, and some room for 'Schrebergarten' (allotment or family garden). In the children's houses 6–8 children of different ages live together with a 'mother' figure who in theory is available day and night for most of the week and most of the year, assisted by an 'aunt' who helps with cleaning and cooking. The villages try to be open to the wider community by providing opportunities for education and medical care. SOSCV also provides support for foster and adoptive parents, and besides institutional care, they have preventive programmes for strengthening families at risk of child abandonment.

Meta-analytic evidence for delayed development in SOSCV

A crucial question is whether the SOS villages offer indeed a special type of family-like institutional care and provide a good alternative for children without permanent parental figures. Do children raised in SOS institutions show better physical, cognitive, and socioemotional development than those growing up in typical institutions? Furthermore, do SOS institutions promote child development adequately so that the children are comparable to children reared in their family of birth or alternative family-type arrangements such as foster or adoptive care? To address these two questions, we searched for pertinent published empirical studies comparing developmental outcomes of children in SOS villages with those of their peers in either traditional institutions or family type of care. The literature search revealed eight unique studies on developmental outcomes of children in SOSCV. Five of these studies included various domains of child development, whereas three papers focused on oral health assessing caries, and one of these three studies also presented physical growth data (see Van IJzendoorn & Bakermans-Kranenburg, 2021; 2022).

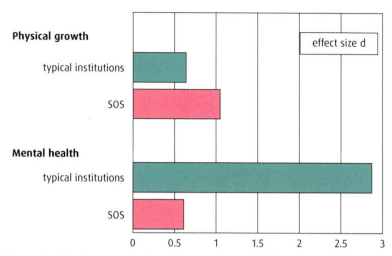

Figure 14.1 Despite small-group care in SOS Children's Villages, meta-analytic evidence shows the delays of SOSCV children in physical and mental development compared to their peers raised in families (baseline, $d = 0$) or in large institutions.
Source: Authors.

We compared SOS children's growth and development with those of children growing up in typical institutions and in families; see Figure 14.1. We found a combined effect size $d = 0.92$ for the comparison of mental health of SOS children with children in typical institutions, indicating that SOS children were better functioning than children in typical large institutions. We also compared SOS children's mental health with those of family-reared children and found a combined effect size of $d = -0.61$, which shows lower mental health for SOS children compared to family-reared children. For physical growth the comparison of SOS children with those from typical institutions amounted to $d = -0.43$, meaning that SOS children lagged behind children in typical institutions, but this comparison was based on only one study (Lassi et al., 2011; $N = 330$). They also lagged behind children growing up in families, with a large combined effect size of $d = -1.17$. Of course, the small number of studies that could be included in this meta-analysis imply large confidence intervals around the point estimates, but the outcomes are not reassuring for the SOS villages.

Growing up in one of the SOSCV does not lead to the same developmental levels as being raised in families. Physical growth of SOS children is lagging behind their peers in families. Moreover, their mental health, assessed with measures of psychomotor and socio-emotional development, shows significant delays compared to family-reared children. Only their dental health was found to be better than the dental health of children reared in families. Comparing SOS children with their peers in typical large-group institutional settings, we found that SOS children do better in the psychomotor and socioemotional domains of development but do worse in physical growth.

Recently, some alarming reports on severe child abuse and neglect in SOSCV were published. In 2023, Verinorm published a study on 30 years of child abuse in the Surinamese SOSCV in which throughout the years 1972–2006 five managers of the institution were involved (Van Wijk, Olfers, & Vloemans, 2023). The report presented atrocious abuse incidents. For example, one of the managers committed sexual abuse and had been sentenced to 3.5 years in prison. The Verinorm team studied documents and interviewed survivors and perpetrators of maltreatment, but they noted explicitly to have uncovered only the tip of an iceberg. Their conclusion was that because managers were involved in the maltreatment, structural maltreatment seems plausible.

In 2023, a so-called Independent Special Commission (ISC) published their report on 10 SOSCV in India, Nepal, Cambodia, Kenya, Panama, Sierra Leone, and Syria (Independent Special Commission, 2023). After less than a year of investigations the ISC had to conclude that 'serious allegations of incidents of child sexual and physical abuse … have occurred in several MAs (children's villages) in Africa, Asia and Central America, based on the reasonable grounds evidential standard applied by the ISC' (p. 12). The commission also concluded that these instances of abuse did not just happen in the past but that 'safeguarding failures persist within SOSCV with instances of omissions to act and report' (p. 8). Most disturbingly, the commission 'observed, and received reports of, numerous cases of pregnancies among children and youth cared for and supported by SOSCV, which occurred as a consequence of sexual abuse' (p. 13), leading in several cases to coercing children to undergo abortion.

It should be noted that both Verinorm and ISC were commissioned and paid by SOSCVI, the international federation of SOS Children's Villages, and thus cannot be considered truly independent. In fact, ISC explicitly complained about attempts of SOSCVI to influence their work, which might have led to underestimates of the maltreatment prevalence. Furthermore, the methods used in both the Verinorm and ISC investigations failed to meet criteria of transparency and reproducibility, as reliability of data collection and coding were absent, and sampling of villages did not provide a representative review of maltreatment in SOSCV around the world. Lastly, the commissions did not have sufficient child developmental research expertise or maltreatment-related credentials to conduct valid studies on historical and present incidences of abuse. One might argue that in alternative care settings such as in adoptive or foster families child maltreatment also occurs. However, we showed in an epidemiological study on maltreatment of atypically developing children in Dutch institutional versus foster care that maltreatment was significantly more prevalent in institutions (Euser et al., 2013; 2014; 2016). What is needed is a truly independent, representative, and valid epidemiological study of child abuse and neglect in SOSCV worldwide.

In general, the evidence base for our conclusions should be considered preliminary because even after 70 years of SOSCV, scientifically sound empirical studies on their efficacy are still rare. The preliminary narrative and meta-analytic evidence support the grounded hypothesis that SOS children show considerable developmental delays compared to family-raised children, and that they fare better than children in large institutions in the domain of mental health but stay behind with respect to physical growth. More and better studies are needed, but unfortunately the overall picture fits in the meta-analyses of non-SOSCV institutions (Chapter 5). The burden of proof is on SOSCV to refute this firmly grounded hypothesis. Only independently and carefully conducted studies of high quality would be able to pivot the current negative evaluation. For the time being we conclude that the SOSCV small-group facilities are not comparable to family-type child-rearing environments.

It is disappointing that after 70 years since SOSCV was founded only about one empirical study per decade evaluating the effects of this type of care could be found. That is a remarkably low number. SOSCV is part of a larger NGO with a variety of activities. The total preliminary budget of 2018 was estimated to be €1,261,028,000, of which the institutions, youth, foster families, and 'transit homes' were estimated to receive €577,847,000 (SOS Children's Villages International, 2018, p. 64). In 2021 the Dutch National Postal Codes Lottery proudly advertised that they donated €1.2 million to SOSCV to provide children with 'the protection they deserve'. Even after SOSCV admitted serious child maltreatment at several SOSCV locations, donations kept running towards this organisation that seems to want to hold on to institutionalisation, which is also highlighted in their brand name of SOSCV. It is therefore puzzling that so little research on the returns of these major investments has been conducted. Such studies are necessary and should be published in peer-reviewed papers in established scientific journals.

SOSCV recently sponsored a so-called 'rapid evidence review' of institutional care which suggested some advantages of small-group homes, without specifically focusing on institutional care provided by SOSCV (Porter, Mitchell, & Giraldi, 2020). This rapid review, however, had serious limitations, such as a very brief time window of 5 years (2015–2019) and a merely narrative approach, with the risk of biased description of selected studies and findings. In general, rapid reviews run the risk of being quick and dirty narrative summaries of selected studies. In contrast, meta-analytic evidence following the PRISMA or PROSPERO guidelines for selection of studies and intercoder reliability for the effect sizes and moderators of the individual studies requires more investments but such meta-analyses yield transparent, reproducible results. If the SOSCV organisation would spend only 1% of its budget on independent research on the efficacy of its small-group homes in comparison to family-type care, some €10 million would be available on a yearly basis to create a firm evidence base for this core component of their business.

Despite the small-group SOS arrangements and favourable staffing, they still do not seem to foster child development in similar ways as (biological, foster, adoptive, kinship) family-type arrangements, and they do not seem to do much better than large institutions in every domain. How can this be explained? We speculate that structural neglect, inherent to institutional care, is not only about size but also about the essential components of good-enough care. Contact comfort, continuity of caregivers, and a small network of attachment relationships for a child to be able to rely on in times of (di-)stress, illness, or potentially traumatic experiences are essential for children (Van IJzendoorn, Bakermans-Kranenburg, Duschinsky, & Skinner, 2020).

SOSCV leading de-institutionalisation?

The time may have come to use the enormous resources of SOSCV, the largest NGO for children without parental care worldwide, to help facilitate the transition from institutional care to genuine family-type care. The organisation is in an excellent position to contribute to this transition because it represents the whole continuum of care, from preventive programmes strengthening families at risk of child abandonment to institutional care and support programmes for foster and adoptive parents. This allows for a coherent research programme, including addressing the issue of how the transition to family-type care arrangements can best be made. If the organisation would spend part of its budget on truly independent research on the transition from institutional to family-type care, this would provide an opportunity to create a firm evidence base for the route to achieve the core goal of SOSCV: to make the group care division of the organisation superfluous. It is time to translate our knowledge about the detrimental effects of large and small institutions into policy and practice by supporting de-institutionalisation (Goldman et al., 2020) with all valorisation means that states, institutions, NGOs, and researchers can invoke. Let us take Herman Gmeiner, the founder of SOSCV, seriously. It was this man who called several decades ago to 'tear down your institutions'.

References

Bowlby, J. (1951). *Maternal Care and Mental Health*. World Health Organization.

Euser, S., Alink, L. R. A., Tharner, A., Van IJzendoorn, M. H., Bakermans-Kranenburg, M. J. (2013). The prevalence of child sexual abuse in out-of-home care: A comparison between abuse in residential and in foster care. *Child Maltreatment, 18*(4), 221–231. https://doi.org/10.1177/1077559513489848

Euser, S., Alink, L. R.A., Tharner, A., Van IJzendoorn, M. H., Bakermans-Kranenburg, M. J. (2014). Out of home placement to promote safety? The prevalence of physical abuse in residential and foster care. *Children and Youth Services Review, 37*, 64–70. https://doi.org/10.1016/j.childyouth.2013.12.002

Euser, S., Alink, L. R. A., Tharner, A., Van IJzendoorn, M. H., & Bakermans-Kranenburg, M. J. (2016). The prevalence of child sexual abuse in out-of-home care: Increased risk for children with a mild intellectual disability. *Journal of Applied Research in Intellectual Disabilities, 29*(1), 83–92. https://doi.org/10.1111/jar.12160

Goldman, P. S., Bakermans-Kranenburg, M. J., Bradford, B., Christopoulos, A., Ken, P. L. A., Cuthbert, C., & et al. (2020). Institutionalisation and deinstitutionalisation of children 2: Policy and practice recommendations for global, national, and local actors. *Lancet Child & Adolescent Health, 4*(8), 606–633. https://doi.org/10.1016/s2352-4642(20)30060-2

Independent Special Commission (2023). *Summary Report of the Work of the Independent Special Commission*. SOS Children's Villages International.

Lassi, Z. S., Mahmud, S., Syed, E. U., & Janjua, N. Z. (2011). Behavioral problems among children living in orphanage facilities of Karachi, Pakistan: Comparison of children in an SOS Village with those in conventional orphanages. *Social Psychiatry and Psychiatric Epidemiology, 46*(8), 787–796. https://doi.org/10.1007/s00127-010-0248-5

Nelson, C. A., Fox, N. A., & Zeanah, C. H. (2014). *Romania's Abandoned Children: Deprivation, Brain Development, and the Struggle for Recovery*. Harvard University Press. https://doi.org/10.4159/harvard.9780674726079.fm

Nobis, E. (2023). *Hermann Gmeiner. Oprichter SOS Kinderdorpen*. Oostenrijk Magazine Online. www.oostenrijkmagazine.nl/deelstaat/tirol/hermann-gmeiner/

Porter, R. B., Mitchell, F., & Giraldi, M. (2020). *Function, Quality and Outcomes of Residential Care: Rapid Evidence Review*. Glasgow, UK: CELCIS.

SOS Children's Villages International. *International Annual Report. 2018*. Available from: www.sos-childrensvillages.org/Publications/Reports/Annual-Report-2018

United Nations General Assembly (2019). Resolution adopted by the General Assembly on 18 December 2019. Rights of the Child with a focus on children without parental care. Available from: https://undocs.org/en/A/RES/74/133; see also: https://bettercarenetwork.org/library/social-welfare-systems/child-care-and-protection-policies/key-recommendations-for-the-2019-unga-resolution-on-the-rights-of-the-child-with-a-focus-on-children.

Van Wijk, A., Olfers, M., & Vloemans, I. (2023). *Historical Abuse Cases in SOS Children's Villages Suriname*. Verinorm. Downloaded on July 2, 2023 from www.verinorm.nl/wp-content/uploads/2023/06/binnenwerk_v4_ENG_small.pdf

Van IJzendoorn, M. H., Bakermans-Kranenburg, M. J., Duschinsky, R., Goldman, P. S., Fox, N. A., Gunnar, M. R., Johnson, D. E., Nelson, C. A., Reijman, S., Skinner, G. C. M., Zeanah, C. H., & Sonuga-Barke, E. J. S. (2020). Institutionalisation and deinstitutionalisation of children I: A systematic and integrative review of evidence regarding effects on development. *Lancet Psychiatry, 7*, 703–720. https://doi.org/10.1016/S2215-0366(19)30399-2.

Van IJzendoorn, M. H., & Bakermans-Kranenburg, M. (2021, April 8). 'Tear down your institutions': Empirical and evolutionary perspectives on institutional care in SOS Children's Villages. *PsyArXiv* https://doi.org/10.31234/osf.io/ye7jh.

Van IJzendoorn, M. H., & Bakermans-Kranenburg, M. J. (2022). Tearing down or fixing up institutional care for abandoned children? Comment on Rygaard (2020). *American Psychologist, 77*(1), 135–137. https://doi.org/10.1037/amp0000912

Van IJzendoorn, M. H., Bakermans-Kranenburg, M. J., Duschinsky, R., & Skinner, G. C. M. (2020). Legislation in search of 'good-enough' care arrangements for the child: A quest for continuity of care. In J. G. Dwyer (Ed.), *The Oxford Handbook of Children and the Law* (pp. 129–153). Oxford University Press. https://doi.org/10.1093/oxfordhb/9780190694395.013.5

15
Is adoption a modern, unethical in(ter)vention?

Controversial adoption

Adoption is a human behaviour that seems to defy evolutionary explanations. It incurs costs for the adoptive parents and losses for the birth parents and brings benefits only to the adopted child. Only adoption by kin might make evolutionary sense, using the concept of 'inclusive fitness'. Kinship adoption increases the chance of transmission of adoptive parents' genes into the next generation. From a socio-cultural perspective, adoption has been criticised as a form of neo-colonialism, with the wealthy taking children away from the poor on 'black markets of adoption'. Although we argue that this metaphor is misleading, a crucial ethical issue remains: how to balance the rights of the children against the rights of the birth parents if they are still alive, and the rights of the adoptive parents. We use Rawls' (1980) theory of justice to indicate a possible way out of the ethical dilemmas in the 'adoption triangle'.

Adoption is not a modern invention

Throughout recorded history children had to cope with loss to death of their parents or abandonment due to poverty or the threat of social exclusion when the child was born out of wedlock. Many abandoned children were rescued and raised as adopted members of another family (Boswell, 1988). At the same time, however, infanticide remained a rather common destiny of children in poor families which stimulated the rise of 'baby hatches' in the 12th century (Chapter 5) and foundling homes in the early 13th century (Boswell, 1988; Hrdy, 1999). Foundling houses were often breeding grounds for deadly infectious diseases, and in poor families wet-nursing children from privileged backgrounds led to severe neglect. In the 18th century the majority of these children did not survive for long (Boswell, 1988). Between 10% and 40% of children in European cities were estimated to be abandoned or placed with wet nurses, with high mortality in both cases.

In the 20th century several waves of increased numbers of children without permanent parents and related (international) adoption can be observed (Altstein & Simon, 1991; see also Selman, 2000; Tizard, 1991; Palacios et al., 2019). A first driver was World War II, which resulted in a large number of homeless Greek and German children waiting to be adopted. A second era began with the Korean War, leading to a large group of mixed-race children with Asian birth mothers and American birth fathers, resulting in more than 100,000 Korean adoptees in the USA (Lieberthal, 1999). In the following decades deteriorating socio-economic conditions in Latin America forced many poor parents to abandon their children who became street children if they were not adopted, fostered, or put in institutional care. The fall of communism opened countries like Romania and Russia for adoptive parents from abroad (Van IJzendoorn & Juffer, 2006). A last wave was rooted in the strict birth control policies in China in the 1990s, which led to the abandonment and subsequent adoption of infant girls (K.A. Johnson, 2004; Van IJzendoorn & Juffer, 2006).

In recent times a sharp reduction of the number of international adoptions set in, maybe due to the increase in prosperity in some of the largest 'donor' countries like China, India, and South American countries. The increase in number of babies born with assisted reproductive technologies might be another reason for the decline in adoptions (Palacios et al., 2019). In several receiving countries concerns about bad and illegal practices around adoptions in the past have been raised, among others, by adoptees reaching adulthood and searching for their roots, which decreased international adoptions drastically. It remains to be seen whether the downwards trend in adoptions will continue its trajectory. The HIV/AIDS and COVID-19 pandemics and raging wars in several parts of the world might once more increase the numbers of biological orphans (Goldman et al., 2020). The negative impact of the pandemics and wars on the economy and climate change in low- and middle-income countries might push children into social abandonment and need for alternative family care (Hillis et al., 2021).

Adoption is rooted in evolution

Adoption is not a uniquely human parenting behaviour but is shared with many non-human primates (e.g., Champoux et al., 1995; Hrdy, 1999). Surprisingly, adoption has been observed in over 120 species of mammal species and 120 species of bird (Avital et al., 1998), although it seems to defy evolutionary explanations (Avital et al., 1998; Hrdy, 1999; Van IJzendoorn & Juffer, 2006) except as an accidental by-product of evolution similar to a 'spandrel' in a cathedral (Gould & Lewontin, 1979). At first glance indeed, adoption seems to only incur costs for the adoptive parents who raise a child who is not their own offspring. Adoption would bring benefits only to the adopted child who gets a better life, and to its birth parents who transmit their genes to next generations without much investment after pregnancy and delivery – which, of course, does not erase the great emotional costs if birth parents are forced to abandon their child because of dire living conditions or cultural taboos (e.g., Brodzinsky & Schechter, 1990; Van IJzendoorn & Juffer, 2006).

Hrdy (1999) notes that many adoptions in non-human species involve offspring of genetically related parents (e.g., Kraaijeveld, 2005), and the concept of inclusive fitness can easily account for the advantages of this type of kinship adoption. In the case of non-kin adoptions reproductive error might play a role, where the adoptive parents fail to recognise the adopted egg or offspring as non-kin (Brown, 1998). Hrdy (1999) suggests that the universal fascination with babies in primates ('babylust') can lead to parenting behaviours towards abandoned or orphaned children. Furthermore, from the perspective of reciprocal altruism adoptive primate parents may invest in other's offspring with the expectation of receiving some form of support in return, such as assistance in parenting their own offspring or protection against predators.

As an example, adoption is observed rather frequently in forest chimpanzees in the Taï National Park in Côte d'Ivoire (Boesch et al., 2010), where chimpanzees share their habitat with a large population of leopards, their natural predators. The situation promotes strong within-group solidarity in the chimpanzees, with care for injured animals and adoption of young orphans. Not only females adopt these youngsters, but also males, which is remarkable as male chimpanzees are not at all active co-parents of their own offspring. Nevertheless, males were seen to adopt as often as females, sometimes caring for their unrelated adopted children for years. Such caregiving included food sharing, sharing their nest during the night, carrying the child or waiting for them during travel, and providing protection during conflicts. These costly parenting behaviours did not pay off for the males themselves (they had no more biological offspring than non-adoptive males) but had huge benefits for the adopted: orphans younger than 5 years of age normally do not survive or show up to 6 years delay in their physical development, whereas adopted orphans display almost normal physical development (Boesch & Boesch-Achermann, 2000). A rationale might be that helping offspring survive to maintain a critical group size is essential in an environment with high predation pressure.

In birds, four explanations for adoption have been suggested: (i) adoption by mistake, where parents do not recognise their young; (ii) active seeking of alloparental care by older fledglings whose parents provide low parental care (e.g., when the biological parents start building a new nest for a second brood); (iii) adults' 'kidnapping' of younger fledglings to protect their own young, as predators will more easily hunt the weakest or youngest birds; and (iv) stealing fledglings by adult birds whose breeding failed (Wysocki et al., 2018). In their 17-year-long observation of blackbirds in a city park in Szczecin (Poland), Wysocki and colleagues found most support for the first two hypotheses: adoption occurred more often when the nests were close and included fledglings of similar age (in line with the first explanation), or when the fledglings were the initiators (in line with the second explanation). Adoption occurred quite frequently, in almost 20% of the broods, and more often when the nests of neighbours were close. When older fledglings (who actively sought parental care) were adopted by neighbours, they were usually older than the adoptive parents' own fledglings; thus taking care of them was not by mistake. The adoptive parents less often produced a second brood, demonstrating the costs of their altruistic behaviour (Wysocki et al., 2018).

Adoption to secure family lineage

In ancient Rome, adoption was a way for the upper class to secure their succession and family legacy. The Roman inheritance laws excluded females as heirs, so it was essential to have a capable son who could inherit the family's name and estate and, in the case of emperors, their role as head of the state. The survival rates of children were low and average families had few children, making adoption of boys or even adult men an attractive and sometimes necessary alternative for high-ranking families. Augustus, the first emperor of the Roman Empire, is perhaps the most famous adoptee. Augustus adopted his grandsons and his stepson, the latter being the next emperor (Tiberius), who in turn adopted his nephew Germanicus as his successor. Germanicus' own son Caligula succeeded him. Caligula is known as a cruel tyrant and an ineffective emperor, as were some of the other emperors-by-birth. Emperors who got their 'job' through adoption, usually from somewhere in the family, were chosen for their capacities and often had a better fit for their role.

Elsewhere, adoptive parents acted as 'match-makers' to provide their own children with socially similar but genetically unrelated mates when they would reach adulthood (Avital et al.,1998). The Chinese practice of adopting a girl to serve as a 'tongyangxi', or future daughter-in-law and wife for an infant son, is an example of adoption with such motivation. In some cases, even childless couples would adopt a 'tongyangxi', believing that adoption would increase the chances of giving birth to a boy (K.A. Johnson, 2004; Van IJzendoorn & Juffer, 2006). Another explanation, derived from cultural evolution, may be the moral choice for the benefit of other human beings especially in the case of adoptions of children with special needs (Palacios et al., 2019).

The adopted child

Benefits for the adopted children are obvious, e.g., improved survival and development through the transfer to a more stimulating and protective family. As in birds, offspring may actively seek adoptive parents who are in a better position to enhance their life chances than their birth parents could do (Dolhinow & DeMay, 1982). Children in orphanages may try to influence the choices of prospective adoptive parents by acting more vigorously and friendly towards them during visits (Storsbergen, 1995). However, following the Hague Convention on Protection of Children and Co-Operation in Respect of Intercountry Adoption (1993), matching of child and adoptive parent should always be done by child protection professionals before a court decision about permanent adoption may be taken (Palacios et al., 2019).

Of course, adopted children may not always benefit from adoption, particularly when it involves transitioning to a different country, culture, and ethnic environment and elevated risks of discontinuity and fragmented (foster) care (Palacios et al., 2019). Concerns about the developmental prospects of adoptees date back some 70 years or more. During World War II, John Bowlby, Emanuel Miller, and Donald Winnicott argued in a public statement that the evacuation of young children out of besieged London would result in severe, life-long personality disturbances. They even cited preliminary findings from Bowlby's retrospective pilot study on 44 juvenile thieves to show that the 'emotional blackout' of evacuation and prolonged separation from the parent would later lead to increased delinquency (Bowlby, 1944). This concern is still present in current ideas about adopted children's delinquency (Smith, 2001). In fact, however, in a population-wide study we showed that criminality among adopted youth in the Netherlands did not substantively differ from their non-adopted peers (Van Ginkel et al., 2018).

Adoption is not a black market

While the benefits of adoption for the adopted children are clear, it is less clear what emotional costs are involved for the birth parents, in particular when they had to separate from their child involuntarily. Adoption has sometimes been criticised as a form of exploitation, with the wealthy taking children away from the poor. 'Black markets of adoption', where children are treated as commodities, have caused great concern in the media and public opinion (Balk et al., 2022). Of course, children should not be viewed as economic commodities whose value is determined by supply and demand (Palmer, 1986; Medoff, 1993). In their paper on the history of international adoption in the Netherlands, Balk et al. (2022) argue that abuses related to international adoption have been frequent, long-standing, and persistent until today. They suggest that these abuses are 'endemic' or 'systemic', and inevitably part of an 'adoption market' and its 'perverse financial stimuli', driven by global disparities between rich and poor countries and the corresponding disparity between the large demand for adopted children and the small supply.

It is worth noting that the use of the market metaphor in this context is seductive but also somewhat misleading, as the millions of institutionalised children far outnumber the estimated 400,000 children adopted into Western countries between 2004 and 2012, including 9,114 adopted into the Netherlands across this period (Selman, 2022; Van IJzendoorn & Bakermans-Kranenburg, 2022). For example, in 2016, Ukraine had almost 800 orphanages housing over 100,000 children (Dobrova-Krol & Van IJzendoorn, 2017), whereas in that year only 399 Ukrainian children were adopted internationally. Small demand in conditions of large supply does normally not increase the supply. Despite the flawed market metaphor, the questions raised by Balk and colleagues remain important, questions whether illegal adoptions and other adoption abuses were frequent, in the Netherlands and elsewhere, and whether these abuses are sufficient reason to call for a halt on international adoptions. Unfortunately, no reliable and exact figures on abuse of adoption are currently available (Van IJzendoorn & Bakermans-Kranenburg, 2022). The market may play a role in some (expensive international) adoptions but there is insufficient evidence for a decisive one in the majority of adoptions.

Ethics of the adoption triangle

Adoption evidently creates ethical issues within a social context of inequalities, and the key question is how to serve the interests of the child and the birth parents in a world where too many parents are unable to care for their children. If we broadly divide adoptions into two categories – adoption of orphans and adoption of abandoned or relinquished children (see Figure 15.1) – it is clear that adoption of orphans is always justified when it provides them with a home and a safe family life that they have lost due to the death of their parents. It is also generally accepted that adoption by relatives (kinship adoption), which often results in domestic adoptions, should be preferred over adoptions by non-kin (national or international adoptions) if the former is available. Humans have an evolutionary bias towards caring for genetically related children (inclusive fitness; Hamilton, 1964; Hrdy, 1999).

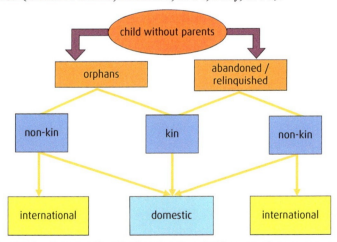

Figure 15.1 International adoption is a child protective measure and a last resort to raise biologically or socially orphaned children without available parents or other (kin) caregivers in a safe, stable and shared (Triple S) caregiving environment.
Source: Authors.

The ethical dilemma in adoption arises when children have been abandoned or relinquished by their parents because they were unable to meet the children's basic needs and provide basic protection and safety. In this case, the 'adoption triangle' (Sorosky, Baran, & Pannor, 1978) emerges, with at least three parties: the birth parent, the adopted child, and the adoptive parent (Van IJzendoorn & Juffer, 2006). The question then is how to balance diverging claims of the three parties and to ensure that the justifiable rights of each are secured. In this case, the preferred option is to enable the birth parents to protect their right to raise children in a 'good-enough' environment (Van IJzendoorn et al., 2020). Psychological, social, or economic problems that underlie separation of children from their birth parents should be addressed. That requires structural and personalised investments, and acceptance of children born out of wedlock in all cultures. If, in spite of such efforts, some parents cannot or will not raise their children, the crucial ethical issue is how to balance the rights of the children, birth parents, and adoptive parents, especially when the life chances of adopted children are significantly better than those of their siblings or peers left behind in adverse circumstances.

To address this ethical dilemma, we can apply Rawls' (1980) theory of justice and the procedures for resolving ethical dilemmas (see Van IJzendoorn & Juffer, 2006). Using Rawls' concept of the 'original position', we try to imagine what our moral choice would be – adoption or not – if we did not know beforehand what role we would play in the adoption triangle in real life (under the so-called 'veil of ignorance'); see Figure 15.2. Rawls (1980) argues that in this original position rational decision makers would choose a general conception of justice based on the maximin rule: 'All social primary goods – liberty and opportunity, income and wealth, and the bases of self-respect – are to be distributed equally unless an unequal distribution of any or all of these goods is to the advantage of the least favoured' (Rawls, 1980, p. 303). He also states that 'the parties in the original position would wish to avoid at almost any cost the social conditions that undermine self-respect' and nullify the chance to lead a more or less fulfilling life (Rawls, 1980, p. 440).

One of the most important bases of self-esteem and the ability to strive for one's life goals – whatever they may be – is the 'experience of a secure family life and the "unconditional" love of parents' (Rawls, 1980, pp. 463–464). Applying the decision rule of maximising the minimum return would mean that the rights and life chances of the weakest party should be given special consideration. No rational decision maker would want to end up in the position of a maltreated or neglected child whose parents had to relinquish or abandon them, without the opportunity for

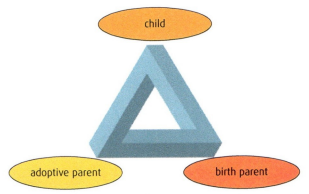

Figure 15.2 The adoption triangle illustrates that in cases of possible adoption of abandoned children, the potential interests of at least three parties are at stake: adoptive parents, birth parents, and the child. Rawls' original position requires the readers to imagine that they do not know their role in the adoption triangle.
Source: Authors.

adoption. Even the potential birth parent would agree that the most vulnerable position is that of the abandoned child, and they would agree that they should prioritise this child's right to a safe and continuous family life to prevent finding themselves in the hopeless position of the abandoned child. Having said that, the rights of the adoptive parents before the adoption are and should be minimal; there is no 'right' to have (adoptive) children.

How to safeguard the best interests of the child?

In their consensus statement about international adoption in the service of child protection, Palacios and his colleagues (2019) list a series of treaties, laws, and declarations for safeguarding the rights of each party in the adoption triangle. 'These include the UN Convention on the Rights of the Child (CRC; United Nations, 1989), which is the universal expression of consensus on the rights of the child. Also, the 1993 Hague Convention on Protection of Children and Cooperation in respect of Intercountry Adoption (HC; HCCH, 1993), which establishes minimum safeguards for the protection of children in intercountry adoption. At the European level, the European Convention on the Adoption of Children (EC; Council of Europe, 1967) and the European Convention on Human Rights (ECHR; Council of Europe, 1950) establish safeguards for children in care and adoption'.

These documents all emphasise the importance of children growing up in their own family (Arts 9, 10 CRC, Preamble HC, Art. 8 ECHR) and stress that children should not be separated from their parents except when competent authorities and professionals determine that such separation is in the child's best interest (Art. 9 CRC). International adoption can only be justified when a suitable family cannot be found within a child's country of origin. International adoptions should be guided by the best interests of the child and conducted ethically. The documents are a powerful universal expression of the rights of children to grow up in a safe family environment.

Some issues with the current formalised safeguards for children without available parents should, however, be mentioned. For example, the position of birth fathers has not been secured in the Hague Convention that does not address the question of birth fathers' consent. The consent of the birth mother seems to be the only important legally recognised voice in this matter. The consensus statement of Palacios et al. (2019) does not even mention birth fathers. If the father's identity is known and they are able to give informed consent, why would that right be restricted to birth mothers only? From a Rawlsian perspective, anyone in the 'original position' might be troubled by the thought of being a birth father and not being allowed to participate in the adoption consent process.

Troubling also is the concept of 'best interests of the child'. The best interests might easily infringe on the right of the birth parent to raise his or her own child. It might be argued that it would be in the best interests of almost all children in deprived families to be transferred to families with more material, educational, and cultural resources. In the original position, however, every child would be assigned an environment where basic physical and mental needs would be met, without maltreatment or neglect, and with sufficient means to strive for one's life goals. Rawls (1980) even suggests that this would entail the experience of a secure family life and 'the unconditional love' of a parent. Secure attachments, however, are observed in only a small majority of families around the globe (Madigan et al., 2023; see Chapter 11). To avoid a massive migration of children to other, more ideal families, we propose that the maximin rule in the original position is interpreted as maximising the minimal standards for leading a respected life. This maximin outcome would better be labelled a right to a 'good-enough' childrearing environment instead of a healthy and happy life as seems to be the focus of the 'quality of life' approach in health economy (see Chapter 8). The original position applied to the adoption triangle would prioritise the needs of the weakest party in the triangle and at the same time ensure that the rights of birth parents are also protected.

In the original position, rational decision makers would likely be concerned about the potential role of poverty or ideology in forcing birth parents to abandon or relinquish a child. Of course, in the original position, there should be no doubts about the genuine inability of the birth parents to care for the child (excluding personal, social, economic or cultural impediments), and adoption should not be a choice at all in the case of a 'good-enough' parent who provides the child with less than optimal but still minimally safe, stable and shared (Triple S) childrearing conditions. In this case, the fundamental rights of the birth parents may take priority even if the child may be better off in another family. We stress this requirement not only because 'the best might be the enemy of the good' but most importantly because the evidence base is lacking for 'professionals who are trained and competent in understanding adoption … responsible for delivering adoption services … (Art. 32 HC; HCCH, 2015b, as cited in Palacios et al., 2019) who are able to responsibly and accurately diagnose parenting and attachment in individual families' (see Chapter 13). The chances of false positive assessments of best interests ('the child should be placed in a different family') are too high to decide about the child's and the birth parents' life course (Chapter 13). It should be noted that there is also a risk of false negatives. Motivated adoptive parents might be assessed as unfit for adoption of a child based on invalid observations and measures leading to potentially more discontinuous foster care – which would not be in the best or even good-enough interest of the child.

Seventy years after Bowlby's (1951) WHO report on institutional childcare it is evident that adoption is a crucial part of a child protection system to save children without permanent parents from maltreatment and structural neglect. Bowlby (1951) advocated adoption as the preferred alternative to institutional care, but he acknowledged the lack of empirical evidence supporting the effectiveness of this intervention. We closed that gap with massive, replicable evidence of the huge positive impact of adoptive care (Van IJzendoorn et al., 2020; see also Chapter 5). Whether (international) adoption can be justified in cases of parents who are unable to raise their own children due to psychological, social, or economic adversities is dependent on structural and personalised investments in empowering the birth parents to be good-enough parents.

References

Altstein, H., & Simon, R. J. (Eds.) (1991). *Intercountry Adoption: A Multinational Perspective*. Praeger Publishers.

Avital, E., Jablonka, E., & Lachmann, M. (1998). Adopting adoption. *Animal Behaviour, 55*, 1451–1459. https://doi.org/10.1006/anbe.1998.0729

Balk, Y., Frerks, G., & de Graaf, B. (2022). Investigating historical abuses. *Journal of Applied History, 5*(1), 19–46. https://doi.org/10.1163/25895893-bja10020

Boesch, C., & Boesch-Achermann, H. (2000). *The Chimpanzees of the Taï Forest: Behavioural Ecology and Evolution*. Oxford University Press.

Boesch, C., Bolé, C., Eckhardt, N., & Boesch, H. (2010). Altruism in forest chimpanzees: The case of adoption. *PLoS One, 5*(1), e8901. https://doi.org/10.1371/journal.pone.0008901

Boswell, J. (1988). *The Kindness of Strangers: The Abandonment of Children in Western Europe from Late Antiquity to the Renaissance*. Pantheon Books.

Bowlby, J. (1944). Forty-four juvenile thieves: Their characters and home life. *International Journal of Psycho-Analysis, 25*, 19–52 and 107–127. https://doi.org/10.1176/ajp.105.11.879

Bowlby, J. (1951). *Maternal Care and Mental Health*. World Health Organization.

Brodzinsky, D. M., & Schechter, M. D. (Eds.). (1990). *The Psychology of Adoption*. Oxford University Press.

Brown, K. M. (1998). Proximate and ultimate causes of adoption in ring-billed gulls. *Animal Behaviour, 56*, 1529–1543. https://doi.org/10.1006/anbe.1998.0913

Champoux, M., Boyce, W. T., & Suomi, S. J. (1995). Biobehavioral comparisons between adopted and nonadopted rhesus-monkey infants. *Journal of Developmental and Behavioral Pediatrics, 16*, 6–13. https://doi.org/10.1097/00004703-199502000-00002

Council of Europe. (1950). European Convention on Human Rights. www.echr.coe.int/Documents/Convention_ENG.pdf

Council of Europe. (1967). European Convention on the Adoption of Children. www.coe.int/en/web/conventions/full-list/-/conventions/treaty/058

Dobrova-Krol, N. A., & Van IJzendoorn, M. H. (2017). Institutional care in Ukraine: Historical underpinnings and developmental consequences. In A. V. Rus, S. R. Parris, & E. Stativa (Eds.), *Child Maltreatment in Residential Care: History, Research, and Current Practice* (pp. 219–240). Springer International Publishing. https://doi.org/10.1007/978-3-319-57990-0_11

Dolhinow, P., & DeMay M. G. (1982). Adoption – the importance of infant choice. *Journal of Human Evolution, 11*, 391–420. https://doi.org/10.1016/s0047-2484(82)80094-8

Goldman, P. S., Van IJzendoorn, M. H., & Sonuga-Barke, E. J. S. on behalf of the Lancet Institutional Care Reform Commission Group (2020). The implications of COVID-19 for the care of children living in residential institutions. *The Lancet Child & Adolescent Health* (Correspondence) April 21, 2020 https://doi.org/10.1016/ S2352-4642(20)30130-9.

Gould, S. J., & Lewontin, R. C. (1979). The spandrels of San Marco and the Panglossian paradigm: A critique of the adaptationist programme. *Proceedings of the Royal Society of London, Series B, 205*, 581–598. https://doi.org/10.1098/rspb.1979.0086

Hamilton, W. D. (1964). The genetical evolution of social behavior. *Journal of Theoretical Biology, 7*, 1–52. https://doi.org/10.1016/0022-5193(64)90038-4

Hague Convention on Protection of Children and Cooperation in Respect of Intercountry Adoption. (1993, May 29).

Hillis, S. D., Unwin, H., Chen, Y., Cluver, L., Sherr, L., Goldman, P. S., Ratmann, O., Donnelly, C. A., Bhatt, S., Villaveces, A., Butchart, A., Bachman, G., Rawlings, L., Green, P., Nelson, C. A., & Flaxman, S. (2021). Global minimum estimates of children affected by COVID-19-associated orphanhood and deaths of caregivers: A modelling study. *Lancet Child and Adolescent Health, 398*(10298), 391–402. https://doi.org/10.1016/S0140-6736(21)01253-8.

Hrdy, S. B. (1999). *Mother Nature: A History of Mothers, Infants, and Natural Selection*. Vintage.

Johnson, K. A. (2004). *Wanting a Daughter, Needing a Son: Abandonment, Adoption, and Orphanage Care in China*. Yeong & Yeong Book Company.

Kraaijeveld, K. (2005). Black swans *Cygnus atratus* adopt related cygnets. *Ardea, 93*, 163–169.

Lieberthal, J. K. (1999). *Adoption in the Absence of National Boundaries*. Paper presented at the 25th Conference of the North American Council on Adoptable Children, NACAC 1999.

Madigan, S., Fearon, R. M. P., Van IJzendoorn, M. H. et al. (2023). A meta-analysis of the first 20,000 Strange Situation Procedures. *Psychological Bulletin, 149*, 99–132. https://doi.org/10.1037/bul0000388

Medoff, M. H. (1993). An empirical analysis of adoption. *Economic Inquiry, 31*, 59–70. https://doi.org/10.1111/j.1465-7295.1993.tb00866.x

Palmer, J. (1986). The social cost of adoption agencies. *International Review of Law and Economics, 6*, 189– 203. https://doi.org/10.1016/0144-8188(86)90003-7

Palacios, J., Adroher, S., Brodzinsky, D. M., Grotevant, H. D., Johnson, D. E., Juffer, F., Martínez-Mora, L., Muhamedrahimov, R. J., Selwyn, J., Simmonds, J., & Tarren-Sweeney, M. (2019). Adoption in the service of child protection: An international interdisciplinary perspective. *Psychology, Public Policy, and Law, 25*(2), 57–72. https://doi.org/10.1037/law0000192

Rawls, J. (1980). *A Theory of Justice*. Belknap Press.

Selman, P. (2000). The demographic history of intercountry adoption. In P. Selman (Ed.), *Intercountry Adoption: Developments, Trends and Perspectives* (pp. 15–39). British Agencies for Adoption and Fostering.

Selman, P. (2022). *Global Statistics for Intercountry Adoption: Receiving States and States of Origin 2004–2020*. https://assets.hcch.net/docs/a8fe9f19-23e6-40c2-855e-388e112bf1f5. February 2022 (accessed March 10, 2022).

Smith, J. (2001). The adopted child syndrome: A methodological perspective. *Families in Society, 82*, 491–497. https://doi.org/10.1606/1044-3894.173

Sorosky, A. D., Baran, A., & Pannor, R. (1978). *The Adoption Triangle*. Anchor Press/Doubleday.

Storsbergen, H. E. (1995). Geadopteerd zijn is ... Geadopteerden van Griekse afkomst over hun leven, hun achtergrond en beleving van hun adoptie [Being adopted means ... Greek adoptees on their lives, background and the perception of their adoption]. In R. A. C. Hoksbergen, H. E. Storsbergen, & C. Brouwer-Van Dalen (Eds). *Het begon in Griekenland [It started in Greece]* (pp. 47–193). Utrecht, The Netherlands: Utrecht University.

Tizard, B. (1991). Intercountry adoption: A review of the evidence. *Journal of Child Psychology and Psychiatry, 32*, 743–756. https://doi.org/10.1111/j.1469-7610.1991.tb01899.x

United Nations. (1989). Convention on the Rights of the Child. United Nations Treaty Series, 1577, 3. https://treaties.un.org/doc/Treaties/1990/09/19900902%2003-14%20AM/Ch_IV_11p.pdf

Van Ginkel, J., Juffer, F., Bakermans-Kranenburg, M. J., & Van IJzendoorn, M. H. (2018). Young offenders caught in the act: A population-based cohort study comparing internationally adopted and non-adopted adolescents. *Children and Youth Services Review, 95*, 32–41. https://doi.org/10.1016/j.childyouth.2018.10.009

Van IJzendoorn, M. H., Bakermans-Kranenburg, M. J., Coughlan, B., & Reijman, S. (2020). Child maltreatment antecedents and interventions: Umbrella synthesis and differential susceptibility perspective on risk and resilience. *Journal of Child Psychology and Psychiatry, 61*, 272–290. https://doi.org/10.1111/jcpp.13147

Van IJzendoorn, M., & Bakermans-Kranenburg, M. J. (2022). Intercountry adoption is a child protection measure. *Journal of Applied History, 5*(1), 75–84. doi: https://doi.org/10.1163/25895893-bja10022

Van IJzendoorn, M. H., & Juffer, F. (2006). The Emanuel Miller Memorial Lecture 2006: Adoption as intervention: Meta-analytic evidence for massive catch-up and plasticity in physical, socio-emotional, and cognitive development. *Journal of Child Psychology and Psychiatry, and Allied Disciplines, 47*, 1228–1245. http://dx.doi.org/10.1111/j.1469-7610.2006.01675.x

Wysocki, D., Cholewa, M., & Jankowiak, Ł. (2018). Fledgling adoption in European Blackbirds: An unrecognized phenomenon in a well-known species. *Behavioral Ecology, 29*(1), 230–235, https://doi.org/10.1093/beheco/arx147

Part 4
Protecting academic freedom promotes replication and translation

In the fourth section we discuss some of the assaults on academic freedom, which is one of the necessary conditions for replicable research and responsible translation (see Figure 0.4). According to UNESCO's 1997 'Recommendation Concerning the Status of Higher-Education Teaching Personnel', academic freedom is defined as follows: 'Academic freedom includes the right, without restriction by prescribed doctrine, to freedom of teaching and discussion, freedom in carrying out research and disseminating and publishing the results thereof, freedom to express freely their opinion about the institution or system in which they work, freedom from institutional censorship and freedom to participate in professional or representative academic bodies' (see Figure 0.4). We add that academic freedom is restricted to the scholar's area of scientific expertise. Outside of that area general freedom of speech is relevant.

Based on some personal experiences we illustrate the crucial role of academic freedom with examples of assaults on the freedom of researchers to determine the design, data-processing, and publication of their investigations. Sponsors of a study might want to block or delay publication of unwelcome findings. Patient and public involvement in research is currently required by several funding agencies but we argue that it may lead to biased results. A growing number of journals require authors to disclose not only their financial interests in research products but also their political, religious, or sexual/gender preferences and practices that 'might cloud objectivity'. We argue that these requirements may lead to severe collateral damage. Last, we believe that safe working environments are crucial. However, a friendly atmosphere should not be given priority over candid scientific discourse about theories, methodologies, vocabularies, and measures.

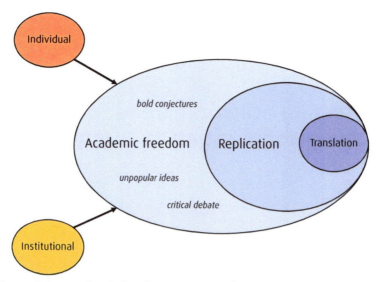

Figure 0.4 Academic freedom is required for scholars in their area of expertise. Individual academic freedom is not only under siege of powers outside academia but is also threatened by the university as a hierarchical organisation.
Source: Authors.

16
Limits to participant, public, and policymaker involvement

Participant involvement in data collection

In biomedical and mental health research, 'Patient and Public Involvement' (PPI) is becoming more and more important, as a way to make research more responsive to the needs and priorities of participants, patients, and the public. PPI would improve the quality and relevance of research by making sure that the research question leads to actionable answers. Patients and participants are requested to be included in translating outcomes to policy or (clinical) practice. In a similar vein, Citizen Science (CS) is meant to democratise scientific research, allowing participants from diverse backgrounds and various knowledge levels to engage in scientific activities.

The number of research papers on PPI published in refereed journals has rapidly increased in recent years, from about 40 papers in the year 2000 to more than 200 papers in 2020. 'In the search for truth man makes two steps forward and one step back', suggested the philosopher Laevsky in Anton Chekhov's novel *The Duel* (1891). In contrast, the communist leader Vladimir Lenin preferred to talk about 'One step forward, two steps back' (Lenin, 1930), which might be called prophetic with the wisdom of hindsight. How can involvement of non-trained individuals in scientific research be realised without repeating failures of the past that resulted in academic freedom under attack?

But first a few examples of PPI. Citizen science projects in the natural sciences mostly focus on data collection with help of the public. A popular example is the Great Backyard Bird Count that asks volunteers to identify and count birds in one's backyard during a specific stretch of time. Biologists use the data collected to better understand population trends and migratory patterns of different bird species. Another example is Zooniverse, a platform that hosts a variety of citizen science projects, such as Galaxy Zoo. In Galaxy Zoo, non-specialist volunteers are asked a standard set of questions about the shape of a galaxy, producing data for astronomers to learn about the astrophysical processes in the galaxy's evolution.

This type of participant involvement does not differ much from the use of respondents in the behavioural sciences who are asked to complete questionnaires about their own behaviour or observe other individuals' behaviour. For example, in our epidemiological studies on the prevalence of child maltreatment in the Netherlands we asked more than 1100 so-called 'sentinels' working with children (e.g., teachers, general practitioners, police) to report suspected maltreatment cases over a period of 3 months. The reports were rated by trained coders with a set of pre-established criteria to compute the maltreatment prevalence, which was estimated to be 33.8 per 1,000 children in the year 2010 (Euser et al., 2013). The study received much attention in the media and in the Dutch parliament and had policy consequences for child protection and family support. The study was shaped after the National Incidence Studies on child maltreatment in the USA (Sedlak et al., 2010), but the methodology is not different from the Great Backyard Bird Count or Galaxy Zoo in terms of involvement of the public in data collection, with instructions about what child maltreatment is and how it can be monitored. So, is it Citizen Science? If it is, it seems to be a new label for an old research method.

In psychology, digital recording instruments such as phone apps or wristwatches to collect data begin to belong to the core set of measures. For example, in the Emotional Brain Study presented as a CS study, Blakemore and Schweizer use an app with games to motivate young citizen scientists across the world to provide data on their cognitive development and to monitor changes in their emotion regulation. The promise is that eventually 'this information can be fed back to participants with personalised recommendations that may range from getting more sleep to contacting a health care professional' (Schweizer et al., 2019). This approach is not much different from the use of the phone app diary method across 14 days in our study with Cuyvers et al. (2022) on state and trait attachment in 9- to 13-year-old children. However, this study is not deemed a CS project. Therefore, it is important to outline the defining core of CS and PPI.

PPI and CS as participatory action research?

PPI and CS share some features with the Germany-rooted participatory action research methodology ('Handlungsforschung', Van IJzendoorn & Van der Veer, 1983) that was popular in the 60s and 70s of the last century. Action research has a cyclical process, in which data collection, analysis, and action are iteratively implemented and improved by researchers and participants, with the aim of promoting social change. It was most frequently used in the fields of education and social work. It aligns with the American philosophy of pragmatism (Biesta, Miedema, & Van IJzendoorn, 1990) and the idea of validating the truth of (causal) propositions by effectively changing reality.

In practice action research often resulted in non-reproducible processes and findings, with the difference between scientific research and social activism fading away (Van IJzendoorn, 1984). Hart (1992) stresses that in 'action research' action and research should go together and be carried out by the same people, and he argues that this is not a 'de-professionalisation' but a 're-professionalisation' of research, with new roles for the researcher as a democratic participant and the participants as co-researchers in all stages of the research cycle. This leads, however, to erosion of the boundary between social activism and scientific inquiry within a research project and, as such, can become a threat to academic freedom. In our view (see Chapter 18) academic freedom is restricted to the specific area of scientific expertise, and translation to policy or practice should be rooted in replicated evidence. Political or social activism cannot be part of research, although it might be a plausible 'activist' translational follow-up of replicated research, e.g., in actions against institutional child-rearing. Thus, academic freedom also implies avoiding using the professorial prestige to initiate or support political action outside the area of scientific expertise or within an area of expertise with a still brittle evidence base. Scholars may of course take part in political activism as ordinary citizens, and in that context, they will be protected by the universal right to have freedom of speech. But it is essential that within a research programme the boundaries between the area of scientific expertise and the common citizen roles are clearly visible and respected.

The Just Community project for moral education, developed by Lawrence Kohlberg and his colleagues, is an example of educational action research. It aimed to foster democracy and a just society by stimulating moral development in young people through immersion in a just and fair school community (see Bakermans-Kranenburg & Van

IJzendoorn, 2019, and Chapter 12). The project was conducted in one high school and emphasised the importance of providing students with positive role models, clear rules and interactions, and well-defined norms of behaviour. Peers within the school community served as embodiment and enforcers of these socio-moral norms. Key components were community meetings for democratic decision-making, a discipline committee for addressing misbehaviour, and a curriculum that included moral dilemma discussions to promote critical thinking.

Researchers collected data on the students' moral development and community functioning and used those data to make adjustments to the programme. They also trained the students in data collection and analysis, allowing them to reflect on the programme and make their own recommendations for improvement. There was no control group. Short-term effects on students' moral judgement levels were reported, but no long-term effects. One year after the end of the study, none of the teachers had continued with the programme (Power, 1988; Bakermans-Kranenburg & Van IJzendoorn, 2019). The Just Community project is thus a telling example of failed generalisability across time and context that appears to be inherent to action research (Van IJzendoorn, 1984) and some other forms of qualitative studies (Van IJzendoorn & Miedema, 1986).

A more recent example of action research is presented by Clements and Harding (2023) who conducted a study on reducing the frequency of sanctioning pupils with withdrawal of playtime. At one primary school two teachers volunteered to be involved in collaborative action research (CAR, Messiou, 2019). With focus group meetings and individual consultations, the reasons for using playtime withdrawal were discussed and potential solutions were explored and implemented. Data analysis of the three recorded and transcribed consultations was subjected to an inductive thematic analysis process in search of common themes across the teachers and sessions. Validity of the data was checked with the teachers. This type of action research can be considered an extreme form of PPI, with replicability possibly problematic because of the unique school setting.

Indeed, Clements and Harding (2023) explicitly labelled their project as an exploratory study, and in Chapter 1 we argued that in the context of discovery anything might go (Feyerabend, 1975) as long as testable hypotheses for further empirical scrutiny are proposed before translation to practice is recommended. However, similar to the Just Community project, the boundaries between researcher and practitioner roles seem to have become rather permeable. This would be problematic in the justification phase of research from our perspective on the relations between replication, translation, and academic freedom. We argue that replicated results instead of exploratory conjectures are a necessary condition for translation to practice or policy.

Viable alternatives with PPI

We have positive experiences with PPI in at least two types of studies. First, when the VIPP-SD intervention (see Chapter 4) is adapted for use with a new target group (e.g., ethnic minority groups, or school teachers; Starreveld et al., 2023), a focus group is established to discuss the intervention procedures and settings and to consider and try out any adaptations for optimal fit with the specific target group, within the boundaries of the VIPP-SD approach. An example is the pragmatic randomised controlled video-feedback intervention trial (see Chapter 4) with parents and their infants at risk for developing externalising problems, Healthy Start, Happy Start (O'Farrelly et al., 2021). PPI was realised by involving representatives of the target population, participants from a pilot study, and others recruited through community and healthcare services. The group included parents of children in the relevant age range, as well as educational and childcare professionals. They met on an annual basis and provided valuable advice on participant materials, recruitment strategies, and ways to disseminate the study's findings to participants. The group's insight was especially valuable in identifying settings and services that were most effective for recruiting difficult-to-reach parents and in developing strategies for engaging and retaining participants.

A second type of PPI involvement was in the phase of the interpretation of findings of an umbrella meta-analysis. In an umbrella study of meta-analyses on the sequelae of child maltreatment, expert-by-experience groups of The National Children's Bureau were consulted about the results of our synthesis (Coughlan et al., 2022). We found that child maltreatment considerably increased the risks of later mental health issues, but the effect sizes were more modest than one might expect, suggesting that some survivors of maltreatment were relatively unaffected by their experiences. According to the experts-by-experience some of this apparent resilience might reflect social desirability bias in their reports of psychological needs. Survivors of child maltreatment may be hesitant to be open about their need for support or treatment for fear of retribution from perpetrators, negative impact on their family, or because of mistrust of professionals or researchers. Their suggestions were included in the final manuscript and their contribution was acknowledged in the paper.

Damaging influence of stakeholders

While participants can valuably contribute in some stages of a study, research must also be protected against interference from non-scientific stakeholders in other parts of the research cycle. We illustrate this position with a study on the quality of centre day-care in the Netherlands (see Van IJzendoorn, 2007, translated in Van IJzendoorn, & Vermeer, 2014, for a detailed case report). In the nineties, Dutch day-care for infants and toddlers transited from state-supported facilities to private enterprises. However, the Dutch parliament wanted to monitor the quality of centre day-care, and the Dutch Consortium for Childcare Research (NCKO; a group of researchers initiated and paid by the Ministry of Social Affairs and Employment) was committed to monitoring the quality of care every five years. An advisory board was installed with thirteen members, some of them with financial interests in centre day-care. Only one member had doctoral training, though not in the field of education or psychology. Nevertheless, the advisory board provided comments on the research question, methods, and results of the research.

In a period of 10 years, three national monitors took place. For each monitor, the quality of care was determined in 40 to 50 day-care centres, based on several hours of careful observation per centre, with internationally accepted instruments. The third monitor, in 2005, showed a steep decline in quality of centre day-care, also compared to countries like Germany, Canada, and the United States. The scores for total quality were on average slightly higher than 3 on a scale ranging from 1 to 7. None of the centres scored in the internationally accepted 'good' range (scores higher than 5), and 36% were in the 'insufficient' (lower than 3) range. In the first monitor no day-care of insufficient quality was observed; in the second monitor 6% scored insufficient, using the same criteria (Vermeer et al., 2008). The decline in childcare quality between 1995 and 2005 could be attributed to a rapid increase in children attending childcare centres and an increasing shortage of qualified staff. Furthermore, changes in vocational training for caregivers, shifting from specialised training to broader social pedagogical training, may have negatively impacted the quality of care provided.

The outcomes of the NCKO research were extensively discussed in the national media, causing commotion among parents and day-care practitioners. Policymakers and politicians were also concerned and requested a fourth and more extensive national monitoring of childcare quality. At the same time, a commercial consultancy was hired without any expertise in the behaviour sciences or day-care to re-analyse the data of the third monitor and to check the NCKO conclusions. The consultancy confirmed the findings and conclusions of the monitor, adding that some informants did not recognise the reported low quality of care while others did. The NCKO proposed a replication of the quality monitor but with a more extensive instrumentation, with an intended start in early 2006.

However, one of the members of the advisory board of the study, a representative of the private sector of day-care centre businesses, published a negative evaluation of the third NCKO monitor on the worldwide web, and his organisation (the MO group) called for a boycott of the NCKO follow-up study and advised affiliated childcare centres to close their doors to NCKO researchers. The minister urged the NCKO to break off and delay the follow-up study. Governmental representatives in the advisory board pushed for changes in the research design to accommodate the private sector interests. We decided to refuse further funding (some millions of euros) and to disengage from the compromised quality monitor study. The interfering MO group received a substantial subsidy for work on quality improvement.

Academic freedom is under attack when civil servants, often less familiar with science than professional scientists, roughly outline research projects on which commercial and university research groups can bid, exercising their administrative influence as a 'fourth power'. The selection of the winning research proposal is in the hands of the government. The fierce competition leads to stranglehold contracts with overly tight funding, adapted short-cut procedures, or conditional publication of the results. When findings are disappointing or unexpected, such as in our case with the day-care quality monitor, interest groups may try to use their influence, which is a blatant transgression of the academic freedom to publish whatever unwelcome results have been found. Media attention causes panic in policy and practice. Rushed policymakers start setting up another study without drawing conclusions from the previous one; unwanted outcomes lead to a request for new research and postponement of policy changes.

Adversarial research

The NCKO project illustrates a clear-cut threat to academic freedom, defined as the right of scholars in their area of expertise to engage in research without fear of censorship, retribution, or persecution. Academic freedom encompasses the ability of individuals to challenge existing beliefs, express controversial opinions, and publish unwelcome results without fear of reprisal from government, special interest groups, or other influencers. We suggest that the follow-up of the NCKO study might have been more constructive and exciting by incorporating an adversarial approach. Researchers with more sceptical versus more optimistic views of day-care quality at the time of the third monitor might have been asked to work together on a design to settle the dispute, again without interference of commercial or political stakeholders.

Adversarial research can indeed be a more elegant way to deal with contrasting perspectives. In the USA the 'child-care war' had been raging at the start of the National Institute of Child Health and Human Development (NICHD) Study of Early Child Care and Youth Development (SECCYD), a $150-million cohort study of 1,364 US children that began in 1991 and officially ran until 2008 but is still continuing into these children's adulthood. Researchers with opposite interpretations of the literature on the effects of quality and quantity of centre day-care on child development were requested to collaborate in an adversarial research project (Crosnoe & Leventhal, 2016; see Preface; Chapter 18). The project developed into one of the most productive studies in developmental science and its data have been used by many (young) researchers in hundreds of papers on a large variety of hypotheses. Sometimes the empirical data left room for contrasting interpretations such as whether elevated scores on externalising behaviour related to day-care should be interpreted as aggression or assertiveness. Unfortunately, Jay Belsky with his contrarian view on the (negative) impact of quantity of day-care was criticised for ignoring the right of mothers to combine child rearing with work outside of the home instead of being considered a scientist who let the data tell the story (Belsky et al., 2020, Chapter 8).

A Cooperative Practitioners-Researchers Model

The pressure on researchers to work closely together with industrial or commercial stakeholders, policymakers, patient interest groups, or future targets of potentially actionable discoveries has been steadily growing, up to the point that large grant foundations such as the Wellcome Trust include such involvement as standard requirement in their funded research. PPI and CS are meant to democratise scientific research, allowing participants from diverse backgrounds and various knowledge levels to engage in scientific activities. Overall, the sympathetic aim is to make science more accessible to the public. But again we wonder: should the voice of the participants and other stakeholders be heard in all types of studies and in all stages of the research cycle?

In a graphical display Te Brinke and colleagues (2022) present the differences between traditional studies and a citizen science research process. Under the umbrella of active engagement of participants in multiple phases of the research process, the adolescent participants advised about relevant questions for research and collaborated on the development of design and methods and on recruitment of subjects. They provided data and advised on the interpretation and dissemination of the results to peers via social and other media. Two important differences with the researcher roles were that the citizen scientists did not participate in the data-analysis phase, and that they were absent as (co-)authors of the scientific publication.

In this study the involvement of three adolescents in the development of measurements for risk taking during COVID-19 was the most remarkable deviation from 'traditional' research. Their input led to re-labelling non-adherence to COVID-19 measures in contact with peers as 'positive risk taking', because transgressions of the social distancing rules would have a positive impact on their own and others' mental health (Te Brinke et al., 2022). In his essay on 'Children's participation: From tokenism to citizenship', Hart (1992) mentions the risk of selecting only a few articulate youth to participate on a conference panel. On the 'Ladder of Participation' (Arnstein, 1969) this would not count as genuine participation (Hart, 1992).

In our Cooperative Practitioners-Researchers Model we propose a somewhat different synergy. Practitioners (including clinicians and policymakers) may be involved in the beginning and end stages of the research process. They initiate the topic or help formulate relevant research domains and questions, which the researchers translate into testable research questions and hypotheses and link these to valid measures, adequate designs, and data-analytic plans. At the end of the research process, practitioners collaborate with researchers to interpret the findings, with a focus on the translational value and ethical implications of the results, and on ways to disseminate the study results to the public and to support implementing the findings in a responsible way in policy or practice (see Figure 16.1).

The ethical considerations in the phase of interpreting and translating research findings to policy or clinical practice are complex. Involving participants and the wider public in the research process allows those who are the subjects and targets of intervention studies to have a voice in shaping the research agenda and addressing translational issues

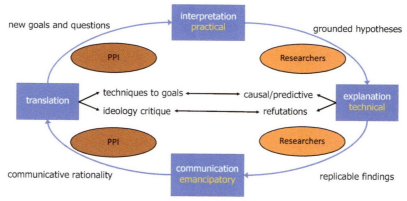

Figure 16.1 A Cooperative Practitioners-Researchers Model. Researchers are responsible for designing and conducting transparent and replicable research. Practitioners are involved in open communication about relevant research questions and about ethical implications of translating findings to policy or practice. Source: Authors.

(Liabo et al., 2018). Ideally the testing and replication stage leads to insight into causal or predictive associations that are the basis for technical means to translate to policy or practice, whereas refutations emerging from this stage lead to ideology critique as a translational revenue (see Figure 16.1). The three knowledge interests articulated by Habermas (1968) drive cooperation between practitioners and researchers in different stages of the research programme, with a practical interest stimulating interpretation of relevant questions for research, a technical interest driving explanatory studies, and an emancipatory interest connecting replication to translation via open communication about ethical obligations and boundaries (see Bohman & Rehg, 2017, Habermas, 1968 and Lempert, 1971, and the Epilogue of this book for the theoretical background of *Erkenntnisinteressen*).

A citizen assembly, based on 'sortition' or random selection of citizens, may be consulted and asked to propose a normative framework for social policy or application of the results (Van Reybrouck, 2016). This may provide an effective and democratic way to promote open communication and civic participation. Ethicists can facilitate the discourse between researchers, practitioners, and the public about the moral choices that inevitably arise. For example, instead of having risk-taking behaviours labelled in a normative way ('positive' versus 'negative') by fewer than a handful of participants (Te Brinke et al., 2022), a citizen assembly based on sortition might create a firmer basis for such complicated value-laden issues.

Last but not least, the research process is iterative, and practitioners are actively involved throughout the development of a research programme, consulting with researchers and offering insights into evolving research questions and findings. The key feature of this cooperative model is the recognition of the distinct and complementary responsibilities of researchers and practitioners, based on their specific areas of expertise. Current participatory or action research projects seem to aim for identical contributions of researchers and participating youth to the research process in most, if not all, stages, including the application of the results to policy or practice. According to its proponents, action research should really be research intertwined with action to change policies and practices. For example, in published projects using participants in research McCabe et al. (2022) reported a majority of these projects involving them in almost all stages of research, including data analysis. Crucial question is how replication as a necessary condition of translation can be established in action research with blurred boundaries between intertwined research and action.

In a 'contemporary narrative review' (i.e., without systematic search) Racine et al. (2023) discuss the importance of studies on child maltreatment involving 'experts by experience' despite the risk of re-traumatisation. They present five studies with various levels of involvement of participants as victims of sexual abuse. In three studies youth were members of a community advisory board, took part in designing participatory sessions, or were involved as research consultants to help identify priorities and develop a survey. But their participation in data analysis and writing was limited or non-existent. Only two ('holistic') studies involved youth in all stages of the research and considered them co-researchers. In the participatory action research on youth 'aging out of care' conducted by Doucet et al. (2021), three of eight participating youth shared their personal narratives as care leavers and became co-authors of the resulting publication. The action research was explicitly aiming to build advocacy capacity and contribute to transformative social change. Another 'holistic' participatory action research is the study of Matthew et al. (2019) about confidentiality concerns in survivors of sexual abuse. In total, 8 of 140 participants volunteered to be co-researchers and after some training in qualitative research they were involved in all parts of the research, including thematic data analysis. Except for some discussion about transparency of the thematic coding approach, the challenges for replicability and validity of the research process and results were not addressed. No experts by experience were co-author of the Matthew et al. (2019) publication, which might be understandable in a study on confidentiality and disclosure of sexual abuse.

To address the challenges of participatory action research in establishing replicability and validity, we emphasize a sharp differentiation of responsibilities between participants and other stakeholders on the one hand and researchers on the other hand. This role differentiation is crucial for maintaining the integrity of the research process, that was violated in our study on day-care quality, but also in the holistic action research projects where intersubjectivity of process and product were insufficiently ensured. In our view researchers should be responsible for the scientific validity by safeguarding strict adherence to transparency and replicability. Replicability is the *sine qua non* of translatability and is therefore prioritised in the cycle of research and implementation. Practitioners cannot be held responsible for the overall research process. From the perspective of our Cooperative Practitioners-Researchers Model, calling them 'co-researchers' would be incorrect. The same goes for assigning them co-authorship, which would be at odds with the current author guidelines of most scientific journals (see, e.g., the International Committee of Medical Journal Editors (2023) definitions of the role of authors and contributors).

In their research, scholars on their part should resist the temptation to become 'policymakers' or even 'politicians' at the same time (Van IJzendoorn, 2019), as blurring the boundaries between science and politics is infringing on academic freedom. We argued that in collaborative research the division of expertise and responsibilities between researchers and participants or other stakeholders should be made explicit and safeguarded. We propose three criteria for the complicated relation between academic freedom, action, and research. First, academic freedom can only be enjoyed in the scholar's specific area of scientific expertise; second, any translation through action to policy or practice should be rooted in replicated evidence; and third, political or social activism cannot be part of research which aims at establishing the evidence base needed for translation. Academic freedom may be balanced by scholars avoiding using their professorial prestige for political action outside the area of scientific expertise, or within an area of expertise with a still brittle evidence base. Of course, scholars are also ordinary citizens who can take part in political or social activism, where the universal right of freedom of speech should protect them.

References

Arnstein, S. (1969). A ladder of citizen participation. *Journal of the American Planning Association*, *35*(4), 216–224. https://doi.org/10.1080/01944366908977225

Bakermans-Kranenburg, M. J., & Van IJzendoorn, M. H. (2019). Dimensions, determinants, and development of prosocial behavior: A differential susceptibility hypothesis on attachment and moral character. In E. Harcourt (Ed.), *Attachment and Character: Attachment Theory, Ethics, and the Developmental Psychology of Vice and Virtue* (pp. 44–70) Oxford University Press. https://doi.org/10.1093/oso/9780192898128.003.0003

Belsky, J., Caspi, A., Moffitt, T. E., & Poulton, R. (2020). *The Origins of You: How Childhood Shapes Later Life*. Harvard University Press. https://doi.org/10.4159/9780674245143

Biesta, G. J. J., Miedema, S., & Van IJzendoorn, M. H. (1990). John Dewey's reconstruction of the reflex-arc concept and its relevance for Bowlby's attachment theory. In W. J. Baker, M. E. Hijland, R. van Hezewijk, & S. Terwee (Eds.), *Recent Trends in Theoretical Psychology, Volume 2* (pp. 211–221). Springer. https://doi.org/10.1007/978-1-4613-9688-8_19

Bohman, J., & Rehg, W. (2017). Jürgen Habermas. In E. N. Zalta (Ed.), *The Stanford Encyclopedia of Philosophy* (Fall 2017 ed.). Retrieved from https://plato.stanford.edu/archives/fall2017/entries/habermas/

Chekhov, A. (1891). *The Duel. The Complete Short Novels*. Vintage Classics.

Clements, T., & Harding, E. (2023). Addressing the withdrawal of playtime: A collaborative action research project. *Educational Psychology in Practice*, *39*(3), 257–272, DOI: 10.1080/02667363.2023.2194610

Coughlan, B., Duschinsky, R., Bakermans-Kranenburg, M., Bakkum, L., Skinner, G., Markham, A., Beckwith, H., & Van IJzendoorn, M. H. (2022, December 19). Sequelae of child maltreatment: Umbrella synthesis on mental health correlates in over 11 million participants. *PsyArXiv*. Retrieved from https://doi.org/10.31234/osf.io/zj7kb

Crosnoe, R., & Leventhal, T. (2016). The child care wars. In R. Crosnoe & T. Leventhal (Eds.), *Debating Early Child Care: The Relationship between Developmental Science and the Media* (pp. 1–26). Cambridge University Press. doi:10.1017/CBO9781316144855.001

Cuyvers, B., Verhees, M., Van IJzendoorn, M. H., Bakermans-Kranenburg, M. J., Rowe, A. C. M., Ceulemans, E., & Bosmans, G. (2022). The effect of attachment priming on state attachment security in middle childhood: The moderating roles of trait attachment and state attachment volatility. *Journal of Early Adolescence*, *43*(2), 164–193. https://doi.org/10.1177/02724316221099871

Doucet, M., Pratt, H., Dzhenganin, M., & Read, J. (2021). Nothing about us without us: Using participatory action research (PAR) and arts-based methods as empowerment and social justice tools in doing research with youth 'aging out' of care. *Child Abuse & Neglect*, 105358. https://doi.org/10.1016/j.chiabu.2021.105358

Euser, S., Alink, L. R. A., Pannebakker, F., Vogels, T., Bakermans-Kranenburg, M. J., & Van IJzendoorn, M. H. (2013). The prevalence of child maltreatment in the Netherlands across a 5-year period. *Child Abuse & Neglect*, *37*. https://doi.org/10.1016/j.chiabu.2013.07.004

Feyerabend P. (1975). *Against Method: Outline of an Anarchistic Theory of Knowledge*. New Left Books. https://doi.org/10.1007/bf02383263

Habermas, J. (1968). *Erkenntnis und Interesse [Knowledge and Human Interests]*. Suhrkamp.

Hart, R. A. (1992). *Children's Participation: From Tokenism to Citizenship*, Innocenti Essay, No. 4, International Child Development Centre, Florence, Italy.

International Committee of Medical Journal Editors (ICMJE). (2023, April 8). *Defining the Role of Authors and Contributors*. Retrieved from www.icmje.org/recommendations/browse/roles-and-responsibilities/defining-the-role-of-authors-and-contributors.html

Lempert, W. (1971). *Leistungsprinzip und Emanzipation. Studien zur Realität, Reform und Erforschung des beruflichen Bildungswesens* [Principles of Achievement and Emancipation]. Suhrkamp Verlag.

Lenin, V. I. (1930). *One Step Forward, Two Steps Back*. Lenin Collected Works.

Liabo, K., Boddy, K., Burchmore, H., Cockcroft, E., & Britten, N. (2018). Clarifying the roles of patients in research. *BMJ British Medical Journal*, *361*, k1463. https://doi.org/10.1136/bmj.k1463

Matthew, L., Barron, I., & Hodson, A. (2019). Participatory action research: Confidentiality and attitudes of victimized young people unknown to child protection agencies. *International Journal on Child Maltreatment*, *2*, 79–97. https://doi.org/10.1007/s42448-019-00020-x

McCabe, E., Amarbayan, M., Rabi, S., Mendoza, J., Naqvi, S. F., Thapa Bajgain, K., & Santana, M. (2022). Youth engagement in mental health research: A systematic review. *Health Expectations*. https://doi.org/10.1111/hex.13590

Mesman, J., Janssen, S., & Van Rosmalen, L. (2016). Black Pete through the eyes of Dutch children. *PLOS ONE, 11*(6), e0157511. https://doi.org/10.1371/journal.pone.0157511

Messiou, K. (2019). Collaborative action research: Facilitating inclusion in schools. *Educational Action Research, 27*, 197–209.

O'Farrelly, C., Barker, B., Watt, H., Babalis, D., Bakermans-Kranenburg, M., Byford, S., Ganguli, P., Grimås, E., Iles, J., Mattock, H., McGinley, J., Phillips, C., Ryan, R., Scott, S., Smith, J., Stein, A., Stevens, E., Van IJzendoorn, M., Warwick, J., & Ramchandani, P. (2021). A video-feedback parenting intervention to prevent enduring behaviour problems in at-risk children aged 12–36 months: The Healthy Start, Happy Start RCT. *Health Technology Assessment, 25*(29).

Power, C. (1988). The Just Community approach to moral education. *Journal of Moral Education, 17*(3), 195–208. https://doi.org/10.1080/0305724880170304

Racine, N., Greer, K., Dimitropoulos, G., Collin-Vézina, D., Henderson, J. L., & Madigan, S. (2023). Youth engagement in child maltreatment research: Gaps, barriers, and approaches. *Child Abuse & Neglect, 139*, 106127. https://doi.org/10.1016/j.chiabu.2023.106127

Schweizer, S., Leung, J. T., Kievit, R., et al. (2019). Protocol for an app-based affective control training for adolescents: Proof-of-principle double-blind randomized controlled trial [version 2; peer review: 4 approved]. *Wellcome Open Research, 4*, 91. https://doi.org/10.12688/wellcomeopenres.15229.2

Sedlak, A. J., Mettenburg, J., Basena, M., Petta, I., McPherson, K., Greene, A., & Li, S. (2010). *Fourth National Incidence Study of Child Abuse and Neglect (NIS–4):* Report to Congress, Executive Summary. U.S. Department of Health and Human Services, Administration for Children and Families, Washington, DC.

Starreveld, K. M., Overbeek, M. M., Willemen, A. M., & Bakermans-Kranenburg, M. J. (2023). Adapting a video-feedback intervention to support teacher–child interaction and behavior regulation of young children at school: A qualitative pilot study. *School Psychology International*. https://doi.org/10.1177/01430343231184001

Te Brinke, L. W., Van der Cruijsen, R., Green, K. H., & Crone, E. A. (2022). Positive and negative risk-taking in adolescence and early adulthood: A citizen science study during the COVID-19 pandemic. *Frontiers in Psychology, 13*, 885692. https://doi.org/10.3389/fpsyg.2022.88569

Van IJzendoorn, M. H. (2019). Addressing the replication and translation crises taking one step forward, two steps back? A plea for slow experimental research instead of fast 'participatory' studies. In S. Hein & J. Weeland (Eds.), Alternatives to Randomized Controlled Trials (RCTs) in Studying Child and Adolescent Development in Clinical and Community Settings. *New Directions for Child and Adolescent Development, 167*, 133–140. https://doi.org/10.1002/cad.20308

Van IJzendoorn, M. H. (1984). Enkele hardnekkige paradoxen van kritisch-psychologisch actieonderzoek [Some paradoxes of critical action research]. *Tijdschrift voor Agologie, 13*, 95–106.

Van IJzendoorn, M. H. (2007). Onderzoek, beleid, praktijk: pleidooi voor gescheiden verantwoordelijkheden geïllustreerd aan de hand van de casus kinderopvang. In A. Soeteman & F. Van den Born (Eds.), *Ethiek van empirisch sociaal-wetenschappelijk onderzoek* (pp. 43–52). Koninklijke Nederlandse Akademie van Wetenschappen (KNAW).

Van IJzendoorn, M. H., & Bakermans-Kranenburg, M. J. (2021). Replication crisis lost in translation? On translational caution and premature applications of attachment theory. *Attachment & Human Development, 23*, 422–437. https://doi.org/10.1080/14616734.2021.1918453

Van IJzendoorn, M. H., & Miedema, S. (1986). De kwaliteit van kwalitatief onderzoek [The quality of qualitative studies]. *Pedagogische Studiën, 63*, 498–505.

Van IJzendoorn, M. H., & Van der Veer, R. (1983). Holzkamp's critical psychology and the functional-historical method: A critical appraisal. *Storia e Critica della Psicologia, 4*, 5–26.

Van IJzendoorn, M. H., & Vermeer, H. (2014). How to protect scientific integrity under social and political pressure: Applied day-care research between science and policy. In R. J. Sternberg & S. T. Fiske (Eds.), *Ethical Challenges in the Behavioral and Brain Sciences Case Studies and Commentaries* (pp. 212–216). Cambridge University Press.

Van Reybrouck, D. (2016). *Against Elections: The Case for Democracy*. Bodley Head.

Vermeer, H. J., Van IJzendoorn, M. H., De Kruif, R. E. L., Fukkink, R. G., Tavecchio, L. W. C., Riksen-Walraven, J. M. A., & Van Zeijl, J. (2008). Child care in the Netherlands: Trends in quality over the years 1995–2005. *Journal of Genetic Psychology, 169*, 360–385. https://doi.org/10.3200/GNTP.169.4.360-385

17
Caution: personal conflicts of interest

Various conflicts of interest

A growing number of journals require authors to disclose not only their financial interests in their research but also their non-financial interests. Questions are asked about personal political, religious, sexual, and gender preferences and practices that 'might cloud objectivity' (Editorial of 31 January 2018, *Nature* journals). Instead of promoting objectivity, we argue that such disclosure requirements endanger academic freedom and even infringe on authors' universal human rights.

Many scientists who did great work also expressed debatable or even abject ideas and prejudices. Whatever we feel about the extreme left or right, woke or anti-woke beliefs, as scientists (authors, reviewers, editors) we should evaluate only their work. Not the author but the text and the data reported in the text are the objects of scrutiny through secondary analysis and replications. We argue that the reproducibility and replicability crisis in science will not be solved with transparency about the authors' personal lifestyle and beliefs. Potential non-financial conflicts of interest cannot be reliably identified in self or others nor sanctioned adequately, because standards for non-financial conflict of interest are absent.

Non-financial conflicts of interest

In March 2018 Marinus was required to sign a *Full Conflict of Interest Disclosure Form* for a paper to be published in *Child Development*, the flagship journal of the Society for Research on Child Development (SRCD).

The experience triggered this chapter. It is difficult to understand *prima facie* why the following stipulation is included in the Conflicts of Interest form and why it would be relevant for scientific integrity: 'Other non-financial sources of conflict or bias, such as personal or political beliefs in direct conflict with the topic being researched' (www.srcd.org/sites/default/files/file-attachments/srcd_conflict_of_interest_disclosure_form-final.pdf, downloaded 22 February 2023). The question is why political or personal beliefs or (non-financial) affiliations might in any way be relevant to the evaluation of the scientific work on whatever topic. Declaring so-called non-financial conflicts of interest seems to infringe on authors' right to have a personal life, with private political or religious beliefs and activities.

In the original form the disclosure requirement was operationalised in questions 8 and 9 of the disclosure form: '8. Other conflicts: Please identify any political or other personal beliefs or affiliations that may contribute to a perception of bias regarding the topic of the work. 9. Other relationships: Please list other activities and relationships that an editor or reader could perceive to be a potential influence on the research you directly or indirectly referenced in this manuscript'. These explanations were deleted from the most recent form (downloaded on 22 February 2023) but they were replaced by similar text (see Figure 17.1). Indirect influences were added that need not focus specifically on the work to be published. Furthermore, the range of potentially conflicting interests was broadened to the perception thereof: 'Often, the perception of a possible conflict of interest is as important as an actual conflict and therefore any potential conflict must be disclosed, even if the author concludes that there is no actual conflict'. The form is introduced as in Figure 17.1.

The SRCD states that 'in developmental science, as in other scientific disciplines, professional integrity includes a commitment to an objective, unbiased presentation of facts and their interpretation'. The somewhat naïve concept of objectivity in this statement goes back to the obsolete logical positivism of the early Wiener Kreis (Vienna Circle) at the beginning of the last century (Uebel, 2022). Scientific work, however, should be evaluated on its own merits as it is made public in manuscripts, not in light of whether the author would be living together with a partner without being married, or having political ideas considered to be extremely liberal or socialist, or even radical right. Voting behaviour is a personal choice that should not be required to be communicated to scientific editors or made public in any way, and the same is true for religious, anti-religious, or humanist beliefs and persuasions. Scientific authors

> In developmental science, as in other scientific disciplines, professional integrity includes a commitment to an objective, unbiased presentation of facts and their interpretation. Authors' interests have the potential to influence how their work is presented and how it is received by readers. Often, the perception of a possible conflict of interest is as important as an actual conflict, and therefore any potential conflict must be disclosed, even if the author concludes that there is no actual conflict. Conflicts of interest are not limited to direct financial or other economic relationships with other entities.
>
> Various types of conflicts include:
> - *Direct influence on the scholarship itself;*
> - *Indirect influence on the scholarship, such as through family, business or personal relationships, or similar arrangements influencing a person without directly focusing on the specific work;*
> - *Financial influence, such as compensation for any task related to the scholarship, employment-related compensation from an entity with a financial interest in the topic of the scholarship, or any profit from stock or intellectual property impacted by the subject of the scholarship;*
> - *Non-financial influence from a third-party, such as support or assistance during the research or writing process, or professional advancement based on the outcome of research; and/or*
> - *Other non-financial sources of conflict or bias, such as personal or political beliefs in direct conflict with the topic being researched, or a familial relationship with a person at an entity or enterprise that stands to benefit from or be harmed by the research.*
>
> Although potential conflicts of interest do not necessarily constitute actual conflicts of interest, scientific integrity requires disclosure of all affiliations and interests, allowing editors and readers to judge and, if necessary, consider the impact of bias on the scientific information being shared.

Figure 17.1 Full Conflict of Interest Disclosure Form of the Society for Research on Child Development.

should not allow screening for such beliefs during the process of evaluating their scientific work as publishable or in the process of the work to be published. This is at the core of academic freedom and more broadly freedom of speech, or freedom to be silent about personal beliefs.

Newton believed in astrology, Einstein was a pacifist during wartime, Heidegger was a Nazi, Sartre a Maoist, Darwin has been accused of being an atheist and an anti-feminist, and Watson (discoverer of the double helix) a sexist, as were Trivers and many other scientists who did great work. Whatever we feel about such beliefs, as scientists (authors, reviewers, editors) we should try to evaluate their work as part of World 3 in the sense of Karl Popper (1978), independent of the person who conducted a study and wrote a paper. World 1 is the physical world of objects and matter, World 2 is the world of subjective experiences and mental phenomena, and World 3 is the world of ideas, theories, and cultural products such as art, literature, and science. Popper argued that World 3 is a distinct domain of reality that is created by the collective of scientists, artists, and intellectuals and exists independently of individual human minds. In Chapter 1 we discussed the replication crisis in World 3. Not the author but the text and the findings reported in the text are the object of scrutiny, of reproducibility through secondary analysis and replicability through meta-analytic syntheses (see Chapter 3). As an aside, the same notion of separating the work from the author is proposed by Nick Cave who argues against cancelling songs because of the musician's despicable ideas or behaviours: 'We need to understand that the songs themselves are the best of them' and we should not 'eradicate the best of these people in order to punish the worst of them' (Cave, interviewed by Lucy Knight for the *Guardian*, 28 May 2023).

If author and study are conflated, the risk of a new kind of McCarthyism arises (Reichman, 2022) of which Linus Pauling, Robert Oppenheimer, Edward Condon, Joseph Weinberg, and many other scientists suffered in the 1950s, being accused of communist sympathies. Less famous scientists were also forced to resign from their jobs, blacklisted from employment, or saw their careers and reputations destroyed because of false accusations and politically motivated investigations. If one of John Bowlby's most important sources of inspiration, the ethologist, attachment researcher, and pacifist activist Robert Hinde (Hinde & Rotblat, 2003) would have lived in the USA in the 1950s he would certainly have been a target of the overzealous Joseph McCarthy, leader of the infamous House Committee on Un-American Activities. Closer to modern times, we should remind ourselves of the risks of the Erdogan-type persecution experienced by our scientific colleagues in Turkey in the wake of the failed coup in 2016. Hundreds of university professors and administrators were dismissed without due process from their tenured positions because of their political ideas, even without any participation in the coup. Due to the stigma of 'terrorists', many have been unable to find any alternative work at all; they lost housing and health care benefits and their passports (Amnesty International, 2017).

When the issue of (collateral) abuse of the disclosure form was brought to attention of the Managing Editor of the SRCD, she responded: 'If an author is publishing a paper on political engagement and has made it his/her lifelong goal to promote political activism, that is something that should be disclosed. We want to support the transparency of readers having all available information, not police and judge researchers'. We disagree and we draw a parallel to clarify why we disagree. If an author is an active but 'closeted' or private homosexual and submits a paper to one of the SRCD journals on homosexual couples with children and the (lack of) effects on child development, he or she is required to report his or her homosexuality on the Full Conflict of Interest Disclosure Form – even though he or she may have come from a country (where their family may still live and to which they might want to return) in which such a personal orientation is forbidden by law (for example, in Iran and in Saudi Arabia same-sex sexual activity is illegal and punishable by death under Islamic law). Note that also in some Western countries individuals sometimes choose to not go public with their homosexual orientation because they are afraid of discrimination.

Should they be forced to come out on the Full Conflict of Interest Disclosure Form? If not reporting being homosexual on the form they would sign a lie. One could think of numerous examples of a similar kind, e.g., being abused in childhood and studying the prevalence of child abuse, or having AIDS and reporting on a study on HIV-infected children's development, or being active in Amnesty International and presenting a scientific critique on a flawed study on Black Pete. Even if an author does not consider a personal interest to be an example of potential conflicts of interest the SRCD still requests disclosure because it is left to the reader to decide whether any conflict exists.

Requiring to declare potential non-financial conflicts of interest concerning private beliefs and practices in case of scientific writing might infringe on basic privacy rights and be in conflict with the Universal Declaration of Human Rights (United Nations General Assembly, 1948) for example, with Article 12 ('No one shall be subjected to arbitrary interference with his privacy, family, home or correspondence, nor to attacks upon his honour and reputation'), Article 18 ('Everyone has the right to freedom of thought, conscience and religion'), and Article 19 ('Everyone has the right to freedom of opinion and expression; this right includes freedom to hold opinions without interference'). Furthermore, the admission of such personal beliefs and activities is a useless requirement for a disclosure form because these potential conflicts of interest cannot be defined accurately, be reliably identified in self or others, or be sanctioned adequately, because standards for non-financial conflicts of interest are simply too vague.

Fifteen years ago, the *PLoS Medicine* Editors (2008) acknowledged this problem in their paper *Making Sense of Non-Financial Competing Interests*. They wrote:

> Establishing such a standard is by no means easy. The BMJ abandoned attempts to require declarations of non-financial competing interests (it now simply encourages disclosure) because the definitions were disputed and the policy unworkable … Neither JAMA, Nature Medicine, The New England Journal of Medicine, nor Science require disclosure of private interests. A recent discussion on the listserv of the World Association of Medical Editors (WAME), whose editorial policy committee … is currently updating its Conflict-of-Interest policy, affirms how difficult it is to define and regulate private interests. In the end, because WAME members felt that non-financial conflicts were so nebulous and unquantifiable, WAME decided that the policy should remain focused on financial interests.

Recent developments

Despite these reservations, in recent years journals and scientific societies seem to change course and to move in the opposite direction of an ever more important place for disclosure of possible non-financial conflicts of interest in their publication guidelines. The publisher Taylor & Francis requires declaration of potential non-financial conflict of interest defined as 'Personal, political, religious, ideological, academic and intellectual competing interests which are perceived to be relevant to the published content' (Taylor & Francis website https://authorservices.taylorandfrancis.com/editorial-policies/competing-interest/ consulted on March 14, 2023). Recently the WAME 'has also included non-financial conflicts of interest (or the appearance of one) related to scholarly commitment: "intellectual passion" (the tendency to favour positions that one has already espoused or perhaps even established); personal relationships (the tendency to judge the works of friends/colleagues or competitors/foes differently because of the relationship); political or religious beliefs (the tendency to favour or reject positions because it affirms or challenges one's political or religious beliefs); and institutional affiliations (the tendency to favour or reject results of research because of one's institutional affiliations)' (www.wame.org/about/wame-editorial-on-coi). For the International Committee of Medical Journal Editors (ICMJE), Ferris and Fletcher (2010, 2019) list the following non-exhaustive conflicts of interest as examples: (a) Financial ties, (b) Academic commitments, (c) Personal relationships, (d) Political or religious beliefs, and (e) Institutional affiliations. In their updated Recommendations for the Conduct, reporting, editing, and publication of scholarly work in medical journals (International Committee of Medical Journal Editors, May 2022) it is stated that other interests than financial interests 'may also represent or be perceived as conflicts, such as personal relationships or rivalries, academic competition, and intellectual beliefs' (p. 3). Such vague descriptions potentially open a can of worms hampering adversarial research and critical analysis because publication of the results of such work could easily be blocked by reference to this guideline.

In an Editorial of 31 January 2018, the *Nature* journals are announced to 'tighten rules on non-financial conflicts' as authors 'will be asked to declare any interests that might cloud objectivity'. The reasoning points explicitly to the transparency and reproducibility crisis: 'Numerous studies have demonstrated that financial competing interests in industry-sponsored research have the potential to introduce bias into study design, analysis and reporting; by comparison, the impact of non-financial competing interests has been much less well studied. Nevertheless, it is fair to expect that these associations could colour study design, interpretation and the subsequent reception of published findings; to guard against that, a number of clinical and biomedical journals have required disclosures of non-financial interests for several years. At a time when there is increasing scrutiny of the scientific process, transparent disclosures that allow readers to form their own conclusions about the published work are the best way to maintain public trust' (www.nature.com/articles/d41586-018-01420-8).

What seems to happen here is that one tries to solve the reproducibility and replication crisis in science with transparency about the authors' personal life and beliefs. Public trust instead of scientific progress seems to become the main goal even for the prestigious *Nature* journals. However, the only solution for reproducibility is detailed description of research design and procedures and, on that basis, the independent conduct of replication after replication after replication, to establish whether we have a real finding or a false-positive result. In the context of bold conjectures and tenacious refutation efforts (sensu Karl Popper, 1959) we do not need confessions about the authors' private lifestyles and belief systems. Should we now feel that Darwin's evolutionary theory is suspicious because he had Victorian beliefs about women (albeit progressive ones for his time and age)? We hope not, as his theory deserves to be critically scientifically evaluated independent of his personality, religious beliefs, and personal life. Whether such evaluation is conducted by atheists or creationists should not matter for the final scientific verdict resulting from scientific research and debate (see Chapter 3). It would be a chutzpah if researchers of the aftermath of the Holocaust were forced to report on their race or religion (see Chapter 6).

The impossibility to report all potential conflicts of interests

A crucial problem is also that we do not know the role of belief systems in the production and reproduction of scientific knowledge, especially when we assume – on empirical grounds – that implicit biases that we are not aware of might influence our behaviour. We are unaware of them, so we are unable to report on them. We may have distanced ourselves from explicit Victorian ideas about women, but there might still be more covert and implicit prejudices that we are unaware of. If it is impossible to report potential non-financial conflicts of interest exhaustively, we would better make our science independent of such necessarily failing efforts to list these conflicts in disclosure forms. We better rely on programmatic replication efforts to enhance transparency, reproducibility, and replicability of our research. Of course, the case for declaring financial conflicts of interest is much better validated (Fontanarosa & Bauchner, 2017) and easier to examine (Zavalis & Ioannidis, 2022).

Although PLoS ONE threatens with the strongest sanctions ('Failure to declare competing interests can result in immediate rejection of a manuscript') the PLoS ONE editors seem to acknowledge the problem of self-disclosure: 'Everyone has competing interests; financial or private, or both. The main problem with competing interests is nondisclosure ... As with all competing interests, it is not possible to reliably judge our own biases. Instead, declaring them allows others to make informed judgments about whether the competing interests are relevant or not'. This latter part of the reasoning is a classic non-sequitur: if we cannot disclose all our potential conflicts of interest because the cultural or political context makes it too dangerous to disclose, or because we have implicit biases that we are unable to recognise, the readers will not be able to make informed judgments. A final argument against the request for authors' declaration of non-financial Conflicts of Interest is that Declaration of Conflict of Interest forms are formatted like self-report questionnaires (see Society for Research in Child Development, April 10, 2023). In Chapter 2 we have argued that biased answers to such questionnaires are inevitable and a reason to stop such measures of complex traits in the developmental sciences.

Research in non-WEIRD countries

Instead of requiring declarations of non-financial Conflicts of Interest, journals should focus on identifiable research behaviour. For example, empirical studies should be in agreement with ethical guidelines regarding the way in which participants are invited, how informed consent is organised, and how protection of data and personal security and integrity are guaranteed. In designing a study in a non-WEIRD environment (WEIRD being Western, Educated, Industrialised, Rich, and Democratic, Henrich et al., 2010), the opportunities for involving and educating junior researchers in methods and substantive components of the study should be considered a necessary component. Collecting data in LMICs and then exporting them to WEIRD academia without local students, professionals, and researchers benefitting from the work should not be allowed. Such export is not much different from Shell exporting crude oil from Nigeria to the Netherlands to be processed there, leaving pollution behind. Two-thirds of the authors of studies on COVID-19 in Africa during the first 9 months of 2020 were not from Africa, and a quarter of the papers had no African author at all (Horn et al., 2023). More in line with the Cape Town Statement on Fostering Research Integrity Through the Promotion of Fairness, Equity, and Diversity (Horn et al., 2023), our work with Zambian and Kenyan students and junior faculty supported by the Lolle Nauta Foundation led to doctoral dissertations defended at local universities and papers first-authored by the local PhD candidates (see www.LolleNautaFoundation.eu).

Conclusion

The only way out is to scrutinise and replicate studies of colleagues whose personal beliefs we feel to be strange or even despicable, to find out whether findings are reproducible and replicable. As a consequence, studies should only be evaluated on the basis of the coherence of the theories involved, the validity of the data collected, and the logic of the reasoning used to connect theories and data. In World 3 the authors' personal beliefs or lifestyles are obsolete, and the academic freedom to conduct critical debates and replications without retaliation is essential.

References

Amnesty International. (2017). No end in sight. Purged public sector workers denied a future in Turkey. Retrieved February 22, 2023, from www.amnestyusa.org/wp-content/uploads/2017/05/No-End-In-Sight-ENG.pdf

Ferris, L. E., & Fletcher, R. H. (2010). Conflict of interest in peer-reviewed medical journals: The World Association of Medical Editors position on a challenging problem. *Journal of Young Pharmacists: JYP, 2*(2), 113–115. https://doi.org/10.4103/0975-1483.63143

Ferris, E., & Fletcher, R. H. (2019). WAME Editorial on Conflict of Interest: Conflict of Interest in Peer-Reviewed Medical Journals: The World Association of Medical Editors (WAME) Position on a Challenging Problem. Retrieved February 22, 2023, from www.wame.org/about/wame-editorial-on-coi

Fontanarosa, P., & Bauchner, H. (2017). Conflict of interest and medical journals. *Journal of the American Medical Association.* https://doi.org/10.1001/jama.2017.4563

Henrich, J., Heine, S. J., & Norenzayan, A. (2010). The weirdest people in the world? *Behavioral and Brain Sciences, 33*(2–3), 61–135. https://doi.org/10.1017/S0140525X0999152X

Hinde, R., & Rotblat, J. (2003). *War No More: Eliminating Conflict in the Nuclear Age.* Pluto Press.

Horn, L., Alba, S., Gopalakrishna, G., Kleinert, S., Kombe, F., Lavery, J. V., & Visagie, R. G. (2023). The Cape Town Statement on fairness, equity and diversity in research. *Nature, 615*, 790–793. https://doi.org/10.1038/d41586-023-00855-y

International Committee of Medical Journal Editors. (2022). Recommendations for the conduct, reporting, editing, and publication of scholarly work in medical journals. www.icmje.org/recommendations/

PLoS Medicine Editors. (2008). Making sense of non-financial competing interests. *PLoS Medicine, 5*(9), e199. https://doi.org/10.1371/journal.pmed.0050199

Popper, K. (1959). *The Logic of Scientific Discovery.* Routledge.

Popper, K. (1978). *Three Worlds.* In *The Tanner Lecture on Human Values.* The University of Michigan.

Reichman, H. (2022). *Understanding academic freedom.* University of Chicago Press.

Society for Research in Child Development. (2023). Conflict of interest disclosure form. www.srcd.org/sites/default/files/file-attachments/srcd_conflict_of_interest_disclosure_form-final.pdf

Uebel, T. (2022). Vienna Circle. In E. N. Zalta & U. Nodelman (Eds.), *The Stanford Encyclopedia of Philosophy* (Fall 2022 Edition). https://plato.stanford.edu/archives/fall2022/entries/vienna-circle/

United Nations General Assembly. (1948). *Universal Declaration of Human Rights* (UN General Assembly Resolution 217 A).

Zavalis, E. A., & Ioannidis, J. P. A. (2022). A meta-epidemiological assessment of transparency indicators of infectious disease models. *PLoS ONE, 17*(10), e0275380. https://doi.org/10.1371/journal.pone.0275380

18
Academic freedom in 'safe spaces'

Cancel culture in the past

In the roaring seventies of the last century, militant students and young faculty members effectively hindered some professors in their efforts to teach or conduct their research because they would have politically incorrect social or scientific ideas. At the University of Amsterdam, a famous example was political scientist Hans Daudt. He was one of the targets of a group of students who interfered with his lectures in the presence of a majority of 'passive bystanders'. Some of them militant communist students themselves, they opposed the more conservative political views of Daudt. They disrupted his lectures and demanded a less traditional lecture style of teaching as well as more 'anti-capitalist' content. Mobbing was the name of the game (Harper, 2009; Van Esterik, 2016). After several years of student protests and administrative manipulations, Daudt felt forced to abstain from teaching large classes. As an undergraduate of the University of Amsterdam in the 1970s Marinus experienced the spillover effects of this successful mobbing in the Department of Educational Science. It led to the dismantling of some of the best (neurobiological and statistical) parts of the educational curriculum because some vocal students deemed them irrelevant to the study of child development.

The Buikhuisen affair at Leiden University was another example. At the end of the 1970s, the criminologist Wouter Buikhuisen (1979) presented his proposal to conduct biopsychosocial research on criminality in search of the neurobiological basis of criminal behaviour. He was critical of the usual socioeconomic explanation of criminality and wanted to examine a complex model of situational and personal characteristics such as genetic, endocrine, psychophysical, and biochemical factors leading to criminality. Because of these contrarian plans he was rather viciously attacked and condemned in the media. Some opponents even labelled him a 'fascist' because of his emphasis on the biological basis of criminal behaviour. Irrespective of the validity of his plans, which now may sound either naïve or overly ambitious, what happened was a massive assault on academic freedom. The result was that Buikhuisen had to retire before he even could show the (lack of) feasibility of his research programme. Several decades later the respective Amsterdam and Leiden university administrators rehabilitated Daudt and Buikhuisen. But at the time of the assaults on academic freedom the highest administrative echelons of both universities lacked the courage to support them and followed the mob of vocal students and upwards mobile faculty in their fight against the 'dissenting' old guards.

Social safety: a buzzword?

Currently, controversies that touch upon academic freedom are mostly related to social safety. Recently, law students at Stanford University interrupted an invited lecture by a conservative federal judge because they felt uncomfortable with the speaker's 'anti-woke' viewpoints. Students and faculty increasingly complain about feeling unsafe because they feel high pressure to achieve, because they are taught theories they do not like (e.g., evolutionary theory), or because they are confronted with unwelcome feedback on their social skills, scientific achievements, or ideas. Or they feel easy targets of such mostly anonymous complaints. The Max Planck Society conducted a survey among 9,000 employees on the workplace culture in their 86 prestigious research institutes. About 13% of the scientific staff reported having been bullied in the past, such as having opinions ignored or being unfairly blamed, publicly humiliated, or shouted at (Abbott, 2019). The survey was initiated because of some widely publicised cases of institute directors accused of bullying, among others, the director of the Max Planck Institute for the Science of Human History, Nicole Boivin; the director of the Max Planck Institute for Astrophysics, Guinevere Kauffmann; and the director of the Max Planck Institute for Human Cognitive and Brain Sciences, Tania Singer. In 2018, nearly 300 academics including senior professors and lab directors at top universities were accused of bullying students or colleagues in the UK. A culture of harassment and intimidation was said to be thriving in Britain's leading universities, with aggressive behaviours, extreme pressures to deliver results, or career sabotage as examples (Devlin & Marsh, 2018). A culture of so-called 'micro-aggression' seemed uncovered.

What is considered bullying or harassment? One of the largest grant foundations worldwide, the Wellcome Trust in the UK, defined bullying as 'any offensive, intimidating, malicious or insulting behaviour (which) can make the person being bullied feel vulnerable, upset, humiliated, undermined or threatened'. Harassment is defined as 'any unwanted physical, verbal or non-verbal conduct that has the purpose or effect of violating a person's dignity or creating an intimidating, hostile, degrading, humiliating or offensive environment for them. It may be persistent or a single incident' (Wellcome Trust, n.d.). These definitions make clear that bullying and harassment are container terms with heterogenous content. Furthermore, the perceptions and feelings of the 'victims' instead of the actual behaviours are crucial. The implication is that in legal procedures truth- or fact-finding that aims at establishing the evidence related to a particular allegation is impossible. If only the perceptions or feelings of the complainants are taken into account, they cannot be wrong.

In recent years, universities were among a large number of corporations, organisations, and institutions that seemed to offer insufficient social safety for their employees. Social safety might be considered a 'meme' in the sense of Richard Dawkins' (1989) concept of cultural evolution. It spread rapidly through governmental agencies, hospitals, police forces, NGOs, art and sports institutions, the entertainment and hospitality industry, publishers, political parties, the parliament, and academia. In one of his newspaper columns Marcel Levi, current director of the Dutch Research Council (NWO) and former head of the University College London Hospitals, complained that social safety had become a buzzword without precise content and with expanding borders (*Het Parool*, 12 November 2022). He noted that employees sometimes invoke social safety issues when they receive negative but professional feedback on their functioning or products. Other examples pertain to filing safety complaints with the institute's confidential advisor because the complainants felt they experienced a colleague or supervisor as irritating or intellectually dominating. The damning responses in the regular and a-social media were immediate, and several individuals and even organisations rushed to demand Levi's resignation. Which, luckily and wisely, he did not follow. Indeed, the 'silent majority' in academia might have the same concerns as Levi articulated.

Complaints about workplace social safety could also easily be misused to get rid of opponents or competitors in the organisation. Both authors have at some points in their careers observed the chilling effects of vague and irrefutable anonymous complaints used to settle the score in a competitive environment with scarce resources. Because feelings and perceptions of the (anonymous) accusers are at stake, truth-finding becomes impossible. From an administrative perspective truth-finding is even unnecessary because the accusations themselves are sufficient reason for suspension or dismissal of the accused on grounds of 'disrupted relationships' or 'incompatibility of temperaments' (Schliesser, 2023). The absence of due process raises fairness concerns because the accused do not get the opportunity to defend themselves (according to the age-old principle 'audiatur et altera pars'). We even witnessed a case where not only the accuser remained anonymous but also the allegation itself was not disclosed. This violates the requirement of 'nemo tenetur se ipsum accusare' (see Alexievich, 2016, and Keilson,1933, for the devastating social consequences when this is considered acceptable). Convergence of various anonymous complaints might seem to substantiate their truth-value, but in most cases these complaints are products of mobbing and all but independent (Harper, 2009).

Three university features threatening social safety

In academic institutes at least three structural features easily create social safety concerns and would (perhaps even should) elicit justified complaints. The first is the hierarchical structure of academic organisations with full professors, chairs, deans, and vice-chancellors, who supervise the tenured faculty and decide about their promotions, often on subjective, not quantified grounds. The current move towards a system for evaluating and rewarding academic staff based on a qualitative narrative of their performance in teaching, research, and community service might tighten instead of levelling the academic hierarchies as it runs the risk of being irreproducible and non-replicable.

Secondly, way down the ladder we find in many universities as much as 50% of the workforce with a fixed or flexible contract who have to finish their doctoral thesis or post-doc publications in a too short time period, always with an eye on the next temporary grant or job. This is the revolving door policy, damned in a recent report of the European Parliament on academic freedom (Panel for the Future of Science and Technology, 2023). Moreover, several universities, among others, Erasmus University Rotterdam and VU Amsterdam, require PhD students to have four or more published papers included in their dissertation. This is curtailing the academic freedom of faculty that lose their autonomy to decide about quality and quantity of dissertation content. In the last 40 years our policy was explicitly to abstain from setting a minimum number of papers or requiring publication of any papers before the PhD defence. An organisation with unrealistic demands is inherently unsettling, intimidating, and unsafe (Rahal et al., 2023).

The continuously changing team composition of 'flex-workers' not only is often a waste of human capital but also makes it impossible to evaluate and reward the team instead of individual researchers. That leads to the third structural feature of unsafe universities. Modern scientific research is genuine teamwork; it functions like a symphony orchestra in which each member of an excellently functioning team is indispensable for the operation and success of the collective. Nevertheless, the reward structure has not changed in line with this development towards 'cooperative research'. It remains focused on the 'brilliant' front man or woman who is loaded with grants and awards. The most extreme example is the Nobel Prize for a maximum of three scientists working on the same topic, an archaic artefact dating back to the 19th century, and nowadays often leading to heated debates about biased selection of awardees and distressing oversight of prominent candidates. This is fruitful soil for proliferating 'jalousie de métier'. Nobel Prize–winning physicist Martinus Veltman complained that the Nobel Prize was an awful shadow over his life and his relationships with colleagues. He suggested abolishing the prize – albeit after he had received one (Van Delft, 2023).

A more modest example is the Spinoza Prize, which in the absence of worldwide competition sometimes is incorrectly labelled the Dutch Nobel Prize. The similarity is that the Spinoza Prize is also free to be spent on any study without red tape. Marinus was the happy recipient of this award in 2004, but in his opinion it should have been awarded to a steadfast team including colleagues like Femmie Juffer and Marian (e.g., see *Sections 1, 2,* and *3* for the results of this teamwork). The problem is that identifying individuals with outstanding academic achievements in a quantifiable and reproducible way is easier than selecting an outstanding team. Nevertheless, the top five symphony orchestras can be identified with relative consensus among experts (e.g., the *Gramophone* magazine top list based on reviews of performances and recordings). A research team might be evaluated in terms of team citations, number of successfully supervised PhD students and post-docs, and responsible and effective translation of their replicated findings to policy or practice.

Social safety and academic freedom

Social safety is extremely important in organisations facilitating scientific research and teaching. These are places of intense (team) competition with high stakes in terms of patents, publications, and reputations. In such organisations everyone should behave in accordance with non-abusive and non-exploitative interactions and relationships. Any misconduct should be brought to (fair) trial for safeguarding the rights of the victims. There is no place for sexual assault, touching, or coercion, nor for other criminal offences. In this respect, universities and research institutes are no different from other organisations where criminal law procedures are called upon. Evidently, physical or sexual assault is prohibited by law in most countries, and so are libel and slander. In some countries (e.g., France) bullying is prohibited by law, and other violations of social safety might become legally forbidden and may restrict academic freedom of the perpetrator after due process.

Thus, at the very least, academic freedom is limited by law. But 'limited by law' is not a licence for scholars to display any non-forbidden, uncivilised, or nasty behaviour. Institutional and collegial safeguards should be installed to protect and promote a safe work environment for everyone. However, the academic freedom of scholars to pursue research and express opinions in their area of expertise should not be curtailed, even when some criticism is unsettling and may make individuals feel vulnerable, upset, or rejected. Criticism may also pertain to the functioning of the university itself, its administrators, or its faculty. Universities are not communities, not a group of people who share common personal goals, values, ideologies, rituals, and warm relationships. In his 2018 Leiden anniversary lecture (Dies Lecture) Carel Stolker, former vice-chancellor of Leiden University, advocated for academic freedom but considered a safe workplace 'essential' because 'the University (is) much more a community of people than an organization. Good mutual relations are essential for a community' (Stolker, 2018).

We disagree with this prioritising of community values above academic freedom. As stated before, we stipulate academic freedom as the right of scholars in their area of expertise to conduct research, publish their findings, comment, and teach, without political, institutional, or ideological interference and the threat of cancelling, even if – or rather: especially if – their theories or findings run counter to prevailing views. Academic freedom should be a basic right, essential for independent, open, transparent science, only limited by universal human rights and their legal implications such as the right for everyone to be treated equally in equal cases. Discrimination on the grounds of religion, belief, political inclination, race, nationality, or gender should not be permitted. Fortunately, in most countries there are various laws and legal regulations and procedures to maintain this basic anti-discrimination article in any organisation, including universities and research centres.

The guiding principle of scientific practice is the academic freedom to acquire knowledge in a transparent and reproducible way. The core of the argument of Erwin Chemerinsky (dean of the law school at Berkeley) and Howard Gillman (chancellor of the University of California, Irvine) in their book *Free Speech on Campus* (2017) is absolute priority of this principle of academic freedom. Following the 'Report of the Committee on Freedom of Expression at Yale' (December 1974) and the 'Report of the Committee on Freedom of Expression' of the University of Chicago (2014), Chemerinsky and Gillman (2017) advocate for the priority of a principled academic freedom over the pragmatic demands that the university as a 'community' can impose. In their view academic freedom is not the cherry on top of the cake. To quote a famous Yale report (Committee on Freedom of Expression at Yale, 1974): 'For if a university is a place for knowledge … it cannot make its primary … value the fostering of friendship, solidarity, harmony, civility, or mutual respect. … it provides a forum for the new, the provocative, the disturbing, and the unorthodox. Free speech is a barrier to the tyranny of authoritarian or even majority opinion as to the rightness or wrongness of particular doctrines or thoughts'. An excellent university excels in being unsettling, was the answer of the dean of Stanford Law School, Jenny Martinez (letter on March 22, 2023), to her upset students and faculty.

In this context of social safety, it may be useful to be reminded of the way John Bowlby distinguished safety from security in attachment theory (see Chapter 7). He notes that safety is etymologically derived from the Latin word 'salvus', that is, the absence of injury, and security originates from 'se cura', that is, being without a care (John Bowlby cited in Duschinsky, 2020). In attachment theory, the primary evolutionary function of attachment figures and attachment relationships is to provide safety, increasing the child's chances for survival and reproductive fitness. In the optimal scenario, attachment relationships and figures also provide security. However, in an insecure attachment relationship the caregiver may still provide safety, even in the absence of security. The discussion on social safety and academic freedom would benefit from a similar distinction. Currently, social safety and unsafety in academia refer to a myriad of experiences, ranging from sexual assault to (lack of) feelings of harmony and friendship. Universities should provide safety, that is, protect students, administrative staff, and faculty from harm or injury. But it is not their first aim to provide feelings of security to their students, faculty, and other employees.

Academic freedom implies critical debate

Scientific integrity means that substantive arguments dominate the debate, even when they are unwelcome. As Karl Popper (1959), philosopher of science, argued, we can only approach truth by undermining cherished but untrue assumptions. That can indeed be painful, for example, when our study showing a promising association between the oxytocin receptor gene (OXTR) and sensitive parenting did not survive later meta-analytic scrutiny (see Chapter 3). Donald Campbell's evolutionary epistemology shows that the basic mechanism of science is 'variation and selective retention', that is, the production of a diversity of wild ideas, bold hypotheses and daring theories, and a rigorous selection of them in mutual, sometimes fierce, competition. And that can be terribly annoying for those who are committed to an untenable hypothesis and have invested in it for years. Those who cannot bear the pain of a collision of their own cherished conviction with the data and arguments of colleagues will feel more comfortable in organisations where the communitarian importance of good social relationships takes precedence.

Ever since the start of our academic careers, critical debate about our research or studies of colleagues has been part and parcel of our work. In one of the most memorable public clashes between attachment theory and temperamental models of child development in a full Ballroom Hall of the SRCD biennial meeting of 1995, Marinus exchanged opposite views with Nathan Fox about the meaning of adult attachment representations and intergenerational transmission of attachment. The debate was heated. It was published in *Psychological Bulletin* and has been cited frequently (Fox, 1995; Van IJzendoorn, 1995a, b). Yet, the past 15 years saw collaborations between the two opponents. In 2015 we presented an integration of temperament and attachment theory under the umbrella of differential susceptibility theory in the *Handbook of Temperament* (Van IJzendoorn & Bakermans-Kranenburg, 2015). At the same time, Nathan Fox began to do work on attachment, for example, in the ground-breaking Bucharest Early Intervention Project (Nelson, Fox, & Zeanah, 2014).

In the same vein of adversarial but fruitful debate is the example of our meta-analysis on the association between sensitive parenting and attachment security. The editor of *Child Development* invited several senior authors, Jay Belsky, Ross Thompson, and Phil Cowan, for critical commentaries. This led to a rebuttal titled 'In search of the absent father' (Van IJzendoorn & De Wolff, 1997). With Jay Belsky we crossed swords on other topics as well, for example, on sex differences in attachment development (Bakermans-Kranenburg & Van IJzendoorn 2009). But we also published eleven papers together with Jay Belsky. A final example is our elaborate commentary on a series of studies on attachment by Glenn Roisman and his colleagues. We threw doubts on the evidence for a continuous instead of categorical interpretation of attachment (Van IJzendoorn & Bakermans-Kranenburg, 2014). The criticisms did not stand in the way of collaboration, and since 2010 we published twelve papers with Glenn Roisman. These examples demonstrate how critical analysis and debate are not in the way of fruitful collaborative work and point to the benefit of adversarial collaboration (Heyman, Moors, & Rabagliati, 2020; Knudsen, 2015).

The case of Black Pete

Improper or poor research and other violations of scientific standards should be discussed in the academic forum without sanctions or retaliations, regardless of the status, position, or sensitivities of the scientists involved. That is part and parcel of academic freedom. An example illustrates that such academic freedom is not self-evident. On 1 June 2017, the vice-chancellor of Leiden University presented Marinus with an agreement for signature with, among others, the following obligation: 'Prof. Van IJzendoorn will refrain from commenting, in any form, on the research performance and results of employees of the University of Leiden'. The names of the vice-chancellor, Carel Stolker, and Marinus were listed under the contract, and the latter only had to sign the 'agreement' to make it a legal reality, silencing the fundamental right to exercise academic freedom. The obligation was the more absurd because it concerned past, present, and future publications of anyone working in whatever department of Leiden University. Marinus refused to sign.

Bone of contention was a paper titled 'Implicit Racial Bias in Black Pete Study', a critical review of a flawed study on 'Black Pete through the eyes of Dutch children' by Judi Mesman, chair of our department and later dean of Leiden University College. Black Pete is historically rooted in the racist Black Face tradition (see Koning, 2018, for a study on the history of Black Pete). He acts as the simple-minded blackened helper of Saint Nicholas who brings presents to the children. Since the 1970s, around

December 5, Dutch black children and adults sometimes complained about being identified with subservient Black Pete, bullied, and verbally abused. Black Pete had been evaluated by the United Nations Committee on the Elimination of Racial Discrimination that urgently recommended the Netherlands to eliminate this racial stereotyping. Mesman et al. (2016) decided 'to examine children's views on Black Pete' and concluded that children 'evaluate Black Pete very positively' (Mesman et al., 2016).

Surprised by the outcome of the study and the publicity it received even before the paper was being refereed and published, Marinus re-analysed the data set. He found that the 'convenience sampling' had resulted in an overwhelming majority of white children from higher socio-economic backgrounds living in predominantly white neighbourhoods. No wonder they were very enthusiastic about Black Pete as the 'donor of presents'. Marinus published his critical commentary in a later issue of the same journal (Van IJzendoorn, 2016). This critical analysis was part of a series of critical reviews (published on his personal website) of published studies that had received uncritical media attention despite significant theoretical or methodological limitations.

After reading the rebuttal the authors of the study responded immediately and agreed with the need to have a more diverse sample to be able to draw valid conclusions: 'The authors are happy to report that the second part of this study is well under way, and that this part includes exclusively children with dark skin. So both perspectives are definitely integral parts of the larger project, but for practical reasons were split into two waves of data collection'. That is an excellent and constructive response, but unfortunately, after 7 years there has yet to be any follow-up publication (search in Web of Science, 28 February 2023).

The administrators of Leiden University, however, were annoyed by Marinus' 'noncollegial' contribution, and it prompted the attempt to ban him from participation in any scientific debate with scientists at Leiden University. In response to Marinus' refusal to sign the restriction of his academic freedom, Carel Stolker tweeted that this action had nothing to do with academic freedom but only concerned social safety at the workplace, requiring that colleagues should interact with each other in friendly ways.

Academic freedom is unprotected

The recent case of Rosalind Franklin Fellow and Associate Professor of Organizational Behaviour Susanne Täuber is also relevant here. Täuber published a critique of the University of Groningen's failed equal opportunity policy (Täuber, 2020). The dean of her faculty demanded the author and the scientific journal to retract the paper, which of course was denied. In the aftermath of this conflict the dean dismissed Täuber from the university (Upton, 2023). Rock bottom was that a judge supported the dismissal because 'even if Article 10 of the European Convention on Human Rights (freedom of speech) would have been violated, still the work relationship remains disrupted and the present working conditions untenable' (https://uitspraken.rechtspraak.nl/#!/details?id= ECLI:NL:RBNNE:2023:854; our translation). Although Täuber explicitly appealed to her fundamental right of academic freedom to publish a scientific article even if it was critical of her university, in the final judgement only freedom of speech was mentioned and found insufficient. Disrupted relationships in her department were legally allowed to supersede her academic freedom. In the Netherlands, the power of a dean to terminate any employee, including tenured professors, has become almost unlimited. A simple appeal to social unsafety or disrupted working relationships, even when only felt by small part of a department or only at the administrative level, is sufficient. In such situations, tenure has become an empty shell (see also Schliesser, 2023). Of course, most administrators will never misuse this legally sanctioned power. Nevertheless, in legal disputes academic freedom concerns should play a role, but currently they seem to be ignored in court.

This is an issue that deserves attention. In several countries, including the Netherlands, academic freedom is a fragile and undocumented right because it is not anchored in the constitution or the law (Groen, 2017). On the Academic Freedom Index, the Netherlands is ranking a deplorable 24th among the European Union states, and its position has been declining in the past 10 years (Kinzelbach et al., 2023). It is no wonder that in the State of Play of Academic Freedom of the European Union it is advised that The Netherlands should create 'a better legal protection of academic freedom'. We must treat academic freedom across the globe with care, because it has become increasingly under assault in the USA and in several other countries, with disastrous effects (Reichman, 2022). As mentioned before a recent and extremely distressing example is Turkey, where scientists have been dismissed from academia without due legal process only because they had protested non-violently against censorship by administrators and politicians. Academic freedom in Iran is currently even harsher under siege by governmental agencies, particularly victimising female scientists in the wake of the uprising of females against authoritarian oppression in their country (Constitution, 2023).

Conclusion

The power of university administrators – rectors, deans, directors – has grown in parallel to the growth of authoritarian regimes across the world (Repucci & Slipowitz, 2022), at the expense of the freedom of scientists to organise, conduct, and communicate their own research. Across the world, university administrators are increasingly more concerned about the university's image in the (social) media, as is also evident from their ever-expanding public relations teams.

Universities should be inclusive environments where individuals can express themselves freely, discuss their own and others' research, contemplate sensitive or controversial topics, and seek support or advice without retaliation. Academic freedom is by no means incompatible with safe spaces. In fact, considerable overlap exists where free debate of controversial topics without retribution is a major aim. Universities should enable and support such debate. The paramount stature of fragile academic freedom deserves to be protected by law.

References

Abbott, A. (2019). Germany's prestigious Max Planck Society conducts huge bullying survey. *Nature, 571*(7763), 14. https://link.gale.com/apps/doc/A592073047/AONE?u=anon~ecbae0fc&sid=googleScholar&xid=b706f2b8

Alexievich, S. (2016). *Second Hand Time: The Last of the Soviets*. Random House. ISBN 978-0399588808.

Bakermans-Kranenburg, M. J., & Van IJzendoorn, M. H. (2009). No reliable gender differences in attachment across the lifespan. Commentary on Del Giudice: Sex, attachment, and the development of reproductive strategies. *Behavioral and Brain Sciences, 32*, 22–23.

Buikhuisen, W. (1979). An alternative approach to the etiology of crime. In S. A. Mednick & S. Giora Shoham (Eds.), *New Paths in Criminology, Interdisciplinary and Intercultural Explorations*. Lexington Books. https://doi.org/10.1002/1098-2337(1981)7:3<293::AID-AB2480070320>3.0.CO;2-X

Chemerinsky, E., & Gillman, H. (2017). *Free Speech on Campus*. Yale University Press. https://doi.org/10.2307/j.ctv1bvnfnb

Constitution, Ms. (2023). 'Woman, Life, Liberty' in Iran and the role of academia. *Nature Human Behaviour, 7*, 3–5. https://doi.org/10.1038/s41562-022-01504-6

Dawkins, R. (1989). *The Selfish Gene* (2nd ed.). Oxford University Press.

Devlin, H., & Marsh, S. (September 28, 2018). Hundreds of academics at top UK universities accused of bullying. *The Guardian*.

Duschinsky, R. (2020). *Cornerstones of Attachment Research in the Twenty First Century*. Oxford University Press. https://doi.org/10.1093/med-psych/9780198842064.001.0001

Fox, N. A. (1995). Of the way we were: Adult memories about attachment experiences and their role in determining infant-parent relationships: A commentary on Van IJzendoorn (1995). *Psychological Bulletin, 117*(3), 404–410. https://doi.org/10.1037/0033-2909.117.3.404

Groen, J. (2017). *Academische vrijheid: een juridische verkenning [Academic freedom: A legal exploration]* (Unpublished doctoral dissertation). Erasmus University Rotterdam.

Harper, J. (2009). *Mobbed! What to Do When They Really Are Out to Get You*. CreateSpace Independent Publishing Platform.

Heyman, T., Moors, P., & Rabagliati, H. (2020). The benefits of adversarial collaboration for commentaries. *Nature Human Behaviour, 4*, 1217. https://doi.org/10.1038/s41562-020-00978-6

Keilson, H. (1933). *Das Leben geht weiter* [Life Goes On]. Fischer.

Kinzelbach, K., Lindberg, S. I., Pelke, L., & Spannagel, J. (2023). Academic Freedom Index 2023 Update. FAU Erlangen-Nürnberg and V-Dem Institute. https://doi.org/10.25593/opus4-fau-21630

Knudsen, S. H. (2015). Adversarial science. *Iowa Law Review, 1503*. https://digitalcommons.law.uw.edu/faculty-articles/14

Koning, E. (2018). Zwarte Piet, een blackfacepersonage. Een eeuw aan blackfacevermaak in Nederland [Black Pete, a blackface personality]. *Tijdschrift voor Geschiedenis, 131*(4), 551–575. https://doi.org/10.5117/TVGESCH2018.001.KONI

Mesman, J., Janssen, S., & Van Rosmalen, L. (2016). Black Pete through the eyes of Dutch children. *PLoS ONE, 11*(6), e0157511. https://doi.org/10.1371/journal.pone.0157511

Nelson, C. A., Fox, N. A., & Zeanah, C. H. (2014). *Romania's Abandoned Children: Deprivation, Brain Development, and the Struggle for Recovery*. Harvard University Press.

Panel for the Future of Science and Technology. (2023). State of play of academic freedom in the EU member states. Overview of de facto trends and developments. European Parliament Research Service, Scientific Foresight Unit (STOA), PE 740.231.

Popper, K. (1959). *The Logic of Scientific Discovery*. Routledge.

Rahal, R. M., Fiedler, S., Adetula, A., et al. (2023). Quality research needs good working conditions. *Nature Human Behavior, 7*, 164–167. https://doi.org/10.1038/s41562-022-01508-2

Reichman, H. (2022). *Understanding Academic Freedom*. University of Chicago Press.

Repucci, S., & Slipowitz, A. (2022). *Freedom in the World 2022: The Global Expansion of Authoritarian Rule*. Freedom House.

Schliesser, E. (2023, March 22). Academici in Nederland hebben geen effectieve academische vrijheid [Academics in the Netherlands lack academic freedom]. Neerlandistiek.

Stolker, C. (2018). Diversity of views: The university as a safe haven. Dies lecture on 8 February 2018, on the occasion of the 443rd Dies Natalis of Leiden University. Leiden: Leiden University.

Täuber, S. (2020). Undoing gender in academia: Personal reflections on equal opportunity schemes. *Journal of Management Studies, 57*(8), 1718–1724. https://doi.org/10.1111/joms.12516

Upton, B. (2023, April 11). Dutch sacking raises concern on academic scrutiny of universities. Susanne Täuber accuses Groningen of 'making a farce out of the academic way of working'. *Times Higher Education*.

Van Delft, D. (2023). *Verrek, dat is 't. Het strijdbare leven van Nobelprijswinnaar Martinus Veltman [Darnned, that's it! The combative life of Nobel Prize winning Martinus Veltman]*. Prometheus.

Van Esterik, C. (2016). *Jongens waren we. Totalitaire verleiding in de jaren zeventig. [Boys we were. The totalitarian temptation in the Seventies]*. Balans.

Van IJzendoorn, M. H. (1995a). Adult attachment representations, parental responsiveness, and infant attachment: A meta-analysis on the predictive validity of the Adult Attachment Interview. *Psychological Bulletin, 117*, 387–403. https://doi.org/10.1037//0033-2909.117.3.387

Van IJzendoorn, M. H. (1995b). Of the way we are: On temperament, attachment and the transmission gap. A rejoinder to Fox. *Psychological Bulletin, 117*, 411–415. https://doi.org/10.1037/0033-2909.117.3.411

Van IJzendoorn, M. H. (2016). Implicit racial bias in Black Pete study. *PLoS One*. https://journals.plos.org/plosone/article/comment?id=info%3Adoi/10.1371/annotation/a1fb61ba-87f5-47af-829e-ac4b7a5a5a7a

Van IJzendoorn, M. H., & Bakermans-Kranenburg, M. J. (2014). Confined quest for continuity: The categorical versus continuous nature of attachment. *Monographs of the Society for Research in Child Development, 79*(3), 157–167. https://doi.org/10.1111/mono.12120

Van IJzendoorn, M. H., & DeWolff, M. W. E. (1997). In search of the absent father: Meta-analyses of infant-father attachment. A rejoinder to our discussants. *Child Development, 68*, 604–609. https://doi.org/10.2307/1132112

Van IJzendoorn, M. H., & Bakermans-Kranenburg, M. J. (2015). Integrating temperament and attachment: The differential susceptibility paradigm. In M. Zentner & R. L. Shiner (Eds.), *Handbook of Temperament* (pp. 403–424). Guilford Press.

Epilogue: replication, translation, and academic freedom

From our insiders' perspective on the development of attachment theory and research across several decades, we propose slow, programmatic research. Slow science promotes uncovering replicable findings and emphasises translational caution to avoid premature applications to policy or practice. Academic freedom is paramount to protect against administrators' and other stakeholders' pressures to conduct 'agile' studies with immediate media attention and premature valorisation (see Figure 0.5). Our personal experiences with attachment theory and research made us participant observers of an exemplary, vibrant, but fallible paradigm. We hope that this insiders' perspective adds to the validity of our reasoning and its plausibility for researchers, clinicians, practitioners, policymakers, and funders in a wider realm of developmental science.

In his polemic essay on 'A trio of concerns' Jerome Kagan (2007) discussed some of his concerns about the state of the art in (developmental) psychology. In this book we address concerns about the trio of replication, translation, and academic freedom, placed in a wider social and methodological context. We argue that reproducibility and replicability of findings are a prerequisite for translation to reduce the risk of collateral damage to academic reputation and, more importantly, to the stakeholders, citizens, participants, children, or patients involved. Replication is a necessary condition of translation, and academic freedom is a necessary basis and safe haven for both.

Academic freedom is now needed more than ever to make open scientific debate and critical research possible without unlawful repercussions, silencing, and suppressions. However, academic freedom is reported to be under siege and stagnating or even in retreat for more than half the world population, not only in autocratic countries but also

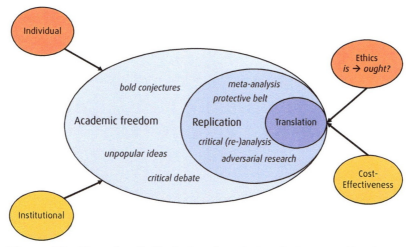

Figure 0.5 Nested ovals displaying the relations between replication, translation, and academic freedom with their various components. Source: Authors.

in WEIRD (Western, Educated, Industrialised, Rich, and Democratic; Henrich et al., 2010) nations (Kinzelbach et al., 2023). The Academic Freedom Index (AFI) is based on five criteria: the freedom to research and teach; the freedom of academic exchange and dissemination; the institutional autonomy of universities; campus integrity; and the freedom of academic and cultural expression. The UK, USA, and the Netherlands are ranking surprisingly low on several indices of academic freedom according to the AFI and in the European Parliament 2023 report on the 'State of play of academic freedom in the EU Member States. Overview of de facto trends and developments'. Nevertheless, academic freedom is paramount in academia and deserves a firm basis in the law.

Replication and translation

Developmental research is plagued by replication crises. For decades, too much emphasis was placed on single, mostly underpowered empirical studies and experiments that ran a great risk of non-replicability and winner's curses. We showed in *Section 1* that scientific evidence gradually accumulates through numerous precise and varied replications, secondary and meta-analyses, followed by umbrella reviews, in a spiralling process that in the end approximates the ever-moving target of truth.

Shortcuts are counterproductive. For example, ethics committees evaluating research have for years insisted on the smallest possible number of animals to be involved in a study, with the laudable intention of saving animals from unnecessary testing and (ultimately) death. But every underpowered study is a waste of all animals because of false positives and false negatives. The same is true for human research, and this damage extends to studies with low-quality designs and sloppy measures that jeopardise the validity of any conclusion.

A replication crisis is naturally followed by a translation crisis, as we documented in *Section 2*. Among the many attachment-based parenting support programmes only a few have been documented to be effective in a series of randomised controlled experiments. Fortunately, one of those interventions is our Video-feedback Intervention to promote Positive Parenting Sensitive Discipline (VIPP-SD, see Chapter 4), although it has not been effective in each and every sample. We argue, however, that applications of methods and techniques to support human development are only a small part of the translational contributions of science to policy or practice. Translation of scientific insights also includes critical analysis of fake facts, findings, and opinions. We unpacked in *Section 3* several untenable ideas about human development, with a special focus on attachment. We concluded that attachment is not determined by specific brain regions or 'love' hormones; it is not a recent, Western invention, and adoption of biological or social orphans is not a recent invention either.

Our critical analysis implies that the use of attachment measures in diagnostic assessments for court procedures or treatment decisions is not defensible. Parenting is not the all-powerful shaper of children's prosocial development. Social context, rules, and nudges seem more important and are only partly under parental control. Unfortunately, many myths originate from developmental science itself, or more precisely, from overly enthusiastic popularisation of developmental theories and research. This is proliferated by overstaffed university public relations offices advertising run-of-the-mill exploratory studies as proving causality and being ground-breaking (Bossema et al., 2019).

To paraphrase John Ioannidis, most technical translations in the area of attachment are false. And this statement might be extended to mental health treatments in general that overestimate the contribution of the technical aspects of treatment compared to the relational components of care (Van Os et al., 2019). One might argue that this leaves the policymaker, clinician, professional, or practitioner with empty hands and that it leaves the public and patients without the support or care they badly need. The provision of untested support or treatment with undocumented, potentially harmful adverse effects for invalidly diagnosed disorders, behaviour problems, or atypical development is, however, ethically unacceptable. *'Primum non nocere':* it is the first and foremost obligation of (mental) health care professionals to avoid causing harm to their clients.

Premature translation is especially problematic if it is seemingly approved and recommended under the aegis of trusted science. Clinician Martinus Langeveld, founding father of the Dutch discipline of (ortho-)pedagogics, argued more than half a century ago that practitioners could not and should not wait for scientists to support or guide them in their daily work. In practice, 'professionals by experience' should prepare the meal for tomorrow and be confident that they are indeed effective coaches. Unfortunately, his verdict may still hold. After some decades of research and clinical work, the Dutch psychiatrist Jim van Os recently suggested a similar approach emphasising that effective support or treatment is based on an empathic, secure relationship between intervener and client, and that type of intervention or professional status and training of the intervener has been proven not to make a substantial difference (Van Os et al., 2019). Even placebo 'treatments' are effective if they mimic the relational component of the real treatment. In his view, laypersons could be perfectly effective coaches in so-called Recovery Academies (Van Os et al., 2019; Zorzanelli & Banzato, 2020).

Academic freedom as the necessary context for critical science

In *Section 4* we discussed assaults on academic freedom. Developmental science is often implicitly guided by three basic human interests embedded in the human condition, 'Erkenntnisinteressen' or knowledge-constitutive interests (Bohman & Rehg, 2017; Habermas, 1968; Lempert, 1971; Miedema, 1994a,b). Their philosophical origins can be traced to the Enlightenment with its emphasis on universality, justice, and the deliberately naïve hope for progress (Neiman, 2023). The *practical* interest is behind the aim to make coherent meaning and narrative understanding of the (social) world and is prominent in the hermeneutical approach of the humanities but also present in some currents of the social and behavioural sciences (see Bruner, 1990). The *technical* interest in predicting and controlling the natural and social environment is the basic driver of the empirical-analytic approach in the natural, biomedical, neurobiological, and behavioural sciences. It is the motivation to search for regularities in and predictors of physical and human interactions and relationships, with a focus on translation to techniques that may improve these interactions and relationships.

The *critical* interest in emancipation from fake facts and false beliefs is driven by the need for self-reflection, self-direction, and agency without unjustifiably constraining bonds of hierarchy, prejudice, and oppression. The critical interest is aimed at reconstructing the ethical and socioeconomic presuppositions behind scientific methods, knowledge claims, and translations to policy or practice. In Wolfgang Lempert's words 'Emancipation opposes constraints which are not only due to material violence, but also to the power of prejudice and ideologies' (Lempert, 1971, p. 318). Social change should be a driver for a just society which does protect and nurture its natural and human resources for a more equitable future for generations to come. We need all three 'Erkenntnisinteressen' and related scientific disciplines in a concerted effort to make sense of why and how we conduct research to acquire replicable and translatable knowledge serving the common good with the aim of increasing social justice in the Rawlsian sense of a liberal society.

This three-pronged approach means that slow science is the main objective of emancipatory research programmes (see Chapter 3), in sharp contrast with the growing movement to 'agile science' (Hekler et al., 2016) that emphasises fast implementation of study outcomes. Instead, we advocate 'slow science' including replications and quantitative syntheses, with a clear division of roles and responsibilities between researchers and practitioners (see Chapter 16) to establish first a strong evidence base and only subsequently strive for implementation in close collaboration with practitioners, clinicians, and policymakers. We submit that what we cannot study in a reproducible way should not be studied at all (or not before a valid method comes around). We need the protection of academic freedom to conduct replicable research in the service of responsible translation to policy or practice.

References

Bohman, J., & Rehg, W. (2017). Jürgen Habermas. In E. N. Zalta (Ed.), *The Stanford Encyclopedia of Philosophy (Fall 2017 ed.)*. Retrieved from https://plato.stanford.edu/archives/fall2017/entries/habermas/

Bossema, F. G., Burger, P., Bratton, L., et al. (2019). Expert quotes and exaggeration in health news: A retrospective quantitative content analysis [Version 2; peer review: 2 approved]. *Wellcome Open Research*, *4*, Article 56. https://doi.org/10.12688/wellcomeopenres.15147.2

Bruner, J. (1990). *Acts of Meaning*. Harvard University Press.

European Parliament. (2023, March). State of play of academic freedom in the EU Member States. Overview of de facto trends and developments. PE 740.231.

Habermas, J. (1968). *Erkenntnis und Interesse [Knowledge and Human Interests]*. Suhrkamp.

Hekler, E. B., Klasnja, P., Riley, W. T., Buman, M. P., Huberty, J., Rivera, D. E., & Martin, C. A. (2016). Agile science: Creating useful products for behavior change in the real world. *Translational Behavioral Medicine, 6*(2), 317–328.

Henrich, J., Heine, S. J., & Norenzayan, A. (2010). The weirdest people in the world? *The Behavioral and Brain Sciences, 33*(2–3), 61–135. https://doi.org/10.1017/S0140525X0999152X

Kinzelbach, K., Lindberg, S. I., Pelke, L., & Spannagel, J. (2023). *Academic Freedom Index 2023 Update*. FAU Erlangen-Nürnberg and V-Dem Institute. https://doi.org/10.25593/opus4-fau-21630

Lempert, W. (1969). Bildungsforschung und Emanzipation. Über ein leitendes Interesse der Erziehungswissenschaft und seine Bedeutung für die empirische Analyse von Bildungsprozessen [Educational research and emancipation]. *Neue Sammlung, 9*, 347–363.

Lempert, W. (1971). *Leistungsprinzip und Emanzipation. Studien zur Realität, Reform und Erforschung des beruflichen Bildungswesens* [Principles of Achievement and Emancipation]. Suhrkamp Verlag.

Miedema, S. (1994a). Kritische pedagogiek [Critical pedagogics]. In S. Miedema (Ed.), *Pedagogiek in meervoud* (pp. 117–169). Bohn Stafleu Van Loghum.

Miedema, S. (1994b). The relevance for pedagogy of Habermas' theory of communicative action. *Interchange, 25*(2), 195–206.

Neiman, S. (2023). *Left Is Not Woke*. Polity Press.

Van IJzendoorn, M. H. (2019). Commentary: Addressing the replication and translation crises taking one step forward, two steps back? A plea for slow experimental research instead of fast 'participatory' studies. In S. Hein & J. Weeland (Eds.), Randomized Controlled Trials (RCTs) in Clinical and Community Settings: Challenges, Alternatives and Supplementary Designs. *New Directions for Child and Adolescent Development, 167*, 133–140.

Van Os, J., Guloksuz, S., Vijn, T. W., Hafkenscheid, A., & Delespaul, P. (2019). The evidence-based group-level symptom-reduction model as the organizing principle for mental health care: Time for change? *World Psychiatry, 18*(1), 88–96. https://doi.org/10.1002/wps.20609

Zorzanelli, R., & Banzato, C. E. M. (2020). Moving beyond psychiatric diagnosis and the medical framework towards social recovery: An interview with Jim van Os. *Revista Latinoamericana de Psicopatología Fundamental, 23*(4), 792–814. https://doi.org/10.1590/1415-4714.2020v23n4p792.7.

Index

Abbott, A., 212
ABC of attachment, 84, 95
Abramson, L., 140
academic freedom, xiv, 7, 185, 186, 187, 189, 191, 193, 198, 201, 203, 210, 212, 214, 216–222, 225, 226, 228, 229
Academic Freedom Index (AFI), 221, 226
ACE modelling of behavioural genetics research, 25–26
Achterberg, M., 13
action and research relation, criteria for, 198
action research, 189–190, 197–198
adoption
   adopted child, the, 171, 173, 175–176, 178
   adoption triangle, 171, 177–179, *179*, 181
   benefits, 171, 173, 174, 175, 176
   best interests of the child, 179–181
   black markets of, 176–177
   controversial, 171
   and evolution, 173–174
   in forest chimpanzees, 173
   history, 171–172
   international adoptions, 172, *177*, 180
   and kinship, 171, 173, 177
   in non-human species, 173
   secure family lineage, 174–175
Adult Attachment Interview, 14, 24, 151, 157
adversarial research, 193–194
Ainsworth, M. D. S., 7, 9, 10, 14, 15, 17, 25, 37, 84, 86
Alexievich, S., 214
alloparents, 130, 141, 174
Alsancak-Akbulut, C., 60
Altstein, H., 172
Amarna family, 126
AMBIANCE-Brief, 157
Armsden, G. C., 25
Arnstein, S., 195
attachment classification and brain morphology, associations between, 120
attachment disorder, 153
attachment networks, 3–5, 130, 131, 155
Attachment Q-Sorts, 83, 145
attachment security, 14, 24, 58, 59, 60–61, 81, 82–83, 89, 92, 128, 129, 133
   and compliance, 146
   and limit-setting promote, 60–61
   and prosociality, 144–146
   and sensitive parenting, 60–61, 144–146, 218

attachment theory and social learning theory, integration of, 56–57
atypically developing children, 152, 166
Augustine of Hippo, 137
Augustus (Roman emperor), 174–175
authors' personal life and beliefs, transparency about, 207
auxiliary hypotheses, 38, 43
Avital, E., 173, 175
avoidant attachment, 127–128

baby hatches, 68
Bachmann, C. J., 92
bad studies, exclusion of, 43
Bakermans, J., 156
Bales, K. L., 130
Balk, Y., 176
Baltimore study, 9, 10, 14, 15
Barel, E., 73
Barocas, H. A., 75
Barone, L., 60
Bartels, M., 103
Bateson, M., 146
Beckwith, H., 151
Bell, S. M., 9, 10
Belsky, J., 85, 95, 105, 107, 157, 194, 219
Ben-Zur, H., 72
Berkeley Adult Attachment Interview, 14
Bernard, K., 95
best interests of the child, 151, 179–181
Biesta, G. J. J., 189
birds, adoption in, 174
birth fathers, 172, 180
Black Pete study, 205, 219–220
Blakemore, 188
Bohman, J., 196, 228
Boivin, N., 212
Bokhorst, C. L., 103
Bolhuis, E., 120
Bonapersona, V., 12
Borenstein, M., 14
Bosmans, G., 10, 37, 38, 82
Bossema, F. G., 227
Boswell, J., 171, 172
Botvinik-Nezer, R., 33, 34
Bowlby, J., 1, 2, 5, 37, 67, 68, 74, 83–84, 86, 87, 94, 161, 175, 176, 181, 204, 217

231

Boyce, W. T., 107
brain
    and behaviour, 119–121
    for benefiting others, 143–144
    brain derived neurotrophic factor (BDNF), 15, 39
    mind over matter, 117–118
Brazil, 133
Brodzinsky, D. M., 173
Broesch, T., 130
Brown, K. M., 173
Bruner, J., 228
Bucharest Early Intervention Project, 64, 119, 161–162, 218
Buikhuisen, W., and Leiden University, 211–212
bullying, 213
Burzynska, A. Z., 119
Bushman, B. J., 35
Button, K., 11

Cadman, T., 145, 157
Calhoun, L. G., 77
Callaghan, B., 105
Campbell, D., 17, 218
cancel culture in the past, 211–212
Carroll, L., 35
Carter, S., 117
causal claims, 121
Cave, N., 204
Champoux, M., 173
Chaudhary, N., 132
Chekhov, A., 187
Chemerinsky, E., 217
child influences on parenting, 105–106
child maltreatment, 5–6, 105–106, 166
    contemporary narrative review, 197
    in the Netherlands, 188
    studies, 40–41
    survivors of, 191
child-caregiver attachment, 131, 162
childless women, 117
chimpanzees, 125–126, 173
China, 133, 172, 175
CHU-9D, 23
Citizen Science (CS), 187, 188, 195
    democratisation of scientific research, 194
    as participatory action research, 189–191
Clements, T., 190
Clevers, H., 16
Clinton, H., 130
cognitive development, of children, 4–5, 12, 64, 125, 132, 162, 188
Cohen, J., 89, 106
Cohen's d criteria, 89, 106
Coles, N., 33
Colombia, 60, 96, 133
community values, prioritising academic freedom above, 216
competence hypothesis, 127
conditioning theory, 10, 38
Condon, E., 204
conflicts of interest, 201
    impossibility to report all, 208–209
    non-financial, 201–208, 209
    non-financial, authors' declaration of, 208–209

recent developments, 206–208
    various types of conflicts, 203
conjectures, bold, 15–17
consensus statements, 36, 44–45, 87, 179, 180
Constitution, Ms., 221
context characteristics, 146–147
context of justification, 42, *42*, 51–16
continuity of care arrangements, 5
contract, concept of, 84
contractualism, 81
Cook, T. D., 41
Cooke, J. E., 157
cooperation, as prosocial behaviour, 139
cooperative breeding, 130, 141
Cooperative Practitioners-Researchers Model, 194–195, *196*, 198
core propositions of attachment theory, 5–6
Cortes Hidalgo, A. P., 120
cost-effectiveness, 89, 91–92, 94, 96
Coughlan, B., 41
COVID-19 pandemic, 66, 90, 195
Cowan, P. A., 3, 219
Cowell, J. M., 140
CpGs, 143
critical debate, and academic freedom, 218–219
critical interest, 229
critical science, and academic freedom, 228–229
Crittenden, P. M., 155, 156
Crone, E., 12, 144
Crosnoe, R., 194
cross-cultural model, 85
culture, and attachment, 125–128
    caregivers, 130–132
    distributions across the world, 128–130
Cuyvers, B., 188
Cyr, C., 129, 152, 157

Dagan, O., 4, 131
Dall'Aglio, L., 109
Danieli, Y. E., 75
Darwin, Ch., 204
Darwinian, 17, 68
Daudt, H., 211, 212
Dawkins, R., 213
Day, C., 16
De Los Reyes, A., 94
de Waal, F. B. M., 28, 141
De Wolff, M. S., 14, 37, 219
de-institutionalisation, 64, 69, 162
    need for, 65–66
    and SOSCV, 167–168
Deneault, A.-A., 145
Desmond, C., 63
Devlin, H., 212
DeVries, M., 68
diathesis-stress model, 107
differential susceptibility models, 38, 82, 106–108, *107*, 218
discoveries, 15, 16, 42, *42*, 190
discrimination, and academic freedom, 217, 220
disorganised attachment, 14–15, 64, 109, 120, 125, 128, 131, 152–153, 157
    and child maltreatment, 152

232   INDEX

coding system, applied to videotaped observations, 152
core criterion for, 152
DNA, 26, 101–102, 110
DNA methylation, 109, 142
Dobbelaar, S., 13, 144
Dobrova-Krol, N., 64, 176
Dogon mothers, study of, 127–128
Dolhinow, P., 175
donating, 140–141, 142
Doucet, M., 197
Duschinsky, R., xv, 2, 14, 15, 83, 84, 87, 167, 217
Dutch Consortium for Childcare Research (NCKO), 192–193, 194
dyadic interactions, 104, 125, 126
Dynamic-Maturational Model of attachment (DMM), 155–156, 157

Eaton, W. W., 72
Eble, A., 158
effect size standards, 43, 89–91
Eichberg, C. G., 14, 15
Einstein, A., 204
Eitinger, L., 71
Elliott, M. L., 11, 152
Ellis, B., 85, 105, 107, 117, 120
Elon, A., 71
emancipatory interest, 99, 196
Emotional Brain Study, 188
epigenome-wide studies (EWASs), 109
EQ-5D approach, 93, 95
EQ-5D for Youth scale (EQ-5D-Y), 23, 93–94
Erasmus University Rotterdam, 214
Erkenntnisinteressen, 99, 196, 228, 229
ethics
 challenges, 86
 guidelines, 209
 implications of supporting parents, 85
 See also is and ought
ethnic minority differences, 129
European Convention on Human Rights, 179
European Convention on the Adoption of Children, 179
Euser, S., 12, 67, 105, 166, 188
evaluation committees for interventions to support families and children, 95–97
event-related potentials (ERPs), 22
evolutionary epistemology, 218
evolutionary models, 141
external morality as social agreement, 83

fathers, 3, 115, 119, 121, 128, 130, 131, 162, 172, 180
Feldman, R., 113, 115, 116, 121
Felix, J., 28
Ferris, E., 207
Feyerabend, P., 16, 190
Fletcher, R. H., 207
Fontanarosa, P., 208
Forscher, P. S., 43
Forslund, T., 36, 44, 87, 151, 152
Fox, N., 38, 218
free speech, 217
freedom of speech, 185, 189, 198, 203, 221

Full Conflict of Interest Disclosure Form, 201, 202–203, 205
Furber, G., 23
Fusar-Poli, P., 40

Galaxy Zoo, 188
Garbage In, Garbage Out, 43
Gardner, F., 95
Gaspelin, N., 22
Geim, A., 16
gene-culture coevolution, 68
gene-environment correlation, 105, 106
gene-environment interaction, 105
Generation R, 24, 105, 120, 143, 144, 146
genetics
 and causal associations, 108–109
 child influences on parenting, 105–106
 counter-arguments against the genomic myth, 102–105
 genetic differential susceptibility, 106–108
 genomic era, 101–102
genocidal trauma. *See* Holocaust survivors
genome-wide association studies (GWAS), 26, 28, 103, 104, 106
Genome-Wide Complex Trait Analysis (GCTA), 142
Germany, baby hatches in, 68
Gewirtz, J. L., 10
Gillman, H., 217
Gillon, R., 92
Gintis, H., 95
Glass, G. V., 34, 35
Gmeiner, H., 162, 168
Goffman, E., 63, 67
Goldberg, S., 22
Goldman, P. S., 44, 65, 66, 161, 162, 168, 172
Goldsmith, H. H., 44
Goodman, R., 22
Goossens, F. A., 131
Gould, S. J., 173
Granqvist, P., xv, 3, 36, 152
Great Backyard Bird Count, 187, 188
Greece, 63, 64, 124
Griffiths, A. W., 24
Groen, J., 221
Groh, A. M., 137, 144, 157
group level, attachment at, 3, 151
Grumi, S., 116
Grunberg, N. E., 140
guiding principle of scientific practice, 217
Guilford, J. P., 152

Habermas, J., 86, 99, 196, 228
Hague Convention on Protection of Children and Co-operation in Respect of Intercountry Adoption (1993), 175, 179
Hamaker, E., 12, 41, 108, 121
Hamilton, W. D., 5, 68, 177
Hamilton's rule, 68
Hamlin, J. K., 140
Hammarlund, M., 151, 153
Handlungsforschung, 189
Harding, E., 190
Harlow, H., 1–2
Harnett, P., 157
Harper, J., 211, 214

Harris, J., 101
harsh parenting, 85, 117
Hart, R. A., 189, 195
Hawks, S., 132
head circumference, 63, 120
Healthy Start, Happy Start, 90, 191
Heckendorf, E., 11
Heckman, J. J., 92
Heidegger, M., 204
Hekler, E. B., 229
Helmreich, W., 78
helping behaviour, 138, 140
Henrich, J., 104, 127, 209, 226
heritability, 102, 110, 142
　estimates for, 102, 103–104, 106
　missing, 103
　and prosocial behaviour, 141–142
　of response bias, 25–29
　twin studies, 13, 101–102
　See also genetics
Hesse, E., 17, 24
Heyman, T., 219
hidden talents model, 85
hierarchy model, 131, 229
Hillis, S. D., 63, 172
Hinde, R. A., 85, 204
Ho, S.-H. S., 113
Hochberg, Z., 85
Hofhuis, S., 17
Holocaust survivors, 71
　effects, *74, 76*
　first generation, *73*
　immigrating to Israel, 77
　living in Israel, 73
　post-traumatic stress symptoms in, 74
　qualities predictive of post-war adaptation in, 78
　second generation of, 75–76, 78
　select and non-select sampling, 72–73, 76
　survival of the fittest, 77
　third generation, 72, 76, 78
Home Visiting Evidence of Effectiveness (HomVEE), 60, 89, 96
Homer, 3, 4, 71
home-visiting programmes, 89–90. *See also* Video-feedback Interventions to promote Positive Parenting and Sensitive Discipline (VIPP-SD)
hormones
　and behaviour, 114–117
　and brain and behaviour, 113, *114*
Horn, L., 209
Horstman, L. I., 119
How, A. R., 86
Hrdy, S. B., 1, 67, 130, 141, 171, 173, 177
Huang, Z. J., 128–129
Hubbard, F., 10, 82
Huffmeijer, R., 11, 22
Hume's law of ethics, 81, 83

Iliad, 3, 71
inclusive fitness theory, 85
independence model, 131
Independent Special Commission (ISC), 165
India, 63, 64, 133, 172
individual children, attachment measures for, 2–3, 151–158

individual participant data (IPD) meta-analysis, 40, 42, 43, 131
Indonesia, 133
infant crying, 101, 139, 153
　and amygdala activation, 119, 121
　and OT, 117–118
　replicating a study on response to, 9–11, 82
infant-father attachment, 130–131
infanticide, 67–68, 171
influence specific behaviour, 147
Innocent III, Pope, 68
institutionalised child-rearing, 43, 63
　brain development studies, 120
　child abuse and neglect in, 68
　and developmental delays, 64
　foster care, 64
　institutionalisation, 63–65
　orphanages against infanticide, 67–68
　prevention and de-institutionalisation needed, 65–66
integration model, 131–132
intercoder reliability of attachment measures, *156*
International Committee of Medical Journal Editors (ICMJE), 198, 207
intervention programmes implementation
　cost-effectiveness, 91–95
　effect size, 91
　scalability, 92
Ioannidis, J., 11, 15, 40, 97, 208, 227
IPPA, 25
is and ought
　ABC of attachment, 84–85
　evolutionary jump, 85–87
　naturalistic fallacy, 81, 83
　replicated evidence, sufficiency of, 82–84
Israeli kibbutzim, 131
iteration, of research process, 197

Johnson, K. A., 172, 175
Jones-Mason, K., 109
Juffer, F., 53, 63, 65, 67, 82, 84, 95, 172, 173, 175, 178, 215
Just Community project for moral education, 189, 190

Kaag, S., 161
Kagan, J., 28, 38, 225
Kahana, B., 73
Kauffmann, G., 212
Keers, R., 108
Keilson, H., 72, 75, 214
Kentrop, J., 12
Khadka, J., 24
Kinzelbach, K., 221, 226
Klein, R. A., 41
Klein Velderman, M., 58
Knight, L., 204
knowledge acquisition, technical interest in, 99
knowledge-constitutive interest, 228
Knudsen, S. H., 219
Kochanska, G., 146
Kohlberg, L., 83, 86, 137–138, 189
Kok, R., 105, 120, 143, 146
Koning, E., 219
Korean War, 172
Kraaijeveld, K., 173

Kraft, M., 89–90, 91, 92
Kreis, W., 203
Kwon, J., 22

Lakatos, I., 10, 36
Lakatosian research programme, 36–38, **37**
Lakens, D., 44
Laland, K., 68
Lamb, M., 3, 130
Langeveld, M., 228
languages, 2, 17, 44
Lassi, Z. S., 164
law, and academic freedom, 216
Leiden Longitudinal Empathy Study, 145
Leiden University, 220
Leiden-Consortium on Individual Development study (L-CID), 12, 13, 144
Lempert, W., 196, 228, 229
Leng, G., 116
Lenin, V., 187
Leon, G. R., 72
Levi, M., 213
Liabo, K., 196
Lieberthal, J. K., 172
life history theory, 38, 85, 86, 105, 120
Lindauer, R., 157
Lolle Nauta Foundation, 209
Londerville, S., 146
Long, M., 121
Lotz, A. M., 116
Luck, S. J., 22
Luo, M., 109, 142, 143
Lyons-Ruth, K., 120
Lytton, H., 42

Madigan, S., 14, 36, 38, 60, 106, 128, 129, 130, 152, 157, 180
Mah, B., 117, 121
Main, M., 15, 17, 24, 86, 87, 146, 152
Mali, 127
Marek, S., 11–12
Marris, P., 3
Marsh, H., 113
Martinez, J., 217
massage, 121
Maternal Behavior Q-Sort, 83
Matthew, L., 197–198
Max Planck Society, 212
maximin rule, 84, 178, 180
Mazor, A., 74
McCabe, E., 197
McCarthy, J., 204
Medoff, M. H., 176
Meehan, C. L., 132
Meehl, P., 10
Mendelian randomisation, 108–109
mental health, 109
Mesman, J., 83, 127, 133, 219, 220
Messiou, K., 190
meta-analyses, 14, 34, 39–40
 attachment research as a Lakatosian research programme, 36–38
 conclusion validity, and availability of pertinent studies, 43
 of cross-cultural patterns of attachment, 35–36
 cumulative, 39
 delayed development in SOSCV, 163, 164
 development of, 35–36
 effects of institutionalisation, 65
 individual participant data (IPD), 40, 42, 43, 131
 process model, 41–45
 replicability and reproducibility, differentiation between, 33–35
 roles in a research programme, 38
 stages in, *34*
 and systematically conducted narrative reviews, compared, 40
 as the three-step identification, 34, 39–40
 of VIPP-SD randomised controlled trials, 58–60
Michalopoulos, C., 89
micro-aggression, 212
Miedema, S., 189, 190, 228
Mileva-Seitz, V. R., 103
militant students, 211
Miller, E., 175
Min, J. L., 109
mobbing, 211, 214
moderators, 22, 34, 40, 42–43
Molendijk, M. L., 15, 39
monotropy, 131
Moore, G. E., 83
moral behaviour, 83, 137, 138
moral dilemmas, 137–138, 190
moral reasoning
 and moral behaviour, gap between, 138
 and prosocial behaviour, 137–129
moral reflection, 138
Morawetz, C., 120
mothers, 3, 54, 83, 104, 115, 117, 127, 128, 130, 132–133, 141, 162, 194
Mortimer, D., 95
Mukuria, C., 23
Mulder, R. H., 109
multilevel modelling, 40
Munn, Z., 45

Naber, F. B. A., 115, 121
National Academy of Sciences, Engineering, and Medicine (NAS), 33
National Institute of Child Health and Human Development (NICHD) Study of Early Child Care and Youth Development (SECCYD), 194
naturalistic fallacy, 81, 83
Nature journals, 207
NCKO. *See* Dutch Consortium for Childcare Research (NCKO)
negative emotions of children, parents' insensitivity to, 94
Neiman, S., 228
Nelson, C. A., 64, 161, 162, 218
Netherlands, the
 academic freedom in, 221
 criminality among adopted youth in, 176
 day-care for infants and toddlers, 192
 dual-earner families, 131
 Dutch Consortium for Childcare Research (NCKO), 192–193, 194
 National Postal Codes Lottery, 166
 Netherlands Youth Institute (NJi), 95–96
Neumann, A., 24

neurobiological effects studies, 73–74
neuroscientific research, 11
Newton, I., 204
Nguyen, T., 121
Niederland, W. G., 72
Nietzsche, F., 29
Nobel Prize, 215
Nobis, E., 162
non-replicability, 7, 11, 21, 24, 34, 214, 226
nonsensical Wildman items, 26, *26*, 27
non-WEIRD countries, research in, 209
normativity hypothesis, 127
Nosek, B. A., 12
Novoselov, K., 16

O'Farrelly, C., 90, 191
O'Neil, D., 95
observational assessments, of attachment, 25
Ohtani, K., 158
Oppenheimer, R., 204
original position, 84, 178, *179*, 180–181
orphanages, 153, 161
　and adoptions, 125–126, 175, 176
　and developmental delays, 64
　against infanticide, 67–68
orphans, 63, 172, 173, 174, 177, 227
Ota, D. W., 3
oxytocin (OT), 113, 114–116
　and activation in the amygdala, 118
　administration, and crying, 118
　and infant crying-in-context, 118
　levels from blood and saliva, 116
　molecule, *115*
　and prosociality, 116
oxytocin receptor gene (OXTR gene), 39, 114, 218

Padron, E., 38
Paine, T., 137
Palacios, J., 172, 175, 179–180, 181
Palmer, J., 176
Pannebakker, F., 145
Pappa, I., 142
parenting dimensions, 145
participants involvement, 195
　damaging influence of stakeholders, 192–193
　involvement in data collection, 187–188
　See also patient and public involvement (PPI)
Pasteur, L., 17
patient and public involvement (PPI), 185, 187–191, 194
　adversarial research, 193–194
　democratisation of scientific research, 194
　as participatory action research, 189–191
　viable alternatives with, 191
　See also participants involvement
Patterson, G., 56
Pauling, L., 204
Pearl, J., 108
Pearson, K., 35
Perpetuo, C., 3
p-hacking, 21–22
phenotyping, 28, 103, 108, 109, 142
physical health, 72, 73, 74, 92, 95, 96, 109

Piaget-Kohlberg tradition, and moral dilemmas, 137–138
Pittner, K., 106
Plomin, R., 101, 102
PLoS ONE, 208
Polderman, T. J. C., 102, 104, 110
Poldrack, R., 14, 155
political activism, and research, 189
polygenetic score (PGS), 108
polygenic scores, 26–27, 39, 106
Popper, K., 17, 42, 204, 207, 218
Porter, R. B., 167
Posada, G., 83, 132–133
post-traumatic stress, 73–74, 75, 77, 78
poverty, 58, 63, 65, 85, 94, 96, 128, 129, 133, 152, 171, 181
Power, C., 190
power failure, 7, 11, 12
　bold conjectures, 15–17
　replication crisis in the cognitive neurosciences, 11–14
　study on response to infant crying, 9–11
　winner's curse, 14–15
practical interest, 196, 228
practical-hermeneutical interest, 99
premature translation, 228
pre-registration, of research design, 12–13, 43–44, 121
Preschool Assessment of Attachment (PAA), 156
Preventive Intervention Team project (PIT), 91–92, 96
primary empirical studies, stages in, *34*
Prince, S. A., 28
privacy rights, 205
process model
　of meta-analysis, 35
　of replications, 43
　of research programmes, 41–45
professional group care, 67
prosocial behaviour
　behaviour dimensions, 138–139
　compliance dimension, 146
　and cortical thickness, 143
　definition of, 138
　developmental context, 137
　general development perspective, 139
　individual differences perspective, 139
　and neonatal DNA methylation (DNAm), 142–143
　Prosocial Cyberball game, 143–144
prosociality
　as an evolutionary-based universal competence, 141
　context characteristics, 146–147
　and contextual factors, 137
　and genes, 141–143
　parenting and attachment security as promoters of, 144–146
　species-wide development versus individual differences in, 139–141
Purnama Sari, N., 91

Q-Sort method, 83, 129, 132–133, 145–146, 157
Quality Adjusted Life-Years (QALYs) measures, 23–24, 92, 94

Time Trade-Off (TTO) approach, 93
  weaknesses of, 95
questionnaires, 21, 41, 92
  in developmental and behavioural research, 28
  EQ-5D for Youth scale (EQ-5D-Y), 23, 93–94
  genome-wide association studies (GWAS), 26, 28, 103, 104, 106
  response bias, 27
  self-report, 21–25, 28–29, 93–94, 209
  Strengths and Difficulties Questionnaire (SDQ), 22–24, 142
  in twin studies, 102–103
Quine W. V., 10

racially minoritised samples, 128–129, 133
Racine, N., 197
Radua, J., 118
Rahal, R. M., 215
rapid and scoping reviews, 45
Rawls, J., ix, 81, 84, 86, 171, 178–180, 229
  maximin rule, 84
  theory of justice, 171, 178
reactive attachment disorder, 153
Recovery Academies, 228
Reichman, H., 204, 221
Repucci, S., 222
response bias, 25–29, 103, 139
responsive care, 125–126
Richards, J. R., 83
Riem, M., 10, 117, 118, 119, 121, 143
Riley, R. D., 40, 42
Rilling, J. K., 141
Roisman, G., 24, 40, 42, 219
Rosenthal, R., 22, 35, 44
Rosnow, R. L., 22
Rousseau, J.-J., 137
Rowen, D., 94
Runze, J., 12, 25, 26, 27
Rushton, J. P., 142
Rust, J., 138
Rutter, M., 74

safe, stable and shared (Triple S) care, ix, xiv, 6, 66, *177*
safe space, 16, 211, 222
safety, 2, 73
  safe haven, 2, 5, 225
  and security, distinguishing between, 84
  social. *See* social safety
Sagi, A., 74, 131, 139, 151
Sagi-Schwartz, A., 76–78, 127
Salvadori, E., 140
Sama-Miller, E., 60, 89, 96
sampling, 28, 41, 165
  convenience sampling, 220
  Holocaust studies, 72–73, 75
Sartre, J.-P., 204
Scheper-Hughes, N., 67, 68
Schliesser, E., 214, 221
Schore, A. N., 120
Schuengel, C., 36, 38, 55
Schwartz, S., 77
Schweizer, S., 188
Schwitzgebel, E., 138
scientific integrity, 202, 203, 218

Sedlak, A. J., 188
Segev, T., 73
self-disclosures, 208
self-reports, 21
  of child maltreatment, 105
  heritability of response bias, 25–29
  and proxy reports, divergence of, 24
  questionnaires, 21–25, 28–29, 93–94, 209
Sellaro, R., 121
Selman, P., 172, 176
sensitivity hypothesis, 75, 127
serendipity, 16
Shanan, J., 74
Shearer, J., 23
Sheridan, M. A., 120
Shmotkin, D., 73
Sigal, J. J., 72
Simmons, J. P., 13, 16, 21
Simonsohn, U., 13, 16, 21, 43, 64
Simpson, J., 139
Singer, T., 212
slow science, 15, 45, 51, 225, 229
Smith, J., 176
Smith, M. L., 35
Smith, P. K., 132
SNP heritability, 28, 106
social activism, and research, 189
social environment, 2, 5, 110, 117, 228
social interactions, 5, 66, 113, 144–145
social learning theory and attachment theory, integration of, 56–57
social network of individuals, 6
social safety, 212–213
  and academic freedom, 216–218
  anonymous complaints, 212, 213–214
societal costs, of insecure attachments, 92
societal impact of interventions, *90*
Society for Research on Child Development (SRCD), 201–202, 203, 205, 218
socio-economic status, 95, 129–130, 133
Soltis, J., 118
Sorosky, A. D., 178
SOS Children's Villages (SOSCV), 161
  child abuse and neglect in, 165
  and de-institutionalisation, 167–168
  delayed development in, 163–167
  sponsorship of 'rapid evidence review' of institutional care, 167
  'Tear down your institutions', 161–163, 168
SOSCVI, 162, 165
Spanjaard, H., 91
species-specific level, attachment on, 1–2
Spieker, S. J., 155, 156
Spinoza Prize, 215
Sroufe, A., 37, 38
Stadhouders, N., 95
Stamkou, E., 146
standard errors and standard deviations, confusion of, 14
Stanford University, 212
statistical significance, 44, 60, 96
Stayton, D. J., 86
Steegen, S., 42
Steele, H., 84, 85
Stein, A., 54
Stevens, E., 90

Stolker, C., 216, 219, 220
Stoltenborgh, M., 105
Storsbergen, H. E., 175
Strange Situation Procedures, 24, 25, 36, 125, 127–128, 152, 155, 157
Strengths and Difficulties Questionnaire (SDQ), 22–24, 142
Suomi, S., 104
support programmes, home-visiting parenting, 89
Surinamese SOSCV, 165
surviving war and genocide, 71–72. *See also* Holocaust
Swaab, D., 91, 113, 119
Swaab, H., 91
Swain, J. E., 113
Szende, A., 93

Tannese dyads, 130–131
Täuber, S., 220–221
Taylor, S. E., 116
Taylor & Francis, 206
Te Brinke, L. W., 195, 196
technical interest, 99, 196, 228–229
temperament theory, 38, 44, 218
Thaler, H., 147
theory of justice, 84, 171, 178
Thijssen, S., 105, 120, 121, 143, 144, 147
three knowledge interests, 196
Time Trade-Off (TTO) approach, for QALYs determination, 93
Tizard, B., 172
Tran, N., 25
transcutaneous vagus nerve (TVN), 121
transmission gap, 17, 38–39
Tricco, A. C., 45
Trivers, R. L., 5, 68, 94, 139, 204
True, M., 127, 128
Tsimane dyads, 131
Tucker, D. M., 141
Turkey, 96, 221
twin studies, 101–102, *102*
 amount of variance molecular genetic studies, 103–104
 environmental context impact on developmental outcomes, 104
 of prosocial behaviour, 141–142
 questionnaires, 102–103
type II errors, 35

Uchiyama, R., 104
Uebel, T., 203
Ukraine
 institutionalised pre-schoolers in, 63–64
 orphanages housing in, 176
umbrella syntheses, 40–41, 42, 43, 44, 106
unclassifiable attachment, 64, 131
United Kingdom
 harassment and intimidation in universities, 212
 Incredible Years, 90–91, 95, 96
 National Children's Bureau, 191
United Nations
 Convention on the Rights of the Child (CRC), 179–180

Intergovernmental Panel on Climate Change (IPCC), 44
UNESCO, 185
Universal Declaration of Human Rights, 205
United States
 child-care war, 194
 Food and Drug Act, 13
 National Incidence Studies on child maltreatment in, 188
universal children's rights, 68
universality, of attachment, 125–130, 132
universities
 administrators, power of, 221–222
 changing team composition of flex-workers, 215
 contract workforce, 214–215
 hierarchical structure of academic organisations, 214
University of Amsterdam, 211
unprotected academic freedom, 220
unpublished dissertations, 44
Upton, B., 221
'utosti' combinations, 41–42

Van Dam, M., 24
Van Delft, D., 215
Van der Asdonk, S., 157
Van der Hal-van Raalte, E. A. M., 77
Van der Mark, I., 140, 145
Van der Meulen, M., 13, 144
Van der Veen, R., 12
Van Esterik, Ch., 211
Van Ginkel, J., 176
Van Os, J., 35, 155, 227, 228
Van Reybrouck, D., 196
Van Rompay, T. J. L., 146
Van Wijk, A., 165
Van Zeijl, J., 58
Van Zonneveld, L., 91
Veltman, M., 215
Verhage, M., 15, 17, 37–40, 42, 129
Verhees, M., 121
Verinorm, 165
Vermeer, H., 192
Vickers, P., 45
Video-feedback Interventions to promote Positive Parenting and Sensitive Discipline (VIPP-SD), 13, 20, 53, *57*, 81–83, 95–96, 191, 227
 and attachment security, 60–61
 attachment theory and social learning theory integration, 56–57
 development of, 53–54
 economic evaluation of pre-registered trial with, 90
 and effective size standard, 89–91
 and Home Visiting Evidence of Effectiveness (HomVEE) review, 60
 intervention sessions, 56
 potential active ingredients in, *55*
 randomised controlled trials, meta-analyses of, 58–60
 specific themes, 56–57
 stilling, repeating, and commenting on fragments tools, 54
 toolbox, 54–56

volunteerism, 138, 139
voluntourism, 161
Vrijhof, C., 22, 94
VU Amsterdam, 214

Wadhwa, M., 41
Wang, Q., 120
Ward, J., 28, 103
Warneken, F., 140
Warrier, V., 106, 109
wars, impacts of, 71
Waters, E., 129
Watson, J., 204
weigh-in procedure, 128
Weinberg, J., 204
WEIRD countries, 104, 127, 130, 132, 161, 226
Wellcome Trust, 194, 213
Wildeboer, A., 143, 146
Wildman, R. W., vii, 25, 26, 27

Wilson, D. S., 83
winner's curse, 14–15, 17, 39, 114
Winnicott, D., 175
within-family polygenic score analysis, 106
Witte, A., 117, 121
Witteman, J., 118, 120, 141
Wong, T. K. Y., 145
World 1, 204
World 2, 204
World 3, 17, 204, 210
World Association of Medical Editors (WAME), 206–207
World War II, 77, 172, 175
Wysocki, D., 174

Yehuda, R., 72, 73

Zavalis, E. A., 208
Zooniverse, 187–188
Zorzanelli, R., 228

Milton Keynes UK
Ingram Content Group UK Ltd.
UKHW050239040724
445115UK00011B/65